ネイティブが教える
英語の句動詞の使い方

デイビッド・セイン *David A. Thayne*
古正佳緒里 *Kaori Furusho*

研究社

Copyright © 2014 by AtoZ

ネイティブが教える
英語の句動詞の使い方

Natural Phrasal Verb Usage for Advanced Learners

PRINTED IN JAPAN

はじめに／本書の内容

　句動詞とはどのようなものでしょうか？
　一般的には、「〈動詞＋前置詞もしくは副詞〉の数単語の組み合わせにより、それを形成する動詞とは異なる意味をもつ表現」とされます。
　句動詞は come, get, take といったごく基本的な動詞と、at や on などのこれまた非常に一般的な前置詞もしくは副詞の組み合わせによって形成されますが、その数は数千とも数万ともいわれます。
　ネイティブは特に日常会話でこの句動詞を多用します。これは「数単語でさまざまな意味を簡単に表現できる」ことが1つにあります。また、1単語の動詞では堅い印象を与えることがありますので、基本的な動詞＋前置詞もしくは副詞からなる句動詞を使うことによって、それを和らげ、より親しみを感じさせる言い方にできることがあります。そのため、ネイティブはあらゆる状況で句動詞を多用するのですが、日本人をはじめとする非ネイティブの人たちは、これを必ずしも簡単であると受けとめることができず、むしろ複雑であると感じてしまうようです。
　句動詞の何が日本人学習者のみなさんを悩ませるかといえば、次の2点に集約されると思われます。

　1．1つの句動詞でもさまざまな意味がある。
　2．基本動詞＋前置詞・副詞の組み合わせは無数にあり、とても覚えきれない。

　1句動詞＝1定義であれば、まだ覚えるのは簡単でしょう。しかし、それが状況によってさまざまな意味で使われてしまうことで、非常にむずかしいと感じてしまうようです。
　たとえば、explode（爆破する）と blow up は、ほぼ同じ意味です。しかし、日常会話であれば、ネイティブはやや堅い響きのある explode より、くだけた印象の blow up を好んで用います。同様に、support よりも back up が、raise よりも bring up が、インフォーマルな場においては使われる傾向があります。
　また、英語では同じ語を繰り返して使わないほうがいい、という共通の認識がネイティブにはあります。同じ言い方をずっとしてしまうと、語彙が豊富でない、教養がない、と相手に思われてしまうことにもなるからです。異なる表現を使わなければな

らない状況では、この句動詞の使用が大変効果的です。

● 句動詞の種類

　句動詞は一般的に品詞の組み合わせで種類分けができます。おおまかに〈動詞＋前置詞〉〈動詞＋副詞〉〈動詞＋副詞＋前置詞〉の３つに分類できます。また、それぞれ「目的語を取るかどうか（自動詞か他動詞か？）」「句動詞を分けられるかどうか（句動詞のあいだに目的語を入れられるかどうか）」といった違いがあります。

１．〈動詞＋前置詞〉の句動詞

　〈動詞＋前置詞〉は他動詞となるため、句動詞のあとに目的語を取ります。この場合、たいてい句動詞のあいだにその目的語を挿入することはできません。

　・I don't ask for coffee.（コーヒーは頼んでいない）

　ほかに come into（…に加わる）, find out（…とわかる）, go on（…をつづける）, live with（…に耐える）, make for（…に急ぐ）などもある。

２．〈動詞＋副詞〉の句動詞

　〈動詞＋副詞〉の場合、句動詞のあいだに目的語を挿入できるため、〈動詞＋副詞＋目的語〉だけでなく、〈動詞＋目的語＋副詞〉の組み合わせも見られます。また、この組み合わせの句動詞は、他動詞としてのみならず、自動詞としても使われます（21ページのコラム「句動詞にも自動詞と他動詞がある」もご覧ください）。

　※本書では、句動詞の基本的な知識と使い方を学んでいただきたいと思い、見出し語で各目的語の位置を … などで示すことはしませんでした。

　・They blew things up. ＝ They blew up things.（彼らがすべてを台無しにした）

　ほかに bring around（…を説得する）, carry out（…を実行する）, drive out（…を追い出す）, make up（…をでっち上げる）, pass around（…を回す）などもある。

　ただし、目的語が代名詞の場合、常に〈動詞＋目的語（代名詞）＋副詞〉の語順となります。

　○ If you keep that up, I'll leave you.（そんなことをしつづけるなら、私は出ていく）
　× If you keep up that, I'll leave you.

3．〈動詞＋副詞＋前置詞〉の句動詞

〈動詞＋副詞＋前置詞〉は他動詞として働き、あとに目的語を取ります。

・The job offer didn't come up to his expectations.（その仕事のオファーは彼の希望に沿うものではなかった）

ほかに do away with（…を処分する），get along with（…と仲よくやっていく），go on with（［仕事などを］どんどん進める），look up to（…を尊敬する）などもある。

●第1章「句動詞の使い方」

冒頭で触れたように、句動詞は無数にあります。よく「こんなにたくさんある句動詞を、ネイティブは全部覚えているのですか？」という質問を受けますが、われわれネイティブは一般的な句動詞はほとんど感覚的に使いこなすことができます。というのは、句動詞は学校の勉強で習うものではなく、日常の会話で実際に使いながら自然と身につけていくものだからです。まわりの人が使う表現を繰り返し耳にし、自分もそれを口にしてみることで、いつのまにか使いこなせるようになるのです。

辞書には性格上、あまりネイティブが使わない句動詞表現もたくさん含まれています。ですから、それを日本人の英語学習者のみなさんが全部覚えるのは大変なことです。そこで本書では、基本100動詞を使った句動詞を679厳選し、その1066の定義と例文を収録しました（そのうち、コラムにあるものは11）。「ネイティブがよく使う句動詞として、これだけは覚えておいてほしい」ものを厳選したのです。動詞別に紹介していますので、基本動詞に前置詞や副詞を組み合わせることによって、意味や使い方がどのように変わるか、きっとイメージしていただけると思います。

また、ネイティブが各句動詞を日常生活でどのように使うか思い浮かべてほしいと思い、用例はすべて会話文で紹介しました。会話のAは女性、Bは男性を想定しています。ネイティブ同士の日常会話の「自然さ」を味わっていただけましたら幸いです。

なお、誠に残念ながら、スペースの都合により、give up（あきらめる），go off（［警報器・目覚まし時計が］鳴り響く），look for（…を探す），check in（［ホテルで］チェックインする），check out（［ホテルで］チェックアウトする），work out（［物事などが］うまくいく）など、ネイティブから見て、日本人のみなさんが比較的よく知っていると思われるものにつきましては、今回は省かせていただきました。みなさんがまだ使いこなせていないと思われるものを中心に選出しました。ご理解のほど、お願いいたします。

●第 2 章「句動詞の問題」
　実際にどのように句動詞が使われているかの参考として、著名人の名言を紹介します。クイズ形式にしましたので、名言を味わいながら、ご自分の句動詞の知識を試してみてください。

●「句動詞和英索引」
　第 1 章で学んだ句動詞を会話や英作文で実際に使いこなしていただくために、日本語で検索できる索引を作成しました。かなり詳細なものになりましたので、ぜひ和英辞典のようにご活用ください。（本索引作成にあたっては、研究社編集部の金子靖さんが都内で開講している「翻訳教室」の受講生の方たちに、大変お世話になりました。）

　本書刊行にあたり、研究社編集部の金子靖さんには、今回も大変お世話になりました。すでに大変な英語の知識と運用能力を身につけておられるにもかかわらず、日々英語学習に邁進される金子さんには、ネイティブの私がいつも非常に刺激を受けています。例文やコラムの執筆、翻訳、そして索引作成まで、金子さんのお力なしでは本書はとても出版できませんでした。
　また、編集段階では、高見沢紀子さんにもお世話になりました。自動詞と他動詞の区別、適切な定義の確認、用例と翻訳のチェックまで、高見沢さんのおかげで、本書の内容はさらに充実したものになりました。お 2 人に深く感謝申し上げます。

　気軽に手に取れる紙数の本にするため、収録を断念しなければならなかった句動詞もありますが、ここで紹介する 679 の句動詞とその 1066 の定義と例文をマスターすることで、「ネイティブ感覚の句動詞の使い方」が身につくはずです。それを日常生活で実際に使いこなしながら、ネイティブとの対話を楽しみ、英語表現の幅を広げていただきたいと思います。本書をきっかけに英語の句動詞に親しみをもっていただければ、著者としてこれほどうれしいことはありません。

2014 年 3 月　デイビッド・セイン

- はじめに／本書の内容　iii
- 本書の使い方　xii

■ 第1章　句動詞の使い方　1

act 2
act as / act for / act on [upon] / act out / act up
add 3
add in / add on / add to / add up / add up to
answer 4
answer back / answer for / answer to
ask 5
ask around / ask for / ask out
back 6
back away / back down / back out of / back up /
beat 7-8
beat down / beat into / beat out / beat to / beat up / beat up on
blow 9-10
blow apart / blow away / blow down / blow in / blow over / blow up
break 11-14
break away / break away from / break down / break for / break in / break into / break off / break out / break out of [from] / break through / break up
bring 15-17
bring about / bring along / bring around / bring back / bring down / bring in / bring on [upon] / bring out / bring through / bring to / bring together / bring up
build 18
build on / build up

buy 19
buy back / buy into / buy off / buy out / buy up
call 20-21
call about / call back / call for / call off / call out / call over / call up
carry 22-23
carry around [about] / carry away / carry back / carry off / carry on / carry out / carry through
catch 23
catch on / catch up
check 24
check in / check into / check on / check out / check over / check with
clean 25
clean out / clean up
clear 26
clear away / clear off / clear up / clear with
close 27
close down / close off / close up / close with
come 28-36
come across / come across as / come after / come along / come around / come at / come away / come back / come before / come between / come by / come down / come down with / come for / come forward / come from / come from behind / come in / come into / come of / come off / come on /

vii

come out / come out against / come (right) out and say [ask] / come out in / come out of / come out with / come over / come through / come to / come together / come up against / come up in the world / come up to /come up with / come with

count 37
count down / count for much / count on [upon] / count up

cry 38
cry for / cry out against / cry over

cut 39-40
cut across / cut back / cut down / cut down on / cut in / cut into / cut off / cut up

die 41
die away / die down / die of / die out

do 42-43
do away with / do for / do in / do over / do up / do with / do without

draw 44-45
draw aside / draw back / draw in / draw into / draw on / draw out / draw up

drop 46-47
drop away / drop behind / drop by / drop in / drop into / drop off / drop out

fall 48-49
fall back on [upon] / fall behind / fall down / fall for / fall in / fall into / fall in with / fall off / fall on [upon] / fall out / fall through / fall under

feel 50
feel like / feel out / feel up to

fight 51
fight back / fight off / fight on / fight over

fill 52
fill in / fill out / fill up

fix 52
fix up

get 53-62
get across / get after / get along / get around / get around to / get at / get away / get away with / get back / get back at / get back to / get back together / get back with / get behind / get by / get down / get down to / get in / get into / get off / get on / get out / get out of / get over / get through / get to / get together / get under / get up / get up to

give 63
give off / give out / give up / give up on

go 64-72
go against / go along / go along with / go around / go away / go back / go back for / go back on / go between / go beyond / go by / go down / go for / go in / go into / go off / go on / go out / go over / go through / go through with / go to / go together / go under / go up / go up to / go with / go without

grow 73
grow into / grow on [upon] / grow out of / grow up

hand 74
hand back / hand down / hand in / hand out / hand over

hang 75-77
hang around / hang around with / hang off / hang on / hang onto / hang out / hang over / hang together / hang up

have 78-79
have against / have around / have back / have in / have off / have on / have out / have over

hear 80
hear about / hear from / hear of / hear out

help 81
help out

hit 81
hit back / hit on [upon]

hold 82-85
hold against / hold back / hold down / hold in / hold off / hold on / hold onto [on to] / hold out / hold over / hold to /

hold up
jump 86
jump around / jump in / jump into / jump on [upon] / jump out at
keep 87-90
keep after / keep around / keep at / keep away from / keep back / keep down / keep from / keep in / keep off / keep on / keep out of / keep to / keep together / keep under / keep up / keep up with
kick 91
kick around [about] / kick back / kick in / kick off
knock 92-93
knock around [about] / knock back / knock down / knock into / knock off / knock out / knock over
laugh 94
laugh about / laugh at / laugh away / laugh off
lay 95-96
lay aside / lay back / lay down / lay off / lay out / lay up
leave 97-98
leave behind / leave in / leave off / leave on / leave out / leave up to
let 99-100
let by / let down / let in / let off / let on / let out / let through / let up / let up on
lie 101
lie ahead / lie around [about] / lie back / lie behind / lie off
live 102-103
live by / live down / live for / live off / live on / live out / live through / live up to / live with
look 104-106
look after / look ahead / look around / look at / look back / look down / look down at [on] / look for / look forward to / look into / look like / look over / look through / look up
make 107
make of / make off with / make out /
make up
mark 108
mark down / mark off / mark up
meet 109
meet up / meet with
move 110
move around / move away / move into / move on / move over
open 111
open out / open up
pass 112-113
pass around [round] / pass away / pass by / pass in / pass on / pass out / pass through / pass up
pay 114
pay back / pay for / pay off / pay up
pick 115
pick on / pick out / pick through / pick up
play 116
play around [about] / play down / play up / play with
pull 117-118
pull apart / pull away / pull back / pull for / pull in / pull into / pull off / pull out / pull out of / pull through / pull together
push 119
push back / push for / push into / push out / push up
put 120-126
put across / put aside / put away / put back / put before / put down / put forward / put into / put off / put on / put out / put over / put through / put to / put together / put toward / put up / put up with
read 127
read into / read on / read out / read through [over] / read up on [about]
run 128-133
run across / run after / run against / run along / run around / run away / run back / run behind / run by / run down / run for / run into / run off / run on / run out / run out of / run over / run through /

run to / run up / run with
see 134-135
see after / see back / see in / see off / see out / see over / see through / see to
sell 136
sell off / sell out / sell out of
send 137-138
send away / send back / send for / send in / send off / send on / send out / send up
set 139-141
set about / set aside / set back / set down / set forward / set in / set off / set oneself against / set out / set up
settle 142
settle down / settle for / settle into / settle on [upon]
shake 143
shake down / shake off / shake out / shake up
shoot 144
shoot down / shoot for / shoot up
show 145
show around / show off / show through / show up
shut 146
shut down / shut off / shut out / shut up
sign 147
sign for / sign on / sign up / sign with
sit 148-149
sit around / sit back / sit by / sit for / sit in / sit on / sit out / sit up
sleep 150
sleep off / sleep on / sleep over / sleep through
speak 151-152
speak about / speak for / speak out / speak to / speak up / speak with
stand 153-155
stand against / stand around / stand at / stand behind / stand by / stand for / stand in / stand out / stand together / stand up / stand up against / stand up for / stand up to
start 156-157
start back / start in on / start off / start (off) with / start out / start over / start up
stay 158-159
stay around / stay away from / stay down / stay in / stay off / stay on / stay out of / stay up / stay with
stick 160-161
stick around / stick at / stick by / stick out / stick out of / stick to / stick together / stick up / stick with
stop 162
stop by / stop in / stop off / stop over / stop up
take 163-166
take after / take along / take around / take away / take back / take down / take for / take in / take off / take on / take out / take out of / take over / take to / take up
talk 167
talk about / talk away / talk back / talk down to / talk out of / talk over
tear 168
tear apart / tear down / tear into / tear off / tear up
think 169
think about / think back / think of / think out / think up
throw 170-171
throw around [about] / throw aside / throw away / throw back / throw in / throw on / throw open / throw out / throw together / throw up
tie 172
tie down / tie up / tie up with
touch 173
touch down / touch off / touch on [upon] / touch up
try 174
try on / try out / try out for
turn 175-178
turn around / turn away / turn back /

turn down / turn in / turn into / turn off /
turn on / turn out / turn over / turn to /
turn up
wait 179
  wait around / wait on / wait up
walk 180
  walk into / walk off / walk off with /
walk through
watch 181
  watch out

wear 181
  wear down / wear out
work 182-183
  work off / work on / work out / work
over / work through / work toward /
work up
write 184
  write down / write off / write out / write
up

■ 第2章　句動詞の問題　185

■ 句動詞和英索引　194

column

- ask 5
- blow 10
- 句動詞にも自動詞と他動詞がある 21
- cry 38
- do 43
- drop 47
- have 79
- leave 98
- pass 113
- set 143
- show 147
- start 157
- wear 179

- beat 8
- break 14
- clean 25
- cut 40
- draw 45
- hang 77
- lay 96
- make 109
- 句動詞はどうしてむずかしい？ 135
- shoot 144
- sit 149
- try 174

本書の使い方

ネイティブが頻繁に使うと思われる句動詞を、コラムのなかのものも含めて、合計 679 紹介しました。

特に句動詞を形成すると思われる 100 の動詞を厳選し、見出し語としてアルファベット順に並べました。

同じ句動詞でも、状況によって異なる意味で使われるものがあります。こうした句動詞は複数の意味と使い方を示しました。

see

□ **see after** …の世話をする
A: I'm stuck in a meeting, but I'm supposed to show a client around the factory.（会議から抜けられない。なのに、お客さんに工場を見せてまわることになっているの）
B: Don't worry. I'll *see after* him.（心配しないで、ぼくがお世話するよ）

□ **see back** （車などで人を）家まで送り届ける
A: Well, it's been a long night. I think I'll turn in.（あー、ずいぶん長くなっちゃった。もう寝るね）→ TURN IN [3]
B: OK, I'll see you *back* to your hotel room.（あぁ、ホテルの部屋まで送るよ）

□ **see in** （人に）よい性質などを認める
A: Is Linda still dating that idiot George?（まだリンダは、あのアホなジョージと付き合ってるの？）
B: Yeah, I just can't understand what she *sees in* him.（うん、彼のどこがいいと思っているのか、わからないな）

□ **see off** （人を）見送る、送り出す
A: Is George flying back to New York today?（ジョージは今日ニューヨークに飛行機で戻るの？）
B: Yeah, I'm going to *see* him *off* at the airport.（うん、空港まで彼を見送りに行ってくるよ）

□ **see out** （人を）玄関まで見送る、…が外に出るのを見送る
A: Is the ABC chairman leaving now?（ABC 社の会長は、今お帰りですか？）
B: Yes. Could you *see* him *out* for me?（そうです、私の代わりに、お見送りしてもらえますか？）

□ **see over** …の向こうが見える
A: I can't believe somebody would wear a hat in a movie theater.（映画館で帽子をかぶるなんて、まったく信じられない！）

B: I know! I can't even *see over* him to watch the film.（まったくだ！ それがじゃまで映画が見られないね）

□ **see through**
[1]（事業など）を 最後までやり通す
A: Why don't you put Linda on the project?（どうしてリンダをプロジェクトに加えないの？）→ PUT ON [1]
B: I don't think she's reliable enough to *see* it *through* to the end.（最後までやり通すほど信頼できないからだよ）
[2]（窓・カーテンなどを通じて）向こうが見える
A: I think Linda needs to put something over her blouse.（リンダはブラウスの上に何か羽織ったほうがいいと思う）
B: I know. You can *see* right *through* it.（そうだね、中が透けちゃうね）

□ **see to** （仕事など）を 引き受ける、世話をする (= undertake)
A: Is somebody going to set up the meeting room for tomorrow's conference?（誰か明日の会議のために会議室を用意してくれる？）→ SET UP [1]
B: Yeah, George and Linda are going to *see to* it.（うん、ジョージとリンダが引き受けるよ）

---

column ▶▶▶ 句動詞はどうしてむずかしい？

「はじめに」でも書きましたが、ネイティブは、論文のような堅い文では collapse（崩壊する）を使うとしても、会話のなかではフォーマルに聞こえてしまうため、この語の使用を避けて、たとえば句動詞 break down で代用しようとします。

しかし、困ったことに、同様に日常会話でも、動詞 analyze（分析する）の代わりに、同じ break down が使われることがよくあるのです。

「ネイティブは簡単な表現だからこそあらゆる場面で使おうとする」のですが、日本人英語学習者にすれば、「句動詞が多用されるよに、同じ句動詞が状況によってさまざまな意味で用いられる」と思えてしまますし、じっさい日本人句動詞初学者をいっそう困惑させているようです。対応策としては、

1 同じ句動詞表現でも、状況に応じてさまざまな意味で用いられることを認識する。
2 その意味を1つひとつ信頼できる辞書で確認し、よく使われる意味の使い方を覚える。

ということになると思います。

2については、研究社の『ルミナス英和辞典』がおすすめです。この辞典には、各動詞の句動詞表現が枠で囲んでまとめられています。意味も、例文も、大変わかりやすく、本書執筆にあたっても、大いに参考にさせていただきました。

句動詞は日常会話でよく使われます。本書では例文はすべて会話文で提示しました。
※音声データは、著者デイビッド・セインが代表を務める AtoZ のサイトからダウンロードできます（有料）。
http://phrasalverbsmip3.blogspot.jp
本書では、句動詞表現を合計 1066!（そのうち、コラムにあるものは 11）紹介しています。

会話文の中で「これも覚えてほしい」という別の句動詞が出てきた場合、クロスレファレンスで示しました。そちらもご参照ください。これによって、句動詞が日常会話で頻繁に使われていることがおわかりいただけると思います。

空きスペースには、コラムを入れました。こちらでも句動詞表現を紹介しています。ぜひご覧ください。

第 1 章

句動詞の使い方

act

☐ act as　…の役を務める

A: I heard George is sick.（ジョージが元気ないと聞いたけど）
B: Yeah, Linda's going to *act as* the manager now.（ああ、リンダが今度マネージャーを務めることになるんだ）

☐ act for　（法廷・取り引きなどで）…の代理を務める、…のために尽くす

A: Can't George go to the conference?（ジョージは会議に行けないの？）
B: No, but I'm going to *act for* him.（行けないけど、ぼくが彼の代理を務めることになっている）

☐ act on [upon]

【1】（主義・忠告・情報などに）基づいて行動する、従う

A: Did you give George any advice?（ジョージに何かアドバイスはした？）
B: Yeah, but he didn't *act on* it.（ああ、でも彼はそのとおりにしなかったんだ）

【2】…に作用する、効く

A: What part of the body does this medicine *act on*?（この薬は体のどの部位に効く？）
B: It helps your eyes.（目に効くよ）

☐ act out　（感情を表に出して）ふるまう

A: I hope Linda doesn't get drunk.（リンダが酔っぱらわないといいな）
B: I know. She *acts out* violently.（そうだね。彼女は乱暴になるから）

☐ act up　（特に子供が）いたずらをする、行儀よくしない

A: Stop *acting up*. Sit down and do your homework.（いたずらはやめて。座って宿題をやりなさい）
B: But I want to play!（でも遊びたいんだ！）

add

□ add in …を足す、加える、入れる

A: This taste is a little flat. (この味はもの足りない)
B: Why don't you *add in* some salt? (少し塩を足したら？)

□ add on …を付け加える、加算する

A: This book is only 15 dollars. (この本はたった15ドルよ)
B: Yeah, but you have to *add on* tax. (ああ、でも税金を足さないと)

□ add to

【1】…を建て増す

A: My house is too small. (うちはあまりに狭すぎる)
B: Why don't you *add* rooms *to* it? (建て増したらどう？)

【2】…を増す

A: Sorry to *add to* your problems, but we lost a client. (問題を増やして悪いけど、顧客をなくしたわ)
B: Everything's going wrong. (何もかもまずい方向に進んでるね)

□ add up …を合計する

A: How much money did we make today? (今日はいくら稼いだ？)
B: Just a minute. Let me *add up* the sales. (ちょっと待って。売り上げを計算させて)

□ add up to

【1】合計…となる

A: I bought a lot of supplies. (消耗品をたくさん買ったよ)
B: How much did it *add up to*? (合計いくらになった？)

【2】結果的に…となる、結局…を意味する

A: How can we fix this problem? (どうやったらこの問題を解決できる？)
B: Whatever we do, it all *adds up to* the same thing. (何をやろうとも、結局は同じことだ)

answer

☐ answer back （特に子供が大人に対して）口答えをする

A: Why did George get fired?（どうしてジョージは解雇されたの？）
B: He *answered back* to his boss.（彼は上司に口答えしたんだ）

☐ answer for

【1】…に代わって答える

A: George agrees with me on this.（ジョージはこのことで私に同意しています）
B: Don't *answer for* me. I don't agree with you.（私に代わって答えないで。きみの意見には同意していません）

【2】（事に対して）責任を持つ［取る］、償う（= account）

A: I'm sorry, but I lost the contract.（申し訳ありませんが、契約書をなくしました）
B: How are you going to *answer for* this?（これに対してどう責任を取るつもりだ？）

【3】…を保証する（= assure）

A: Can we really trust Linda?（本当にリンダは信頼できる？）
B: Yes, I've known her for a long time, and I can *answer for* her.（はい、彼女を長く知っていますし、保証できます）

☐ answer to （人に対して事態の）責任を負う

A: We lost a lot of money on this project.（このプロジェクトでかなりの損失を出した）
B: We're going to have to *answer to* the shareholders.（株主に対して責任を取らなければいけないだろう）

ask

☐ ask around あちこち聞いてまわる

A: George from HR is *asking around* for you.（人事部のジョージがあなたを探しまわっているわよ）

B: I wonder why he wants to talk to me.（どうして彼は私と話したいのかな）

☐ ask for

【1】(物・助けなどを) 求める

A: Where can we get a map?（どこで地図がもらえるかな？）

B: Let's *ask for* one at the convenience store.（そのコンビニで聞いてみよう）

【2】(電話などで) …はいないかとたずねる

A: Mr. Green called and *asked for* you.（グリーンさんが、あなたはいないかと電話をかけてきたわ）

B: Oh, really? Does he want a call back?（へえ、本当に？ 彼は折り返しの電話をほしがっていた？）

☐ ask out …を (食事・パーティなどに) 招く、誘う

A: Are you going to *ask* Linda *out*?（リンダと出かけるつもり？）

B: Yeah, I'm going to take her to a movie.（うん、彼女を映画に誘うつもりだ）

---

column ▶▶▶ ask

人を家に招き入れる場合、よく ask の句動詞を使います。その際、「自分がいる場所」によって副詞を使い分ける必要があります。

- *ask* someone *in*（普通に玄関から招き入れる）
- *ask* someone *over*（近くに住んでいる人を招き入れる）
- *ask* someone *up*（自分が2階以上に住んでいて、階下の人を招く）
- *ask* someone *down*（自分が地下もしくは相手がいる場所より低いところにいて、そこに招き入れる）

いずれも日本語にすれば「…を家に招き入れる、招く」でよいですが、副詞によってニュアンスが異なることに注意しましょう。

back

☐ back away 後ずさりする、後退する

A: *Back away* from the machine. (その機械から下がって)
B: Is it dangerous? (危ないのかい？)

☐ back down （計画から）手を引く、後退する

A: I don't think this project is going to be profitable. (このプロジェクトは儲からないと思う)
B: I see. Do you think we should *back down*? (そのようだね。やめたほうがいいかな)

☐ back out of （企て・契約などから）手を引く、約束を破る

A: Why did you *back out of* the joint venture? (なぜ合弁事業から手を引いたのですか？)
B: We realize it would be better not to do it. (そうしないほうがいいだろうと判断したのです)

☐ back up

【1】（議論・主張などを）支持する (= support)

A: I'm planning to sell our factory. (弊社の工場の売却を計画しています)
B: I can't *back* you *up*. It's a bad idea. (あなたを支持することはできません。それは悪い考えです)

【2】（ディスク・ファイルなどを）バックアップする

A: My computer crashed and I lost all my data. (コンピュータが壊れて、データが全部なくなっちゃった)
B: I told you to *back* it *up*. (データをバックアップするように言ったのに)

【3】渋滞する

A: The traffic is starting to *back up*. (交通渋滞が始まっているわ)
B: I hope we don't get in a traffic jam. (渋滞にはまらないように願ってるよ)

beat

☐ beat down

【1】（太陽が）ぎらぎら照りつける

A: Why did all these plants die?（どうしてこの植物はみんな枯れたの？）
B: The hot sun *beat down* on them.（太陽が照りつけたからだ）

【2】（値段を）値切る、（売り手に）値をまけさせる

A: George wants 300 dollars for his camera.（ジョージはこのカメラを 300 ドルで売りたいって）
B: You can *beat* him *down* to 200 dollars.（200 ドルまで値切れるよ）

【3】（ドアなどを）たたき破って中に押し入る

A: How did the police get inside Linda's house?（警察はどうやってリンダの家の中に入ったの？）
B: They *beat down* the door.（ドアをたたき破って押し入ったんだ）

☐ beat into …をたたいて〜させる

A: Why did you tell the police you robbed the bank?（どうして銀行を襲ったことを警察に話したの？）
B: I was *beaten into* a confession.（殴られて白状させられたんだ）

☐ beat out （競争で相手を）打ち負かす

A: Congratulations on getting the job!（その仕事につけておめでとう！）
B: Thanks. I had to *beat out* 20 other applicants.（ありがとう。ほかの 20 人の応募者に勝たなければならなかったんだ）

☐ beat to

【1】（競争などで）…より先に〜に到着する

A: Did Linda *beat* you *to* the airport?（空港にはリンダのほうが早く着いたの？）
B: Yes, she got there 30 minutes before me.（うん、彼女はぼくたちより 30 分早く着いた）

【2】…より先にやり遂げる

A: Do you have any questions?（何かご質問は？）
B: I did, but George *beat* me *to* it.（ありましたが、ジョージが先に質問しました）

☐ beat up （人を）打ちのめす、さんざん殴りつける

A: My son got *beat up* by a bully. （息子がいじめっ子に殴られました）
B: Was he hurt badly? （ひどくやられたのかい？）

☐ beat up on

【1】…をぶちのめす、徹底的にやっつける

A: Did you *beat up on* George? （ジョージを殴ったの？）
B: Yeah, but he pushed me! （ああ、でもあいつもぼくを押したんだ！）

【2】（人を）責める（beat up on oneself）

A: What I did was so stupid. （私、そんなバカなことをしちゃって）
B: Don't *beat up on* yourself. You didn't do anything wrong. （自分をそんなに責めないで。きみは何も間違ったことをしなかったよ）

---

column ▶▶▶ beat

　たとえば He beat me. は、「彼は私を負かした／たたいた／へとへとに疲れさせた／だました」など、さまざまな解釈が可能なため、前後関係からその意味を判断するしかありません。

　しかし、句動詞を使って He *beat* me *up*. と表現すれば、「彼は私を何度もたたいた（ひどい目にあわせた）」になり、beat（たたいた）より意味が具体的になります。

　また He beat me. はニュアンスが曖昧なこともあって、大人がぼかして言っているようにも聞こえますが、He *beat* me *up*. だと「何度もたたいた」→「ボコボコにたたいた、ボカスカとたたいた」というようにやや幼い表現に感じられ、子供が発言しているようにも聞こえます。

　このように、良きにせよ悪しきにせよ、句動詞は1語の動詞よりも、具体的な意味を伝えることができます。

blow

☐ blow apart

【1】…を爆破する

A: Did the chemical reaction damage the building?（その建物は化学反応によって破壊されたの？）
B: Yes, it almost *blew* it *apart*.（ああ、ほとんど爆破されてしまった）

【2】（うそなどを）完全にあばく

A: How did you know Linda was lying?（リンダがうそをついていると、どうしてわかったの？）
B: It was easy to *blow* her lie *apart*.（彼女のうそをあばくのは簡単だった）

☐ blow away

【1】…を吹き払う

A: Is it too late to see the cherry blossoms?（お花見はもうむりかしら？）
B: I'm afraid so. The wind *blew* them *away*.（そのようだね。風が桜の花を散らしてしまった）

【2】（相手を）完全に負かす

A: I heard the Giants had an easy win.（ジャイアンツが快勝したそうね）
B: That's right. They *blew* the Yankees *away*.（ああ、ヤンキースをこてんぱんにやっつけたよ）

☐ blow down　…を吹き飛ばす

A: What happened to that sign? Where did it go?（あの看板はどうなったの？　どこに行ったの？）
B: The wind *blew* it *down*.（風で吹き飛ばされたよ）

☐ blow in　（場所に）ひょっこり姿を見せる［現わす］

A: What did you do on the weekend?（週末はどうしてたの？）
B: An old friend *blew in*, so I showed him around.（昔の友だちがひょっこりきたので、彼をあちこち案内してたよ）　⇨ SHOW AROUND

☐ blow over （危機・悩みなどが）立ち消えになる、無事におさまる

A: Are George and Linda still fighting?（ジョージとリンダはまだけんかしてる？）
B: No, that *blew over*.（いや、もう終わったよ）

☐ blow up

【1】…を爆破する（= explode）

A: What happened to the bridge?（橋はどうなったの？）
B: It was *blown up* by terrorists.（テロリストに爆破された）

【2】（風船などを）ふくらませる

A: Can I help prepare for the party?（パーティの準備を手伝おうか？）
B: Sure. Could you *blow up* those balloons?（お願いします。風船をふくらませてもらえますか？）

【3】…を誇張する、（写真などを）引き伸ばす

A: I can't believe it! Linda lied to me!（信じられない！ リンダったら、私にうそをついたのよ！）
B: It was just a small lie. Don't *blow* it *up*.（ちょっとしたことじゃないか。大騒ぎするなよ）

【4】 かっとなる

A: Why did you *blow up* at Linda?（リンダにかっとなったのはなぜ？）
B: She forgot about an appointment.（彼女が約束を忘れたからだ）

---

column ▶▶▶ blow

ご覧のとおり、blow の句動詞はさまざまな場面で用いられますが、その派生名詞もよく使われます。ここでは、blowout という名詞を紹介します。

blowout

- I got a *blowout* on my way here.（ここに来る途中でパンクした）[blowout =「パンク」]
- There was a *blowout* and the lights went out.（ヒューズがとんで、明かりが消えた）[blowout =「（ヒューズが）とぶこと」]
- The election was a *blowout*.（選挙で圧勝した）[blowout =「圧勝」]
- The workers couldn't control the *blowout*.（作業員はその［油田やガス田の］噴出を抑えられなかった）[blowout =「（油田やガス田の突然の）噴出」]

break

☐ break away 突然立ち去る

A: Where's your dog? What happened?! (あなたの犬はどこ？ どうしちゃったの？!)
B: He *broke away* from me. (逃げたんだ)

☐ break away from (慣例などと) 異なることをする

A: We always get drunk on Saturday. (土曜はいつも飲んだくれるのよね)
B: I know, but I want to *break away from* that tradition. (ああ。でもその習慣はもうやめようと思う)

☐ break down

【1】…を(打ち)壊す、解体する

A: This room is too small. (この部屋は狭すぎるわ)
B: We could *break down* this wall and make one big room. (この壁を壊せば広い部屋が1つ作れるよ)

【2】…を分解する、…に分類する

A: This is a total of all the costs. (これがすべての費用をまとめたものです)
B: Could you *break* the costs *down* into categories? (項目ごとに分けてもらえますか？)

【3】(偏見・反対などを) 打破する

A: There's a lot of xenophobia in the company. (社内には外国人を嫌っている人たちが大勢います)
B: What can we do to *break* it *down*? (偏見をなくすにはどうすればいいだろう？)

【4】取り乱す、精神的にまいる

A: What did Linda do when you told her the bad news? (悪い知らせを伝えるとリンダはどうしたの？)
B: She *broke down* and started crying. (取り乱して、泣き出した)

【5】(機械・乗物・通信網などが) 壊れる、故障する

A: I'm afraid my computer has *broken down*. (私のコンピュータ、壊れちゃったみたい)
B: Let me see if I can fix it. (修理できるかどうか見てみよう)

B

☐ break for …へ向かって走り［逃げ］出す

A: What happened when the doors opened?（入口を開けたらどうなった？）
B: The shoppers *broke for* the electronics area.（買物客が電気製品コーナーに走って行った）

☐ break in

【1】口を挟む（= interrupt）

A: Sorry for *breaking in*, but I have a question.（お話中にすみません、質問があるのですが）
B: No problem. What is it?（いいですよ。何ですか？）

【2】（動物・車・靴などを）使い慣らす

A: These new shoes are really uncomfortable.（この新しい靴、はきにくいったらありゃしない）
B: It'll take a few days to *break* them *in*.（2, 3日すれば慣れるよ）

☐ break into

【1】…に侵入する

A: While I was gone, a burglar *broke into* my house.（留守中に空き巣に入られた）
B: Oh, no! What did he steal?（そんな！ 何を盗まれた？）

【2】（汗などを）突然吹き出す

A: Do you think George is lying?（ジョージがうそをついてると思う？）
B: Yeah, when I asked him if he did it, he *broke into* a sweat.（ついてるね。おまえがやったのかと聞いたら、あいつ、どっと汗をかいてたよ）

【3】（新しい職業・分野などに）参入する

A: George wants to *break into* singing?（ジョージは歌手になりたいのかな？）
B: I think he can do it. He has a great voice.（彼ならなれると思う。すごくいい声をしているから）

☐ break off

【1】（関係・通信などを）急に断つ、終わらせる

A: Why did Linda *break off* her engagement to George?（なぜリンダはジョージとの婚約を解消したの？）
B: He lied to her.（ジョージがうそをついたからさ）

【2】…をもぎ取る、ちぎり取る

A: How can we start a fire?（火をおこすにはどうすればいい？）
B: First, we need to *break off* the branches from this dead tree.（まず、この

枯れた木から枝を取らなければいけない）

□ break out
【1】（火事・戦争・暴動・病気などが）起こる

A: Where did the fire *break out*?（どこから出火したの？）
B: It started on the third floor and spread from there.（3階から出火して広がった）

【2】（吹出物などが）突然出る、発疹する

A: Don't you like kiwi?（キウイは嫌い？）
B: I do, but when I eat it, I *break out*.（好きだけど、食べるとじんましんが出るんだ）

□ break out of [from] …から逃げ出す［脱出する］

A: Did George get released from prison?（ジョージは釈放された？）
B: No, he *broke out of* prison, so he's running from the police.（いや、脱走して、警察に追われてる）

□ break through
【1】…を突破する

A: It's been raining for five days.（5日間、雨が降りつづいています）
B: I know. I'm worried the river will *break through* the embankment.（そうだね。川の水が堤防を破るんじゃないか、心配だ）

【2】（太陽・月などが）…から現われる

A: Look! The sun is *breaking through* the clouds.（見て！ 太陽が雲のあいだから出てくるわ）
B: It's really beautiful.（とても美しいね）

【3】（困難・偏見などを）克服する

A: How can we *break through* this difficult problem?（この難問をどうやって切り抜けたらいいかしら？）
B: Let's have a brainstorming meeting.（会議でブレーンストーミングしよう）

□ break up
【1】…を粉ごなにする、ばらばらにする

A: How is this old glass recycled?（この古いガラスはどうやってリサイクルするのですか？）
B: It's *broken up* into little pieces and added to cement.（細かく砕いてからセメントに混ぜます）

【2】（群衆・会などを）解散する

A: How did the police *break up* the demonstration?（警察はどうやってデモを解散

B: They used tear gas. (催涙ガスをまいたんだ)

【3】（関係などが）終わる、解消する

A: Do you think George and Linda are going to *break up*? (ジョージとリンダは別れると思う？)
B: Maybe. They're always fighting. (たぶんね。いつもけんかばかりしているから)

【4】（人を）大いに笑わせる

A: Why was everyone laughing? (どうしてみんな笑っていたの？)
B: George's jokes *broke* us *up*. (ジョージが冗談を言ったから、ぼくたちは大笑いしたのさ)

【5】（[ラジオ・携帯電話などで]人の声が）聞き取れない

A: And then.... Because we have to... (それでそのあと…しなければならないので…)
B: I'm sorry, you're *breaking up*. Could you say that again? (申し訳ございません。お電話が遠いようです。もう一度繰り返していただけますでしょうか？)

---

column ▶▶▶ break

break の句動詞は、1語となり名詞として使われることが多いようです。その代表的なものを例文とともに挙げてみましょう。

- There was a *breakdown* in negotiations. (交渉は決裂した) [bereakdown =「（制度・事業などの）崩壊、破綻、失敗」]
- She had a nervous *breakdown*. (彼女は神経衰弱だった) [breakdown =「悪化、衰弱、（特に）神経衰弱」]
- My car had a *breakdown*. (車が故障した) [breakdown =「故障、機能停止」]
- This is a *breakdown* of the total price. (これが総取引額の明細です) [breakdown =「明細、分析」]
- What caused the *breakup* of their marriage? (何が原因で彼らは結婚生活を解消したのか？) [breakup =「別離、解消、絶縁、崩壊」]
- There was a *break-in* in my neighborhood last week. (先週、近所で窃盗があった) [break-in =「窃盗、不法侵入、押し入り」]
- The prison guards couldn't stop the *breakout*. (看守は脱獄を防ぐことができなかった) [breakout =「脱獄、（包囲網からの）強行突破」]
- The vaccine couldn't stop the *breakout*. (そのワクチンは発疹を押さえられなかった) [breakout =「発疹、吹出物」]
- She made a big *breakthrough* in biology. (彼女は生物学で重大な発見をした) [breakthrough =「重大な発見、大きな進歩、躍進」]

いずれも突発的なニュアンスがあり、ややネガティブな意味合いで使われることが多いのが特徴です。

bring

☐ bring about （変化・事故などを）引き起こす、もたらす
A: It seems like the staff lacks motivation. （スタッフはやる気がないみたい）
B: How can we *bring about* a change? （どうすれば、意識を変えられるだろうか？）

☐ bring along …を連れて［持って］くる (= take)
A: Do you mind if I *bring along* one of my coworkers? （同僚を1人、連れていってもいいですか？）
B: Not at all. Bring as many people as you'd like. （もちろん。お好きなだけ何人でもご一緒にどうぞ）

☐ bring around 考えを…へ変えさせる、説得する (= persuade)
A: How can we convince Linda that we're right? （私たちが正しいって、リンダを説得するにはどうすればいいの？）
B: Maybe these statistics will *bring* her *around*. （この統計データを見れば、彼女も納得するだろう）

☐ bring back
【1】（元へ）返す、返却する
A: Do you mind if I take this book home? （この本を家に持ち帰ってもいい？）
B: No, not at all. But make sure you *bring* it *back*. （いいけど、必ず返してね）

【2】（物事が）…を思い出させる (= remind)
A: Look at this photo of us in high school. （高校時代の私たちの写真を見てよ）
B: That *brings back* a lot of memories. （いろんなことを思い出すなあ）

☐ bring down
【1】（人・政府などを）打ち倒す、崩壊させる
A: How did the rebels *bring down* the government? （反対派はどうやって政府を倒したの？）
B: They kidnapped the president. （大統領を誘拐したんだ）

B

【2】…を下へ持ってくる、降ろす

A: Could you go up to my room on the third floor and *bring down* the green file?（3階の私の部屋に上がって、緑色のファイルを持ってきてもらえますか？）　⇨ GO UP TO ［2］
B: Okay, I'll be right back.（いいですよ、すぐに戻ります）

【3】（物価・温度などを）下げる、（人に）値引きさせる

A: How can we get ABC to *bring down* their prices?（ABC社に値引きさせるにはどうしたらいい？）
B: We could offer to buy in bulk.（大量に購入したいと提案できるかもしれない）

【4】（人を）がっかりさせる

A: Why does everyone look disappointed?（みんな、なぜ浮かない顔をしてるの？）
B: The bonus cuts *brought* everyone *down*.（ボーナスカットでみんながっかりしてるのさ）

□ bring in

【1】（収入・利益・利子などを）生む、（人が）稼ぐ（= earn）

A: How much does this branch *bring in* annually?（この支店の年間の売上高は？）
B: It has about 12 million dollars in sales.（約1200万ドルです）

【2】（法律・改革［改革案］などを）導入する、取り入れる（= usher）

A: The current accounting system isn't working.（現行の会計システムが機能していないわ）
B: Should we *bring in* a new system?（新しいシステムを取り入れるほうがいいかな？）

【3】（外部の人を）…に参加させる

A: We don't have the skills to solve this problem.（私たちには、この問題を解決するスキルがない）
B: Why don't we *bring in* a consultant?（コンサルタントにきてもらおうか？）

□ bring on [upon]

【1】（病気・災害などを）引き起こす（= cause）

A: You look like you have a bad cold.（ひどい風邪みたいね）
B: Walking in the rain *brought* it *on*.（雨の中を歩いたせいだ）

【2】…に（災いなどを）招く、もたらす

A: I don't know why I got fired.（クビになった理由がわからない）
B: You *brought* it *on* yourself. You always did as little as possible.（自業自得だよ。きみはいつも最低限のことしかしなかったから）

☐ bring out

【1】…を世間に出す、リリース［出版］する (= produce, publish)

A: When are you going to *bring out* your new camera?（御社の新型カメラの発売はいつですか？）

B: We're going to introduce it next month.（来月発表予定です）

【2】（性質・意味などを）明らかにする、はっきり示す

A: Did you read the consultant's report?（コンサルタントの報告書を読んだ？）

B: Yes, it *brings out* the importance of cutting our costs.（うん、費用削減の重要性がはっきり書かれている）

☐ bring through …に（困難などを）切り抜けさせる

A: How did George get through this huge problem?（どうやってジョージはこの大問題を切り抜けたの？） ⇨ GET THROUGH ［5］

B: The love from his family *brought* him *through*.（家族からの愛情が彼を救ったんだ）

☐ bring to

【1】…を正気づかせる

A: George got drunk and now he's passed out on the floor.（ジョージは酔っぱらって床の上で酔いつぶれているわ） ⇨ PASS OUT ［2］

B: Throw some water on him. That'll *bring* him *to*.（水をかけてやれ。目が覚めるさ）

【2】（勘定などを）合計…にする

A: Oh, one more thing. I'd like to get this gum.（あ、これも。このガムもいただくわ）

B: Okay, that *brings* the total *to* 12 dollars and 45 cents.（では、あわせて12ドル45セントになります）

☐ bring together …を（引き）あわせる、一緒にする

A: How did your parents meet and fall in love?（ご両親はどんなふうに出会って恋におちたの？）

B: A mutual friend *brought* them *together*.（共通の友人が2人を引きあわせたんだ）

☐ bring up （子供を）育てる、しつける (= raise)

A: I've never heard Linda gossip about anyone.（リンダが他人の噂話をするのを聞いたことがない）

B: She said her parents *brought* her *up* not to gossip.（噂話をしないように両親からしつけられたって、リンダが言ってたよ）

build

□ build on （成果などを）基に事を進める

A: Are you going to start a new company? (新しい会社を始めるつもり？)
B: No, my parents have a company, so I'm going to *build on* that. (いや、両親の会社を大きくしようと思う)

□ build up

【1】（次第に）増す、（兵力などを）増強する

A: Why is your country *building up* your military forces? (なぜ、あなたの国では軍備を増強しているの？)
B: We're worried that neighboring countries will attack us. (近隣諸国から攻撃されるのではないかと、われわれは心配している)

【2】（事業・富・信頼などを［徐々に］）築き上げる

A: How can we increase our sales? (どうすれば売り上げを増やせる？)
B: We just need to *build up* our reputation little by little. (少しずつ信用を積み上げていくしかない)

【3】…をもてはやす、宣伝して…にする (build up into)

A: You're going to be a big star someday. (あなたはいつかきっと大スターになるわ)
B: I don't want to be *built up* into someone special. I'm a regular person. (もてはやされて特別な人物になりたいとは思わない。ぼくは平凡な人間さ)

【4】（場所を）建物で囲む、建て込ませる

A: Do you think the lake will flood? (その湖は氾濫すると思う？)
B: That'll be horrible. The area around it has been *built up*. (それは困る。あのあたりは家が建て込んでいるからね)

【5】（交通が）渋滞する

A: Do you want to go by train or car? (電車で行くつもり？ それとも車？)
B: The traffic is *building up*, so the train might be faster. (車は渋滞してるから、電車のほうが早いだろう)

buy

☐ buy back …を買い戻す

A: Linda sold her wedding dress, but now she wants to *buy* it *back*. (リンダはウエディングドレスを売ったけど、買い戻したいんですって)

B: She shouldn't have sold it in the first place. (そもそも売るべきじゃなかったんだ)

☐ buy into

【1】(会社の) 株を買う、…に参入する

A: Are you thinking about *buying into* Linda's company? (リンダの会社を買収するつもりなの？)

B: I'm thinking about it. She's probably going to be successful. (そのつもりさ。彼女は成功するだろう)

【2】(考えなどを) 受け入れる、信じる

A: Do you *buy into* George's proposal? (ジョージの提案を受け入れる？)

B: No, I don't. I don't think it's feasible. (いや、彼の提案はうまくいきそうにない)

☐ buy off …を買収する、金で丸め込む (= bribe)

A: I'm surprised that George didn't get arrested. (ジョージが逮捕されなかったのは驚きだわ)

B: I know. I think he *bought off* the police. (そうだね。警察を買収したんだろう)

☐ buy out (企業などを) 買い取る、…から株や権利を買い取る

A: We're ten times bigger than ABC, but they're causing a lot of headaches for us. (うちの会社は ABC 社よりずっと大きいけど、あの会社は頭痛の種ね)

B: Why don't we just *buy* them *out*? (買収すればいいんじゃないか？)

☐ buy up (土地・商品などを) 買い占める、(会社を) 買い取る (= corner)

A: Why do you think land prices are going up so quickly around here? (このあたりでこんなに地価が急騰しているのはなぜだと思う？) ⇨ GO UP [1]

B: ABC is trying to *buy up* all the land for a shopping mall. (ABC 社がショッピングモールを建てるために、このあたりを全部買い占めようとしているんだ)

call

□ call about …のことで電話する

A: Hello. How may I help you?（こんにちは。ご用件は何でしょうか？）
B: I'm *calling about* your advertisement in the newspaper.（御社の新聞広告の件でお電話したのですが）

□ call back （電話をくれた人に）あとから［折り返し］電話する

A: I'm afraid George isn't here. Would you like to leave a message?（申し訳ありません、ジョージは席を離れております。ご伝言を承ります）
B: Could you ask him to *call* me *back*?（折り返し電話してくれるようにお願いできますか？）

□ call for

【1】 …を求めて叫ぶ、電話で呼ぶ

A: This man is badly injured. Someone, *call for* help!（この男性は大けがをしています。誰か、電話で助けを呼んで！）
B: I already called the ambulance.（もう救急車を呼んであります）

【2】 …を要求する、必要とする（= require）

A: A really big storm is going to hit this area tonight.（今夜、激しい暴風雨がこの地域を直撃する見込みです）
B: I guess that *calls for* caution.（警戒が必要だな）

【3】 （天候に関して）…を予想［予報］する

A: It's really cold today, isn't it?（今日はものすごく寒いわね）
B: Yeah, the weather forecast *calls for* snow tonight.（ああ、今夜は雪の予報が出ている）

□ call off （約束・命令などを）取り消す、取りやめる、中止する（= cancel）

A: Do you know why the meeting was *called off*?（なぜ会議が中止になったか知ってる？）
B: I think it's because George can't come.（ジョージがこられなかったからだと思う）

☐ call out …を大声で呼ぶ［言う］、（名前などを）読み上げる

A: If the teacher *calls out* your name, you have to stand up. (先生から名前を呼ばれたら、起立しなければいけません) ⇨ STAND UP [1]

B: I hope he doesn't call on me. (呼ばれなければいいのに)

☐ call over …を呼び寄せる

A: I can't get this printer to work. (このプリンタ、使えない)

B: Let's *call over* Linda. She knows how to fix it. (リンダを呼ぼう。彼女なら修理の仕方がわかる)

☐ call up …に電話する (= telephone)

A: Let's *call up* the computer company and ask for help. (コンピュータ会社に電話して、問い合わせよう) ⇨ ASK FOR [1]

B: Do they have a customer service number? (カスタマーサービスは、電話でサポートしてくれるかな？)

---

column ▶▶▶ 句動詞にも自動詞と他動詞がある

ご存じのとおり、動詞には自動詞の用法と他動詞の用法があります。そしてそれは句動詞でも同じです。

たとえば、句動詞 get up を考えてみましょう。自動詞では、62 ページで紹介するように、「起床する、起きる」の意味で使われます。

・Sam *got up* early this morning. (サムは今朝は早く起きた)

そして他動詞では、「(人を) 起床させる」の意味で使われます。

・Would you *get* Sam *up* at 6:00 tomorrow? (明日サムを 6 時に起こしてもらえますか？)

hold out はどうでしょうか？ 84 ページで紹介するとおり、こちらも両方の使い方があり、それぞれ意味が異なります。自動詞では、「(食糧などが) もつ、つづく」の意味で使われることがあります。

・Our food will hold out until May. (食糧は 5 月までもつだろう)

他動詞では、「(希望・見込みなどを) 持たせる、与える」の意味で用いられることがあります。

・The parents are holding out faint hope that their son is still alive. (息子はまだ生きているかもしれないと、両親ははかない望みを抱いている)

「句動詞だけでも膨大にあるのに、さらに自動詞と他動詞の用法で意味も違うの？」と驚かれる人もいることでしょうが、これは怠け者（？）のわれわれネイティブが、「簡単な表現だからこそあらゆる場面で使おうとする」ことが原因かもしれません。

日本人の英語学習者のみなさんには、大変なご苦労をおかけしますが、「状況をよく判断」した上で、「目的語があるかないかに注目」し、信頼できる辞書で 1 つひとつ確認していただけたらと思います。

carry

☐ carry around [about] （傘などを）持ち歩く

A: Why don't you have an umbrella?（どうして傘を持ってないの？）
B: Whenever I *carry* one *around*, I lose it.（持ち歩くといつもなくすんだ）

☐ carry away 夢中にさせる、我を忘れさせる

A: George always makes a fool of himself at parties.（ジョージはパーティではいつもおちゃらける）
B: I know, he gets *carried away* and starts singing and dancing.（そう、夢中になって、歌ったり踊ったりし始めるんだよね）

☐ carry back …を元の所に戻す、連れ戻す

A: Are you going to go home from here?（ここから家に帰るつもり？）
B: No, I have to *carry* this box *back* to the office.（いや、この箱を会社に戻さないといけない）

☐ carry off

【1】…を奪い［連れ］去る

A: What happened to your sign? Did someone *carry* it *off*?（おたくの看板どうしたの？ 誰かが持って行ったの？）
B: Yeah, it got stolen last night.（うん、昨日の夜、盗まれちゃって）

【2】（行為・役・義務などを）うまくやってのける

A: Linda is going to be the head of the legal department.（リンダが法務部長になる予定よ）
B: Can she *carry* it *off*? She has no legal experience.（彼女に務まるのかな？ 法務畑の経験はないんだぜ）

☐ carry on

【1】つづける（= continue）

A: Did everyone leave at 6:00 yesterday?（昨日はみんな6時に退社した？）
B: No, Linda *carried on* until around 10:00.（いや、リンダは10時頃まで残業していた）

【2】（泣いたりわめいたりして）騒ぎ立てる

A: I can't believe it! Someone took my pen! (信じられない！ 誰かが私のペンを持って行ったなんて！)
B: Stop *carrying on*. It's just a pen. (大騒ぎするなよ。たかがペンじゃないか)

□ carry out （約束・計画・命令などを）実行する (= achieve)

A: On paper, this plan looks good, but do you think we can *carry* it *out*? (書類上では、この企画はとてもよさそうですが、実行できると思われますか？)
B: Yes, I don't think it'll be hard at all. (できると思います。実行困難とはまったく思いません)

□ carry through （目的・計画を）達成する (carry through with [on])

A: Do you think I should give up? (あきらめるほうがいいかしら？)
B: No, I think you should *carry through* with your plan. (そんなことはない。きみの計画を達成すべきだと思う)

catch

□ catch on
【1】わかってくる、理解する (= understand)

A: How are you doing in your math class? (数学の授業はどう？)
B: It was hard at first, but I'm starting to *catch on*. (最初はむずかしかったけど、だんだんわかってきました)

【2】人気を博する

A: Why do you think this phone is selling so well? (この電話がこんなに売れているのはなぜだと思う？)
B: It *caught on* with teenagers. (10代に受けているんだ)

□ catch up …に追いつく (catch up with, get caught up)

A: George already left for the train station. (ジョージはもう駅に向かいました)
B: Okay, I'll hurry and *catch up* with him. (わかった、急いで彼に追いつくよ)

check

☐ check in （人に）連絡する、知らせる (check in with)

A: Why do you need to call your office on your day off?（どうして休暇中も会社に電話しないといけないの？）
B: I have to *check in* with my boss once a day.（1日1回、上司に連絡しないといけないんだ）

☐ check into （問題などを）調べる

A: It seems like one of the printers isn't working.（プリンタの1台が動かないようです）
B: Could you *check into* that?（原因を調べてもらえますか？）

☐ check on （問題がないか）…の様子を見る、…を調べる (= investigate)

A: Is the air conditioner still on?（エアコンはまだついてる？）
B: I think I turned it off, but I'll *check on* it.（消したはずだけど、見てみるよ）
⇨ TURN OFF [1]

☐ check out （情報が調査の結果）正確であると確認される

A: Do you think we can trust the government reports?（政府の報告書は信じられるかしら？）
B: No, I don't. They don't *check out*.（信じられない。情報が正確かどうか、当局は確認しないからね）

☐ check over …を調べる、点検する、検査する

A: I haven't been feeling very well for the last few weeks.（この数週間、体調があまりよくありません）
B: You need to go to the hospital and have them *check* you *over*.（病院で検査を受けるべきだ）

☐ check with （確認のために）…にたずねる、許可を求める

A: Can you sign this contract today?（本日、この契約書にご署名いただけますか？）
B: No, I need to *check with* my boss first.（いいえ、まず上司の許可が必要なので）

clean

☐ clean out

【1】…の中を（すっかり）きれいにする、…を一掃する

A: I'm going to move, so I have to *clean out* my room. (引っ越そうと思うので、自分の部屋をきれいにしないと)

B: Do you have a lot of things? (持ち物がたくさんあるの？)

【2】…からごっそり盗み出す

A: Did the robbers take everything in your store? (泥棒はあなたの店のものを全部持っていったの？)

B: Yes, they *cleaned* me *out*. I have nothing left. (ああ、ごっそり盗られた。もう何も残ってない)

☐ clean up

【1】…をきれいに（掃除）する

A: Why do we have to *clean up* the factory today? (なぜ今日、工場の清掃をしなくちゃいけないの？)

B: An inspector is coming tomorrow. (検査官が明日くるからだ)

【2】大儲けする

A: Why does Linda have so much money? (リンダがあんなにお金持ちなのはどうして？)

B: She bought a few stocks and really *cleaned up*. (株を買って大儲けしたんだ)

---

column ▶▶▶ clean

I *cleaned* my room. と I *cleaned up* my room. の違いは何でしょうか？

数人のネイティブに聞いたところ、さまざまな答えがありました。「意味はほとんど同じ」という人もあれば、I *cleaned up* my room. は「物を片づける」ニュアンスが、I *cleaned* my room. は「殺菌する」ニュアンスが強いように感じるという人もいました。

この2つの違いに明確な定義はありませんが、「部屋を掃除をした」と表現する際、ネイティブは I *cleaned up* my room. を好んで使う傾向があります。これは副詞の up に「すっかり…し尽くす」というニュアンスがあり、I *cleaned* my room. では何かもの足りなく感じるためだと考えられます。

clear

☐ clear away …を片づける、一掃する、取り除く

A: Where are you going to plant your vegetables?（野菜ははどこに植えるつもり？）
B: Right here, so I have to *clear away* all these rocks.（ここに植えるから、この石を全部どけないと）

☐ clear off （食卓などから）物を片づける

A: Can we use the kitchen table to play cards?（キッチンテーブルでトランプしてもいい？）
B: Okay, let me *clear* it *off*.（いいよ、テーブルの上を片づけるね）

☐ clear up

【1】（空が）晴れ上がる

A: Do you think it's going to keep raining this afternoon?（午後も雨が降りつづけるかしら？）
B: No, I'm pretty sure it's going to *clear up*.（いや、きっと晴れるよ）

【2】（病気が）治る、吹出物が取れる

A: Do you still have a rash?（まだ吹出物が出てる？）
B: No, I changed my diet, and it *cleared up*.（いや、食生活を変えたら、出なくなった）

【3】（問題などを）解決する、解く、…をはっきりさせる

A: Were you able to *clear up* the accounting problem?（経理の問題は解決できた？）
B: Yes, I talked with George, and everything's fixed now.（うん、ジョージと話してもう全部解決したよ）

☐ clear with （上司・本部などに）…を認可[承認]してもらう

A: Why don't we just buy a new computer?（新しいコンピュータを買いましょう）
B: We have to *clear* it *with* the headquarters.（本社の許可をもらわないと）

close

☐ close down

【1】(店・工場などが) 閉鎖される

A: Do you still work at the clock factory? (今も時計工場で働いてるの?)
B: No, they *closed down*, so I'm looking for a job now. (いや、工場は閉鎖したから、仕事を探してるんだ)

【2】(ソフトなどを) 終了する

A: Why is my computer so slow? (どうして私のパソコンは動きが遅いのかな?)
B: If you *close down* some of the applications, it'll help. (ソフトをいくつか終了すれば、速くなるよ)

☐ close off (道路などを) 閉鎖[遮断]する

A: Do you know why the road is *closed off*? (道路が閉鎖されているのはなぜ?)
B: A mudslide took out the road up ahead. (先のほうで土砂崩れがあったんだ)

☐ close up (店などが) 閉まる、(店などを) 閉める

A: What time does that Italian restaurant *close up*? (あのイタリア料理店は何時に閉まる?)
B: They're open 24 hours a day. (あそこは24時間営業だ)

☐ close with (会・映画・手紙などが) …で終わる

A: How did the meeting end today? (今日の会議、最後はどうだった?)
B: It *closed with* an announcement about the budget. (予算案の報告で終わった)

come

□ come across …に出会う、…に出くわす、…をふと見つける

A: That looks like a really nice jacket. (すごくすてきなジャケットね)
B: I *came across* it at a yard sale yesterday. (昨日ガレージセールで見つけたんだ)

□ come across as (相手に)…(である)という印象を与える

A: What did you think about George? (ジョージのこと、どう思った？) ⇨ THINK ABOUT
B: I only spoke to him for a few minutes, but he *came across as* a nice guy. (ほんの数分しか話してないけど、好青年みたいだった) ⇨ SPEAK TO [1]

□ come after
【1】 …につづく

A: What *comes after* Linda's presentation? (リンダのプレゼンのあとは？)
B: We're going to have a Q&A session. (質疑応答になります)

【2】 …のあとからくる

A: Is George going to go with you to the factory? (ジョージはあなたと一緒に工場に行くの？)
B: No, I'm leaving at 10:00, and he's going to *come after* me. (いや、ぼくは10時に出る。ジョージはあとからくる予定だ)

□ come along
【1】 一緒にくる［行く］

A: Is Linda going to *come along* with you? (リンダはあなたと一緒にくる？)
B: No, I'm afraid she's too busy. (いや、残念ながら彼女はすごく忙しくてね)

【2】 (健康が)よくなる (= progress)

A: How's George *coming along*? Is he doing better? (ジョージの調子はどう？ 具合はよくなったかな？)
B: Yes, he's going to check out of the hospital tomorrow. (うん、明日、退院する予定だ)

□ come around

【1】（人が）回ってくる

A: How often does the security guard *come around*?（警備員はどれくらい回ってくる？）
B: He walks around the factory once an hour.（工場を巡回するのは1時間に1度だ）

【2】（相手の考えなどに）同調［同意］する（= agree）

A: Does Linda still disagree with your plan?（リンダはまだあなたの案に反対なの？）
B: Well, I talked to her yesterday and she's *coming around*.（いや、昨日話をしたら、賛成してくれた）

【3】意識を取り戻す、元気になる

A: I heard that George got knocked out.（ジョージがノックアウトされたって？）
B: Yeah, but it only took him a few seconds to *come around*.（うん、でも瞬時に立ち直った）

□ come at …に襲いかかる

A: What did you do when the dog *came at* you?（犬が襲いかかってきた時どうした？）
B: I climbed up a tree to get away from it.（木に登って逃げた）　⇨ GET AWAY［1］

□ come away （ある感情・印象などをいだいて）去る（come away with）

A: How was ABC's exhibition at the trade fair?（見本市でABC社の展示はどうでしたか？）
B: I *came away* with a really good impression of their products.（あの会社の製品はとてもいいと思って帰ってきました）

□ come back

【1】戻ってくる（= return）

A: Are you planning on *coming back* to the office?（会社に戻ってくる予定ですか？）
B: No, I think I'll go straight home.（いいえ、直帰するつもりです）

【2】復活する、再び流行する

A: Do you think miniskirts will ever *come back*?（またミニスカートがはやると思う？）
B: I'm sure they'll be popular in a few years.（ここ数年で、絶対はやるね）

【3】（話題などに）戻る（come back to）

A: We need to talk about the new campaign some more.（新しいキャンペーンについてもう少し話し合う必要があります）
B: Let's *come back* to that in the afternoon meeting.（午後の会議でまたその話をしましょう）

☐ come before

【1】…の前に現れる、…に先立つ

A: Mozart *came before* Bach, didn't he?（モーツァルトはバッハよりも年上よね？）

B: No, Mozart was born five years after Bach died.（違うよ、モーツァルトはバッハが死んでから5年後に生まれたんだ）

【2】…の上位にある、…より重要である

A: We have to increase production. I don't care what we do.（生産高を上げなくては。手段は問わないわ）

B: Well, I think safety *comes before* making money.（そうでしょうか。金儲けより安全第一だと思いますが）

☐ come between …のあいだに割り込む、…の仲を裂く

A: I heard that George and Linda are no longer friends.（ジョージとリンダは絶交したそうよ）

B: Really? I wonder what *came between* them?（ほんとに？ 何が2人の仲を引き裂いたのかな？）

☐ come by

【1】…に立ち寄る (= pass)

A: Why don't you *come by* my house tonight and we can play cards?（今夜うちに寄って、一緒にトランプしようよ）

B: Okay, that sounds like a lot of fun.（うん、すごくおもしろそうだね）

【2】…を手に入れる (= get)

A: Where did you *come by* that old camera?（あの古いカメラ、どこで手に入れたの？）

B: My grandfather gave it to me.（祖父がくれたんだ）

☐ come down

【1】(建物などが) 倒れる、崩れる、倒壊する (= fall)

A: Why do you think the building *came down*?（ビルが倒れたのはなぜ？）

B: The columns weren't strong enough to hold it up.（柱が弱くて支えきれなかったんだ）⇨ HOLD UP [1]

【2】(値段・温度・評価などが) 下がる

A: Do you think I should buy gold right now?（今すぐ金を買うべきかしら？）

B: No, why don't you wait until the price *comes down* a little?（いや、もう少し値が下がるまで待つほうがいい）

【3】（北から）南にくる、（都会から）田舎にくる

A: My friend is *coming down* from Hokkaido next week. （友人が来週北海道からやってきます）

B: Are you going to show him around Tokyo? （東京を案内してあげるの？）
⇨ SHOW AROUND

☐ come down with （病気に）かかる

A: I heard that Linda called in sick. （リンダから、体調が悪いので休むと電話があったそうですね）

B: Yeah, she said she *came down with* the flu. （そう、インフルエンザにかかったと言ってました）

☐ come for

【1】…を取りにくる、迎えにくる

A: By when do I need to box up these parts? （何時までにこの部品を箱に詰めておけばいいでしょう？）

B: The shipping company is going to *come for* them at 3:30. （運送業者は3時半に取りにくる予定です）

【2】…に迫る、襲いかかる、…を連行にくる

A: I think I can hear a police siren. They're *coming for* you. （パトカーのサイレンみたい。あなたを捕まえにくるわ）

B: Oh, no! I have to get out of here! （まずいな！ ここから逃げないと！）
⇨ GET OUT OF ［4］

☐ come forward （問題などが）会議に出される

A: Did you take care of all the problems at the meeting? （会議ですべての問題を扱ったのですか？）

B: Yeah, but some new problems *came forward*. （はい、ただ新たな問題もいくつか出されました）

☐ come from （音などが）…からしてくる、…に由来する

A: Where is that strange noise *coming from*? （あの変な音、どこから出てるの？）

B: I think one of the motors in the factory is having problems. （工場のモーターの1つに問題があるようだ）

☐ come from behind （試合で）逆転する

A: I guess the Giants lost again. （ジャイアンツがまた負けたんでしょ）

B: No, they *came from behind* in the final minutes and won! （いや、最後に逆転して勝った！）

□ come in

【1】到着する、(商品が) 入荷する

A: Are you still sold out of coffee mugs? (マグカップはまだ在庫切れ？) ⇨ SELL OUT OF
B: Yes, but we have some new ones *coming in* tomorrow. (はい、でも明日には新しいものを入荷します)

【2】収入として入る

A: How much do we have *coming in* next week? (来週いくらお金が入るかな？)
B: Our sales will probably reach up around 50,000 dollars. (売り上げはたぶん5万ドルくらいになるだろう)

【3】(仲間として) 加わる、(計画などに) 参加する (= join)

A: We need someone who's up on computers for this project. (このプロジェクトでは、コンピュータに詳しい人材が必要です)
B: Maybe we should get George to *come in* on this. (ジョージに参加してもらうといいだろう)

□ come into

【1】(頭などに) 浮かぶ

A: Why did you turn down ABC's offer? (どうして ABC 社の申し出を断ったのですか？) ⇨ TURN DOWN [2]
B: Something *came into* my mind at the last minute. (土壇場になって、あることが思い浮かんだもので)

【2】(財産などを) 受け継ぐ、…を手に入れる (= inherit)

A: It seems like Linda is throwing money around like crazy. (リンダはむちゃくちゃ浪費しまくっているみたい) ⇨ THROW AROUND [ABOUT]
B: Well, her rich uncle died and she *came into* a lot of money. (うん、金持ちのおじさんが亡くなって、大金を手に入れたんだよ)

□ come of …に生じる、起こる

A: Do you know what *came of* George? I haven't seen him in a long time. (ジョージに何があったかご存じ？　もうずっと彼とはご無沙汰だわ)
B: I heard he moved away a few months ago. (数カ月前に引っ越したそうだ)

□ come off

【1】(ボタンなどが) …から取れる

A: Oh, no! A button *came off* my sweater. (あらやだ！　セーターのボタンが取れてる)
B: Let me sew it back on for you. (付け直してあげるよ)

【2】（うまく）切り抜ける、[副詞をともなって] 結果が…となる

A: How was the seminar? Did everything work out?（セミナーはどうだった？ 万事オーケーだった？）
B: Yeah, it *came off* really well.（ああ、すべてとてもうまくいった）

【3】…と思われる（come off as）

A: What was your impression of Linda? Do you think she'll be easy to work with?（リンダの印象はいかが？ 一緒に仕事をしやすいと思う？）
B: Well, she *came off* as kind of stubborn.（なんていうか、ちょっと頑固な感じでした）

□ come on

【1】[命令文で] おいおい、まさか、そんな、いいかげんにしろ

A: Do you mind if I take off a little early today?（今日、少し早めに帰ってもいいですか？）
B: *Come on*! You've been leaving early almost every day.（おいおい！ ほぼ毎日早退してるじゃないか）

【2】放映される、上演[上映]される

A: Do you have time to come over and watch the Olympics tonight?（今夜うちにきて、オリンピックをテレビで見る時間はある？）　⇨ COME OVER [1]
B: What time do they *come on*?（何時からやるの？）

【3】（電灯・テレビ・ラジオなどが）つく

A: Why did the radio suddenly *come on*?（ラジオが突然鳴ったのはなぜ？）
B: I had the alarm set to go off at noon.（お昼になったら鳴るようにアラームをセットしておいたんだ）

【4】[交替して] 出場する

A: I heard that you got kicked off the field.（あなた、ピッチから出されたんですってね）
B: Yeah, but George *came on* for me.（うん、でもジョージが代わりに出てくれたよ）

□ come out

【1】（製品などが）世に出る

A: Do you know when this camera *came out*?（このカメラ、いつ発売されたか知ってる？）
B: Yeah, it went on sale in June.（うん、6月に発売されたよ）

【2】（しみ・色などが）消える、あせる

A: Sorry! I spilled coffee all over your tablecloth.（ごめんなさい！ テーブルクロスにコーヒーをこぼしちゃった）
B: Don't worry. It'll easily *come out*.（気にしないで。しみはすぐに取れるから）

【3】（花が）咲く、（芽が）出る

A: When do you think the cherry blossoms will *come out*?（桜はいつ咲くと思う？）
B: They usually start to peak out in late March.（いつも3月下旬に満開になる）

【4】結果［順位］が…となる

A: How did your presentation *come out*?（あなたのプレゼンはどうでしたか？）
B: Really good. I picked up a lot of support.（大成功でした。多くの支援を得ました）

come out against …に反対を表明する

A: Why did you *come out against* my suggestion?（なぜ私の提案に反対したの？）
B: I didn't think it would work out.（きみの案はうまくいくとは思えなかったんだ）

come (right) out and say [ask] …と公然と［あからさまに］言う

A: How are you going to get George to back down?（どうやってジョージに手を引かせるつもり？） ⇨ BACK DOWN
B: I'm going to *come out and say* he's making a big mistake.（きみは大きなミスをおかそうとしている、とジョージにはっきり言ってやるよ）

come out in …という状態で出てくる

A: What's wrong with the printer?（プリンタ、どこか悪いの？）
B: Everything I print *comes out in* green.（印刷すると、みんな緑色で出てくるんだ）

come out of （しみ・色などが）…から消える

A: Do you think this stain will *come out of* my shirt?（私のシャツのしみ、取れるかな？）
B: Why don't you drop it off at the cleaners?（クリーニング屋に持っていってみれば？）

come out with

【1】（新製品などを）公表する

A: How do you know ABC is going to *come out with* a new camera?（ABC社が新型カメラを出す予定だって、どうして知ってるの？）
B: I read about it on the Internet.（インターネットでその情報を得たんだ）

【2】（事実などを）すっぱ抜く、（秘密を）漏らす

A: How did the public find out about the scandal?（みんな、どうやってそのスキャンダルに気づいたの？）
B: A newspaper *came out with* the story.（新聞が暴露記事を掲載したんだ）

☐ come over

【1】（ぶらりと）訪問する

A: Do you want to *come over* and watch a movie on TV?（うちに寄ってテレビで映画を見ない？）

B: I wish I could, but I have to finish up some chores.（そうしたいけど、家事を終わらせないと）

【2】（…の）側につく、（相手の考えなどに）同調する

A: Why don't you talk to Linda and get her to *come over* to our side?（リンダに話をして、私たちの味方になってもらえないかな？）

B: OK, I'll bring her around.（わかった、彼女を説得してみるよ） ⇨ BRING AROUND

☐ come through （ビザなどが）おりる

A: When do you think your passport will *come through*?（いつパスポートをもらえると思う？）

B: I'm hoping it'll arrive in the mail any day now.（数日中に郵送されると思うよ）

☐ come to

【1】…に達する、…になる

A: I heard that George got forced out of the company.（ジョージは会社を辞めさせられたそうよ）

B: Oh, really? I didn't think it would *come to* that.（ほんと？ そんなことになるとは思わなかった）

【2】（突然）…の心に浮かぶ

A: How did you come up with the idea for your novel?（小説のアイデアはどうやって浮かんだのですか？） ⇨ COME UP WITH

B: It just *came to* me when I was in the bathtub.（湯船につかっていたら浮かびました）

☐ come together （最終的に）合意に達する

A: It seems like everyone was fighting over everything in the meeting.（みんな会議では、どの議題でも言い争っていたみたいね） ⇨ FIGHT OVER

B: Yeah, but we all *came together* at the end.（ああ、でも最終的には誰もが合意したよ）

☐ come up against （困難・反対などに）遭う

A: Why did you pull out of the joint venture?（合弁事業から撤退したのはなぜ？） ⇨ PULL OUT OF

B: We *came up against* a lot of problems.（多くの問題にぶちあたったんだ）

C

☐ come up in the world　出世する

A: Linda really has *come up in the world*, hasn't she?（ほんとにリンダは出世したわよね）
B: Yeah, for sure. She's known around the world.（ああ、そうだね。彼女は世界的に有名になった）

☐ come up to　…まで達する

A: Do you think the water will *come up to* here at high tide?（満潮になったら水はここまで達すると思う？）
B: I'm sure it will. We'd better move back.（そうなるだろう。退避したほうがいいね）

☐ come up with　（解決策などを）考え出す、見つける

A: We need to *come up with* a way to fix this problem.（この問題の解決策を考えなければ）
B: OK, I'll talk it over with the engineers.（了解、エンジニアと話し合ってみます）
⇨ TALK OVER

☐ come with　…にともなって生じる

A: When I become the team leader, do I have to fill out all of these reports?（チームリーダーになったら、ここにある報告書を全部書き込まないといけないんですか？）
⇨ FILL OUT
B: I'm afraid so. It *comes with* the job.（そうです。それも仕事のうちです）

count

☐ count down 秒読みする、(残りの日数などを) 数えながら待ちわびる

A: Do you still have a long time before the new product launch? (新製品の発売まで、まだしばらくあるの？)
B: Not really. We've already started to *count down* the days. (いや、すでに秒読み段階にある)

☐ count for much 非常に重要である、物を言う

A: Will it help increase our sales if we change our logo? (会社のロゴを変えたら売り上げアップにつながるでしょうか？)
B: No, I don't think that will *count for much*. (ならないでしょう。ロゴを変えてもあまり効果はないと思います)

☐ count on [upon]

【1】…をあてにする、頼りにする、期待する (= depend)

A: Should we ask Linda to help us with the presentation? (リンダにプレゼンを手伝ってもらうほうがいいでしょうか？)
B: I think we should. We can *count on* her. (それがいいでしょう。リンダは頼りになります)

【2】…を予想する

A: Do you think it's going to rain tomorrow? (明日、雨になるかな？)
B: Yeah, it's the rainy season, so you can *count on* it. (うん、梅雨時だからね、降ると思って間違いないだろう)

☐ count up …の (全体の) 数を数え上げる

A: Do you have enough chairs for 200 people? (椅子は200人分ある？)
B: I'll need to *count* them *up*. (数えてみなくちゃ)

cry

☐ cry for …を強く求める、緊急に…を必要とする

A: The design team has been really busy for a long time. (デザインチームは長いこと大忙しです)

B: I know. They're *crying for* more help. (そうだね。さらなる手助けを強く求めている)

☐ cry out against …に激しく反対［抗議］する

A: Do you think we should make everyone work on Saturday this week? (この土曜は全員出勤させるべきでしょうか？)

B: I'm sure everyone would *cry out against* that. (みんな大反対するだろうな)

☐ cry over (不幸・失敗などを) 嘆く

A: I can't believe I lost all my data. (データをすべてなくしてしまったなんて、信じられません)

B: It's not going to help to *cry over* that now. (今さら嘆いてもどうにもならない)

---

column ▶▶▶ cry

イギリスではよく使われるものの、アメリカではほとんど使われない句動詞に cry off, cry down があります。それぞれのイギリス英語での用法を紹介しておきましょう。

- George tried to *cry off* after promising he would do the presentation. (ジョージはプレゼンをやると約束したあとでそれを取り消そうとした) → cry off =「取り消す」
- Linda *cried down* the government's plan to raise taxes. (リンダは増税するという政府の計画を非難した) → cry down「非難する、けなす、やじる」

cut

☐ cut across   …を横切って近道をする

A: We have to get to the train station in 15 minutes.（15分で駅に着かないと）
B: We can make it if we *cut across* the park.（公園を横切って行けば着ける）

☐ cut back   （生産・出費・人員などを）縮小する、切り詰める

A: We're going to have to reduce our expenses to stay in business.（事業を継続するには、支出を削減しなければなりません）
B: I guess we'll also have to *cut back* our staff.（人員も整理せざるをえないだろう）

☐ cut down

【1】（値段を）切り下げる

A: This item isn't selling very well.（この商品はあまり売れません）
B: Do you think we should *cut down* the price?（値下げしたほうがいいかな？）

【2】（文章などを）短くする

A: My report is 90 pages long.（私の報告書は90ページあります）
B: That's too long. Could you *cut* it *down* to 50 pages?（長すぎます。50ページに減らしてもらえませんか？）

☐ cut down on   …の（消費）量を減らす（= reduce）

A: How about something for dessert?（デザートはいかが？）
B: That sounds good, but I'm trying to *cut down on* sugar.（いただきたいのですが、糖分を控えているところなもので）

☐ cut in   話をさえぎる（= interrupt）

A: Excuse me for *cutting in*, but I have a question.（お話し中にすみません、質問があるのですが）
B: No problem. Go ahead.（いいですよ。ご質問をどうぞ）

☐ cut into   （利益・価値を）減少させる

A: Were you able to save up a lot of money?（たくさん貯金できた？）

B: No, I got sick and that *cut into* my savings. （いや、病気になったせいで、貯金が減ったよ）

□ cut off

【1】（ガス・水道などの）供給を止める（= stop）

A: I heard that George's electricity got *cut off*. （ジョージは電気を止められたんだって）
B: Yeah, he doesn't have enough money to pay his electric bill. （うん、電気代を払う金がないんだ）

【2】（人と）交際を断つ

A: Why did Linda *cut* herself *off* from everyone? （リンダが誰とも付き合わないのはなぜ？）
B: She just doesn't like to talk to people. （おしゃべりするのが苦手なだけさ）

□ cut up （野菜などを）切り刻む

A: We need to *cut up* these carrots into little pieces. （にんじんを細かく刻まなくちゃ）
B: Are these pieces small enough? （これくらい細かければいいのかな？）

---

column ▶▶ cut

cut out は「…を切り抜く [切り取る]、（語句などを）取り除く、削る」のほか、さまざまな意味で用いられます。ここではネイティブがよく使う cut out の成句表現を2つ紹介します。

cut out for [to be]... で、「…に（なるのに）適任である」という意味です。普通は受身形で使われます。
A: I heard George wants to quit. （ジョージが辞めたがっているそうよ）
B: He realizes he wasn't *cut out to be* an accountant. （自分は経理に向かないと気づいたのさ）

cut it [that] out で、「やめる」という意味です。命令形で使われることが多いです。
A: Here, let me read the newspaper. （ねえ、新聞を見せて）
B: *Cut it out*! This is my newspaper. （やめてくれよ！ ぼくが読んでるんだから）

die

☐ die away （音が）徐々に聞こえなくなる

A: Can you hear that music? Where's it coming from?（あの音楽、聞こえる？　どこから流れてくるのかしら？）⇨ COME FROM
B: I don't know. It's *dying away*.（さあね。だんだん聞こえなくなってるよ）

☐ die down （興奮などが）さめる、（音などが）小さくなる、静まる

A: Is everyone still talking about the new smartphone?（まだみんな新型のスマホの話題で盛り上がってるわけ？）
B: No, I think the excitement is finally *dying down*.（いや、もう騒ぎは収まりつつある）

☐ die of （…の病気で）死ぬ

A: Did your grandfather *die of* old age?（あなたのおじいさんは老衰で亡くなられたの？）
B: No, he *died of* cancer. He was only 70.（いや、癌で死んだ。まだ70歳だった）

☐ die out

【1】死に絶える、絶滅する

A: I heard that polar bears are almost extinct.（ホッキョクグマはほとんど絶滅しているそうね）
B: That's right. They're *dying out* quickly.（そのとおり。もうすぐ死に絶えてしまう）

【2】（習慣などが）廃れる

A: Are there still a lot of arranged marriages in this country?（この国ではいまだにお見合い結婚が多いのですか？）
B: No, that custom has mostly *died out*.（いいえ、その風習はほぼ廃れています）

【3】（雨・風などが）弱まる

A: Do you think we should leave now?（今すぐ出発するほうがいいと思う？）
B: The rain has mostly *died out*, so it should be okay.（雨はほぼやんだから、出かけてもいいだろう）

do

☐ do away with …を捨て去る、廃止する

A: We should *do away with* making everyone wear business suits. (ビジネススーツの着用を強制するのはやめるべきです)
B: I disagree. We need to keep that policy. (賛成できません。その方針は維持するべきです)

☐ do for

【1】…をだめにする、殺す、罰する

A: Do you think George is going to get fired? (ジョージは解雇されるかしら？)
B: I'm sure he is. He's *done for*. (されるに決まってる。あいつはもうだめだ)

【2】…の身のまわりの世話をする、…のために家事をする

A: When I'm away, you'll have to *do for* our kids. (私がいないときは、子供たちの世話をしないといけないわよ)
B: Of course I will. Don't worry, you can count on me. (もちろんできるさ。心配ない。大船に乗った気でいてよ) ⇨ COUNT ON [UPON] [1]

☐ do in

【1】…を殺す (= kill)

A: If you keep saying stupid things like that, someone's going to *do* you *in*. (そんなバカな言葉かり言ってると、誰かに殺されるわよ)
B: I don't care. I want to say what I think. (かまうもんか。思ったことを言いたいんだ)

【2】…を（へとへとに）疲れさせる

A: I've never been so tired in my life. (こんなに疲れたのは生まれて初めて)
B: Yeah, this physical labor will really *do* you *in*. (ああ、この力仕事をすると、へとへとになる)

☐ do over …をやり直す

A: My boss really didn't like my report. I have to *do* it *over*. (私の報告書、上司に気に入ってもらえなかったの。書き直さなくちゃ)
B: Do you have to rewrite it completely? (全部、書き直さなくちゃいけないのかい？)

☐ do up （ボタン・靴ひも・衣服などを）留める

A: It looks really cold outside. You'd better *do up* your coat. (外はすごく寒そう。コートのファスナーを閉めたほうがいいわ)
B: Oh, my zipper is broken. (ああ、困ったことに、ファスナーが壊れてるんだ)

☐ do with …を処理［処置］する、扱う

A: What do you want me to *do with* these reports? (この複数の報告書を私にどうしろとおっしゃるのですか？)
B: You need to read them over and sort them. (全部読んで、分類してほしい)
⇨ READ THROUGH［OVER］

☐ do without …なしですませる

A: Do you think we can *do without* a printer? (プリンタがなくてもすむでしょうか？)
B: No, we have to have one. (いや、1台必要だ)

---

column ▶▶▶ do

do up はここで紹介した以外にも、さまざまな状況で使われます。次のような言い回しも日常的に使うので、ぜひ覚えておいてください。

- I *did up* my hair. （髪をアップにした）[do up ＝「（髪を）結い上げる」]
- Everyone looks *done up*. （みんなすっかり疲れているようだ）[do up ＝「すっかり疲れさせる」]
- I need to *do up* my shoelaces. （靴ひもを結ばなくちゃ）[do up ＝「（靴ひもを）結ぶ」]
- I need to *do up* my house before I sell it. （家を売る前にきれいにしなくちゃ）[do up ＝「きれいにする」]
- The package was *done up* in wrapping paper. （その荷物は包装紙で包まれていた）[do up ＝「包む」]
- She spends an hour *doing* herself *up* in the morning. （彼女は朝、化粧をするのに1時間かかる）[do up ＝「化粧する、着飾る」]

draw

☐ draw aside （人を）わき［片すみ］に連れていく

A: When did Linda tell you about the defect?（その不具合についてリンダはいつあなたに話したの？）
B: She *drew* me *aside* after the morning meeting and told me about it.（朝礼のあと、ぼくをわきに呼んで話してくれた）

☐ draw back

【1】…を引き戻す、引っ込める、（カーテンなどを）引いて開ける

A: This room is a little dark. Could you turn on the light?（この部屋は薄暗いです。電気をつけていただけますか？）⇨ TURN ON ［2］
B: Okay. Do you want me to *draw back* the curtains too?（はい、カーテンも開けましょうか？）

【2】（事業などから）手を引く

A: Do you think ABC is still interested in this project?（ABC 社はまだこのプロジェクトに関心があるでしょうか？）
B: Not as much as before. They're starting to *draw back*.（以前ほどではないだろう。プロジェクトから手を引こうとしている）

☐ draw in …を引き寄せる、誘い込む

A: How is that restaurant able to *draw in* so many customers?（あのレストランはどうしてあんなにたくさん集客できるのかな？）
B: A lot of customers are attracted by their low prices.（多くの客はあの店のメニューの安さに引かれているんだ）

☐ draw into …を～に引っ張り込む、誘い込む

A: Linda and George are fighting again. Aren't you going to step in?（リンダとジョージはまたけんかしてる。止めたらどう？）
B: No, I don't want to get *drawn into* their quarrel.（2人の口論に巻き込まれたくない）

☐ draw on …に頼る、…を利用する

A: Why do you think we should hire Linda? (なぜリンダを雇わなくちゃいけないの？)
B: I want to *draw on* her years of experience in advertising. (彼女の長年にわたる広告業務の経験に期待したいんだ)

☐ draw out

【1】…を引き伸ばす、(時間的に) 延長する (= stretch, prolong)

A: Should we ask George to make this announcement? (ジョージにこの発表をしてもらうほうがいいですか？)
B: No, he'll *draw* it *out* into a 30 minute speech. (だめだ、彼に発表させると長くなって、30分のスピーチになってしまう)

【2】…にしゃべらせる、(恥ずかしがる人の) 気持ちをほぐす

A: It seems that Linda likes to stay away from people. She's really shy. (リンダは人と距離を置きたいみたい。すごく内気なの) ⇨ STAY AWAY FROM
B: I'll talk to her and see if I can *draw* her *out*. (彼女に話しかけて、おしゃべりするように仕向けてみるよ)

☐ draw up …の草案を作る

A: I think we should open up an online shop. (オンラインショップを開いたらいいと思います) ⇨ OPEN UP [1]
B: I agree. Could you *draw up* a plan to do that? (そうですね。そのためのプランを作ってもらえますか？)

---

column ▶▶▶ draw

drawには「引く」という意味があり、44ページでも句動詞draw back([カーテンなどを]引いて開ける)を紹介しました。しかし、最近は「カーテンを閉める」と言う場合、draw the curtains closed の代わりに、close the curtains と表現するほうが一般的です。また、draw の動詞は「引く」よりも「(絵を)描く」のイメージのほうが強いようです。

ちなみに、draw the curtain over[on] で「(話などを) 終わりにする、秘密にしておく」という意味になります。

drop

☐ drop away （関心・支持などが）なくなっていく

A: Do you think Linda will win the next election? (リンダは次の選挙で当選すると思う？)

B: I doubt it. A lot of her supporters are *dropping away*. (どうかな。多くの支持者が離れつつあるからね)

☐ drop behind （学業などで）ついていけなくなる、…より遅れる

A: If you don't start studying, you're going to *drop behind* the other students. (勉強を始めないと、ほかの生徒に遅れてしまうわよ)

B: Don't worry. I can keep ahead of them. (心配ないよ。いつだってぼくはみんなより進んでるんだ)

☐ drop by （ついでの折などに）立ち寄る、ちょっと訪ねる

A: If you have time tomorrow, why don't you *drop by* for coffee? (明日、時間があったら、うちに寄ってコーヒーを飲んでいかない？)

B: Okay, I'll try to finish up my work early and get there around 4:00. (うん、それじゃあ、仕事を早めに終わらせるようにして、4時頃お邪魔するよ)

☐ drop in ちょっと立ち寄る

A: Do you mind if I *drop in* this afternoon? (今日の午後、お宅にお寄りしてもいいですか？)

B: Not at all. I'm just sitting around anyway. (いいですよ。ぼくはこれといって何もしていませんし) ⇨ SIT AROUND

☐ drop into …に立ち寄る

A: Why don't we *drop into* the bar on our way home today? (今日、帰りにあのバーに寄ってみようよ)

B: Okay, sure. It'll be nice to hang out with everyone. (うん、そうしよう。みんなでのんびり過ごせたらいいね) ⇨ HANG OUT [3]

☐ drop off

【1】減る、減退する

A: Do you think that the stock market will *drop off* this month?（今月、株価は値下がりするかしら？）

B: No, I expect the opposite. It'll go up and up.（いや、その逆だろう。株価は上がりつづけるよ）⇨ GO UP [1]

【2】（うとうと）眠ってしまう

A: Why did Linda keep *dropping off* in the meeting?（リンダはどうして会議中に居眠りしたの？）

B: She stayed up late preparing her presentation.（プレゼンの準備で夜更かししたんだ）⇨ STAY UP [1]

【3】（人・荷物を車から）降ろす

A: If you'd like, I can *drop* you *off* at the airport.（よろしければ、空港まで車でお送りします）

B: That's okay. I'll just pick up a taxi in front of the hotel.（結構です。ホテルの前でタクシーを拾いますから）

☐ drop out （学校を）中途退学する、（競争などから）脱落する

A: Weren't you taking a training course to brush up on your programming skills?（研修コースに参加して、プログラミングのスキルを磨き直してたんじゃなかったの？）

B: I was, but I got busy and had to *drop out*.（してたさ。でも忙しくなって途中でやめざるをえなくなった）

---

column ▶▶▶ drop

drop in（ちょっと立ち寄る）は、あらかじめ予定を伝えず「急に」訪問するイメージがあります。

そのため、She gets angry *at the drop of a hat*. で「彼女はちょっとしたことですぐに怒る」となり、at the drop of a hat は「すぐ、早速、合図ひとつで」という意味になります。

日本人はあまり drop という単語になじみがないかもしれませんが、ネイティブはかなり幅広い意味で使います。Drop it!（やめろ！）, drop a brick（へまなことを言う［やる］）, drop the curtain（緞帳を降ろす、終焉とする）などは、日常的によく使う言い回しですから、覚えておいてください。

fall

☐ fall back on [upon] （最後の手段として）…に頼る、…をよりどころにする

A: I'm not very worried about saving money.（貯金しなくちゃ、とはあんまり思わないの）
B: But don't you need a little money in savings to *fall back on*?（でも、いざという時に困らないように、少しは蓄えが必要じゃないか？）

☐ fall behind （支払いなどに）遅れる

A: Why did you *fall behind* on your rent?（どうして家賃を滞納したの？）
B: I used up my salary on medicine.（給料は薬代に消えたんだ）

☐ fall down 倒れる、転ぶ

A: I heard that Linda can't come in today.（今日、リンダはこられないそうね）
⇨ COME IN [3]
B: Yeah, she *fell down* and hurt herself.（ああ、転んでけがしたんだ）

☐ fall for

【1】…に夢中になる、ほれ込む

A: I'm not surprised that George *fell for* Linda.（ジョージがリンダに夢中なのもむりないわ）
B: I know. They were made for each other.（そうだね、２人はお似合いだよ）

【2】（計略に）はまる、（話などに）だまされる

A: George said I'll get rich if I invest in his company.（ジョージが言ってたよ、彼の会社に投資すればお金持ちになれるんだって）
B: Don't *fall for* that. He's trying to trick you out of your money.（だまされちゃだめだ。あいつ、きみのお金をだまし取ろうとしてるんだ）

☐ fall in （屋根などが）落ち込む、めり込む

A: Do you think that this roof might *fall in*?（この屋根、落ちてこないかしら？）
B: Don't worry. It's held up by steel columns.（大丈夫さ。スチールの柱で支えられてるから）

☐ fall into （急に）…となる、…に陥る

A: I'm worried about the economy *falling into* a recession.（景気が悪くなるんじゃないかしら）

B: Oh, really? Should I get rid of my stocks?（え、ほんと？ 株を売ってしまうほうがいいかな？）

☐ fall in with （人と）一緒になる、偶然出会う

A: Where do you think George went wrong?（ジョージはどこで道を踏み外したのかな？）
B: When he went to college, he *fell in with* the wrong kind of people.（大学時代、悪いやつらとつるむようになったんだ） ⇨ GO TO

☐ fall off 減少する、低下する、衰える (= decrease)

A: Why do you think our sales are *falling off*?（売り上げが落ちている理由は何だと思う？）
B: Our customers are getting tired of our design.（顧客はわが社のデザインに飽きてるんだ）

☐ fall on [upon] （休日・誕生日などが）…にあたる

A: What day does your birthday *fall on* this year?（あなたの誕生日、今年は何曜日？）
B: I'll have to look it up, but I think it's on a Monday.（調べないとわからないけど、たぶん月曜日だと思う） ⇨ LOOK UP ［2］

☐ fall out

【1】 外へ落ちる

A: Just put those old books in the closet.（ここにある古本、全部クローゼットにしまって）
B: It's already too full. When I open it, things *fall out*.（もう満杯だよ。開けたら中の物がどっと落ちてくるよ）

【2】 …と仲たがいする、けんかする (fall out with)

A: I heard that George *fell out* with Linda.（ジョージはリンダとけんかしたそうね）
B: That's right. They got into a big fight.（そうなんだ。大げんかになっちゃって）
⇨ GET INTO ［3］

☐ fall through （計画などが）失敗する、挫折する

A: Why do you think your plan *fell through*?（計画が失敗したのはなぜ？）
B: The president of the company didn't back me up.（社長がぼくを後押ししてくれなかったんだ） ⇨ BACK UP ［1］

☐ fall under …の部門に入る、…に該当する

A: Avocados are a type of vegetable, aren't they?（アボカドは野菜でしょ？）
B: No, they're fruit, so they *fall under* a different category.（違う、果物だよ。違うジャンルに入れられてるんだ）

feel

☐ feel like

【1】(自分が) …のように感じる

A: Did you enjoy staying at the ABC Hotel? (ABCホテルのご宿泊はいかがでしたか？)
B: Yeah, they made me *feel like* a king. (うん、王様みたいにもてなしてくれたよ)

【2】(どうやら) …らしい

A: The economy isn't doing very well, is it? (景気はあまりよくないんでしょ？)
B: No, it's *feeling* more and more *like* a recession. (よくない。どんどん不景気になるみたいだ)

【3】(仕事・行為などを) したい気がする

A: Do you *feel like* taking a break? (休憩したい？)
B: No, let's keep on working a little longer. (いや、もう少し仕事をつづけよう)
⇨ KEEP ON [3]

☐ feel out …に探りを入れる、…の意向を探る

A: Do you think ABC is still interested in this project? (ABC社はまだこのプロジェクトに関心があるでしょうか？)
B: I'm not sure. I'll *feel out* the president and see what he thinks. (どうかな。社長に探りを入れて、彼がどういうつもりなのか見当をつけてみるよ)

☐ feel up to …に耐えられそうな気がする、…をやれそうに思う

A: Do you *feel up to* walking to the train station? (駅まで歩けそうですか？)
B: I'm kind of worn out. Could we take a taxi? (なんだか疲れてしまって。タクシーに乗りませんか？) ⇨ WEAR OUT [2]

fight

☐ fight back

【1】反撃する、抵抗する（= resist）

A: My former employer is taking me to court. I don't know what to do. (以前の雇用者が私を訴えているの。どうしていいか、わからないわ)

B: You should *fight back*, of course. (もちろん反撃しなくちゃ)

【2】（感情などを）抑える（= contain）

A: That movie was so sad, I had to *fight back* the tears. (あの映画、とても悲しかったの。涙をこらえなければならなかったわ)

B: I know. I couldn't stop crying. (わかるよ。ぼくは涙が止まらなかった)

☐ fight off …を寄せつけない、撃退する

A: Three new stores opened up right next to here. (ちょうどこの並びに、新しいお店が3軒オープンしたの) ⇨ OPEN UP [1]

B: I know. It's going to be tough to *fight* them *off*. (そうだね。そうした店との競争に勝つのは大変だろうな)

☐ fight on 戦いつづける

A: Are you going to give up and pay the penalty? (あきらめて罰を受けるの？)

B: Of course not! I'm going to *fight on*. (もちろん、そうはしないよ！ 戦いつづけるさ)

☐ fight over …をめぐって（言い）争う

A: Why do you and George *fight over* everything? (どうしてあなたとジョージは、あらゆることで言い争うの？)

B: I don't know, but there's nothing we agree on. (さあね。でも、ぼくたちは意見が一致することが何もないんだよ)

fill

☐ fill in
【1】(用紙・空所に) 書き込む、(必要事項を) 記入する (= complete)

A: Do I need to *fill in* this form? (この用紙に記入しなくてはいけないのですか？)
B: Yes, it needs to be filled out completely. (はい、もれなく記入してください)
⇨ FILL OUT

【2】(…について) 詳しい知識 [最新の情報] を人に与える

A: I just got back from the morning meeting. (朝礼に出てきたところよ) ⇨ GET BACK
B: Could you *fill* me *in* on what happened? (何があったのか教えてもらえますか？)

☐ fill out (書類などに) 書き込む (= complete)

A: Could I borrow a pen to *fill out* this form? (この用紙に書き込むために、ペンをお借りしてもよろしいでしょうか？)
B: I'm afraid I didn't bring one with me. (すみません、ペンを持ってこなかったんです)

☐ fill up (空間・時間を) 埋める

A: We'll have to wait at the airport for five hours. (空港でこれから5時間待ち)
B: Really? How are we going to *fill up* the time? (ほんとに？ どうやって時間をつぶそうか？)

fix

☐ fix up …を修理する、手直しする (= repair)

A: Do you think I can get a good price for my house? (私の家を売れば、いい値になるかしら？)
B: Yeah, if you *fix* it *up*, you could sell it for a million dollars. (ああ、修理すれば、100万ドルで売れるよ)

get

☐ get across
【1】（橋などを）渡る

　　A: How are we going to *get across* this river?（どうやってこの川を渡るの？）
　　B: If we keep on walking, we'll probably find a bridge.（このまま歩いていけば、たぶん橋があるよ）　⇨ KEEP ON ［3］

【2】（発言などが）伝わる、（考えや話を相手に）わからせる

　　A: We'll need to expand sales or we'll go out of business.（販売を拡張しなければ、倒産してしまいます）
　　B: How can we *get* that *across* to all our employees?（従業員全員に納得してもらうにはどうすればいいだろうか？）

☐ get after　…をしかる、責める

　　A: My boss *got after* me for being late.（遅刻して上司にしかられました）
　　B: You have to be more careful to be on time.（時間厳守するように、もっと気をつけなければいけない）

☐ get along
【1】暮らしていく、（なんとか）やっていく

　　A: How do you *get along* with so little money?（そんなに少しのお金でどうやって暮らしていくの？）
　　B: It's not hard for me to enjoy life without a lot of money.（大してお金がなくても、楽しく生きられる。そんなことぼくにはむずかしくないよ）

【2】仲よくやっていく、（うまく）折り合っていく

　　A: George seems to *get along* with everyone.（ジョージは誰とでもうまくいくみたい）
　　B: I know. It's really easy for him to talk with people.（ああ、誰とでも実にたやすく会話ができる）

【3】（仕事などが）はかどる、（仕事などを）進める (get along in ［with］)

　　A: How are you *getting along* in your new job?（新しい仕事はうまくいってる？）
　　B: Pretty good. I'm picking up a lot of new skills.（上出来さ。新しいスキルもたくさん覚えているところだ）　⇨ PICK UP ［2］

☐ get around …を歩きまわる

A: What's the best way to *get around* this city?（この街を歩きまわるのにいちばんいい方法は何かしら？）
B: The subway will get you almost anywhere.（地下鉄に乗れば、街のほとんどに行けるよ）

☐ get around to …する機会［ひま］ができる、（やっと）…に取りかかる

A: When do you think you'll *get around to* translating that letter?（いつになったら、あの手紙の翻訳に取りかかれるの？）
B: I'll probably be able to get to it tomorrow.（たぶん明日になればできる）⇨ GET TO [2]

☐ get at

【1】（手を伸ばすなどして）…に届く、…を手に入れる

A: Why do we need to lock up these documents?（この書類、どうしてしまっておかなくちゃいけないんですか？）
B: I don't want anyone to *get at* them.（誰の手にも届かないようにしておきたいんだ）

【2】…を暗示する、ほのめかす（= imply）

A: Tell me where you were last night at 10:30.（昨日の夜10時半にどこにいたのか、教えて）
B: What are you trying to *get at*? Do you think I stole the money?（何が言いたいんだ？ あの金をぼくが盗んだと思ってるのか？）

☐ get away

【1】逃げる、逃走する（= escape）

A: How did the suspect *get away*?（容疑者はどうやって逃げたの？）
B: He went to the bathroom and escaped out the window.（トイレに行って、窓から逃げた）

【2】休暇をとる

A: Do you ever get a chance to *get away* from work?（もしかして仕事を休めたりする？）
B: No, I haven't taken a vacation for years.（むりだ。何年も休暇を取っていない）

【3】立ち去る、離れる（get away from）

A: This city is really dangerous.（この街は危険すぎる）
B: I wish I could *get away* from it somehow.（なんとかしてここを離れたいよ）

☐ get away with …を持ち逃げする

A: What did the robber *get away with*?（泥棒は何を盗んでいったの？）

B: He took just about everything I own. (ぼくの所持品、全部取っていったよ)

☐ **get back** 戻る、(家に) 帰る (= return)

A: Do you want me to wait for you here? (私、ここで待ってるほうがいい？)
B: Yeah, I should *get back* in about 30 minutes. (うん、30分ぐらいで戻ってくるから)

☐ **get back at** (人に) 仕返しをする

A: Aren't you angry that George tricked you? (ジョージにだまされて怒ってないの？)
B: Yeah, and I'm going to *get back at* him. (怒ってるよ。だから仕返ししてやるつもりさ)

☐ **get back to** (考えたり調べたりして) あとで (人に) 返事 [連絡] する

A: About when do you think you can give me an answer? (大体いつ頃ご回答いただけますか？)
B: I'll try to *get back to* you early next week. (来週早々にお返事するようにいたします)

☐ **get back together** (男女が) よりを戻す

A: I thought George and Linda broke up. (ジョージとリンダは別れたと思ってた)
 ⇨ BREAK UP [3]
B: They did, but now they're *getting back together*. (別れたけど、今はよりを戻してる)

☐ **get back with** …とよりを戻す

A: I heard John *got back with* Nancy. (ジョンがナンシーとよりを戻したと聞いたわ)
B: That's true, and now they're engaged. (そう、それでもう婚約しているんだ)

☐ **get behind**

【1】(支払いなどに) 遅れる

A: Why don't you just take tomorrow off and relax? (明日は休みを取ってゆっくりすれば？) ⇨ TAKE OFF [3]
B: I'd like to, but I don't want to *get behind* in my work. (そうしたいけど、仕事が遅れるのはいやだから)

【2】(人・事を) 支援する、励ます

A: Do you think your project will get the thumbs up? (あなたのプロジェクト、承認してもらえるかな？)
B: Well, maybe if George *gets behind* it. (うん、ジョージが味方してくれれば、たぶん大丈夫だ)

□ get by

【1】なんとかやっていく［切り抜ける］

A: Do you think I can *get by* on 30 dollars a day?（1日30ドルでやっていけると思う？）
B: Sure. In this country, that's a lot of money.（もちろんさ、この国では30ドルは大金だから）

【2】通り抜ける

A: Excuse me. I need to *get by*.（すみません、通らせてください）
B: Oh, sorry. Let me move my suitcases out of the way.（あ、失礼しました。スーツケースをどけます）

□ get down

【1】（高いところから）降りる (get down from)

A: How did you *get down* from the mountain?（どうやって下山したの？）
B: We put on our skis and skied down.（スキーで滑り降りてきた）　⇨ PUT ON [1]

【2】身をかがめる

A: What should we do if there's an earthquake?（地震がきたらどうすればいい？）
B: You should *get down* on your hands and knees and hide under your desk until it stops.（地震が止むまで、四つんばいになって机の下に隠れるんだ）

【3】…をがっかりさせる、落ち込ませる

A: Why don't you like listening to this song?（この歌を聞きたくないのはなぜ？）
B: It brings back sad memories and *gets* me *down*.（悲しい思い出がよみがえって、落ち込むから）　⇨ BRING BACK [2]

【4】…を書き取る

A: Take a pen and paper and try to *get down* everything George says.
（ジョージの言うことをすべて、ペンと紙で書き取りなさい）
B: Maybe I should just make a recording.（録音したほうがいいかも）

□ get down to　…に本気で［真剣に］取りかかる

A: Stop wasting time and *get down to* work.（ぶらぶらしてないで、仕事に取りかかって）
B: I wish I could, but I'm waiting for Linda to send me some information.（ぼくだってそうしたいけど、リンダが送ってくれる情報を待ってるんだ）

□ get in

【1】…の中に入る (= enter)

A: How did you *get in* your house without a key?（鍵なしでどうやって家に入ったの？）
B: I had to climb through a window.（身をよじって窓から中に入るしかなかった）

【2】（乗用車・タクシー・列車・バスなどに）乗る (= take)

A: ***Get in*** and I'll give you a ride to the train station.（さあ、乗って。駅まで送るわ）
B: Thanks. I'm glad I don't have to walk in the rain.（ありがとう。雨の中を歩かずにすんで助かるよ）

【3】（飛行機・列車などが）到着する (= arrive)

A: What time does your flight ***get in*** to London?（何時にロンドンに着く飛行機なの？）
B: The plane takes off at 3:30, so I'll get there at around 8:00.（3時半に発つから8時頃着くはずだ） ⇨ TAKE OFF ［4］

【4】…を提出する

A: By when do I need to ***get*** this report ***in***?（この報告書の提出期限はいつですか？）
B: If you could put it on my desk by the end of today, that'll be okay.（今日中にぼくの机の上に出してくれればいい）

□ get into

【1】（列車などが）…に到着する (= arrive)

A: What time does your train ***get into*** Tokyo?（何時に東京駅に着く電車？）
B: We should get there at around 3:00.（3時頃、着くはずだ）

【2】（乗用車・タクシーなどに）乗る (= take)

A: Why don't you ***get into*** my car and I'll take you to the airport?（私の車に乗って。空港まで送っていくよ）
B: That's okay. We already bought train tickets.（大丈夫。ぼくたち、もう電車の切符を買ってあるんだ）

【3】（悪い）習慣などが身につく、よくない状態になる

A: When did you ***get into*** the habit of smoking?（タバコを吸うようになったのはいつ？）
B: I started smoking after I got out of college.（大学を出てから吸い始めました）

【4】…を（苦労して）着る［はく］

A: Why are you spending so much money on clothes?（どうしてそんなに洋服にお金を使ってばかりいるの？）
B: I gained some weight, and now I can't ***get into*** my old clothes.（太っちゃって、昔の服が着られないんだよ）

【5】（学校・会などに）入る、（議会の）議員に選出される

A: Do you think Linda will be able to ***get into*** a good college?（リンダはいい大学に入れるかしら？）
B: She's studying hard to keep her grades up, so she should be okay.（一生懸命勉強して、よい成績を保っているから、大丈夫だろう）

【6】…にのめり込む、興味を持つ

A: It seems like you go mountain climbing almost every weekend. (あなたはほとんど毎週末、山登りに行ってるみたいね)
B: Yeah, I really *got into* it. I can't get it out of my head. (うん、登山に夢中なんだ。山のことが頭から離れない)

【7】（ある考えが人に）とりつく、…に影響を及ぼす

A: George sure has been acting strange lately. What's *gotten into* him? (ジョージは最近変だ。どうしちゃったのかな？)
B: Maybe he's fallen in love or something. (たぶん、恋でもしてるんじゃないか)

□ get off

【1】（列車・バス・旅客機などから）降りる

A: Why don't you sit down? (座りませんか？)
B: That's okay. I have to *get off* at the next stop. (ありがとう。でも次のバス停で降りますので)

【2】出発する（= leave）

A: Why isn't Linda here yet? (どうしてリンダはまだなの？)
B: I called her up and she said her train *got off* 30 minutes late. (電話したら、電車が30分遅れだって言ってた) ⇨ CALL UP

【3】（軽い刑罰などで）免れる、逃れる

A: I thought the judge was going to put George away for 20 years. (私、裁判官はジョージを20年の刑に処すると思っていたけど)
B: Yeah, he was lucky to *get off* with only five years. (ああ、たった5年の刑ですんで、あいつラッキーだったな)

【4】（1日の仕事を）終える、退社する

A: Why don't we meet up tonight and have a drink? (今夜一緒に飲もうよ)
⇨ MEET UP [1]
B: Sounds good. I *get off* work at 6:00. (いいね。6時に退社する)

【5】…を取る、外す、脱ぐ

A: I can't *get* this ring *off*. My finger is swollen. (指輪が外れない。指がむくんでる)
B: Put some soap on your finger and then try to pull it off. (指に石鹸をぬってから、指輪をひっぱってみなよ) ⇨ PULL OFF [1]

□ get on

【1】（列車・バス・旅客機などに）乗る

A: Sorry, I have to hang up and *get on* the train now. (ごめんね、電話を切らないと。

もう電車に乗るから）　⇨ HANG UP　[2]

B: Okay, I'll call you up tonight. （わかった、今夜電話するよ）　⇨ CALL UP

【2】仲よく［うまく］やっていく、（なんとか）やっていく

A: How do you think Linda is fittng in? （リンダはなじんでるかしら？）
B: Not too bad. She seems to *get on* well with people. （うん、まずまずだよ。みんなとうまくやってるみたいだ）

【3】（人が）年を取る

A: Is George planning on going skydiving with you? （ジョージはあなたとスカイダイビングするつもり？）
B: Probably not. He's *getting on* in years. （それはないね。彼も年を取ってきたから）

【4】…を着る、身につける

A: It's kind of cold outside. I'd better *get on* my coat. （外はちょっと寒いわ。コートを着たほうがいいわね）
B: Okay, I'll put on mine too. （わかった、ぼくも着るよ）　⇨ PUT ON　[1]

□ get out

【1】逃げ出す、（組織などから）抜け出す (get out of)

A: I have to *get out* of this job. It's too much stress. （この仕事、辞めないと。ストレスがかかりすぎる）
B: It's not so bad when you get used to it. （慣れればそれほど悪くない仕事だ）

【2】（秘密などが）漏れる、知れ渡る

A: We have to make sure this information doesn't *get out*. （この情報は絶対に漏らしてはいけません）
B: Why do we need to keep it a secret from everyone? （なぜ誰にも言ってはならないのですか？）

【3】（本などを）出版する

A: What's it like to work for a newspaper company?（新聞社の仕事ってどんな感じ？）
B: Well, it's really hard to *get out* a paper twice a day. （まあ、1日に2度新聞を出すのは本当に大変だよ）

【4】（言葉を）やっと発する、言う

A: Did Linda tell you why she's planning on quitting? （なぜ仕事を辞めるつもりなのか、リンダはあなたに話した？）
B: Yeah, but she had a hard time *getting* it *out*.（ああ、でもとてもつらそうに話してたよ）

get out of

【1】（衣服などを）脱ぐ

A: Could you help me to *get out of* this coat? It's really tight. (このコートを脱ぎたいんですが、手伝ってもらえますか？ すごくきつくて)
B: How did you manage to put it on? (どうやって着たの？) ⇨ PUT ON [1]

【2】（乗用車・タクシーから）降りる

A: You need to *get out of* the taxi in front of the bank. (銀行の前でタクシーを降りてください)
B: Okay, after I get there, I'll wait for you. (ああ、向こうに着いたら、きみがくるのを待ってる)

【3】…することを免れる、…せずにすませる

A: I wish I could *get out of* going to the meeting this afternoon. (午後の会議に出なくてすめばいいのに)
B: Do you want me to tell everyone you're tied up? (きみは手が離せないって、みんなに言っておこうか？)

【4】…から逃れる

A: We have to *get out of* this building! (このビルの外に出ないと！)
B: Why? Do you think it might fall on us? (なぜ？ ビルが倒れるとでも思ってるの？)

【5】（人から真相などを）聞き出す

A: How did you *get* the truth *out of* Linda? (リンダからどうやって真相を聞き出したの？)
B: I told her she had to tell me the truth to keep her job. (仕事を失いたくなければ、ぼくに本当のことを言わなくてはいけない、と告げたんだ)

get over

【1】…を乗り越える

A: Do you think we can *get over* this mountain before it gets dark? (暗くなる前に山を越えられるかしら？)
B: Probably not. We'd better set up camp here. (むりだろう。ここでテントを張るほうがいいね) ⇨ SET UP [1]

【2】（物事が）終わる

A: Do you know what time the meeting *gets over*? (会議がいつ終わるかわかる？)
B: I think they should finish up in about 30 minutes. (あと30分くらいで終わると思う)

【3】（相手に考えなどを）理解させる、伝える

A: Were you able to *get* your message *over* to the staff? (スタッフにあなたの言いたいことを伝えられた？)
B: Yeah, I think they picked up on what I was trying to say. (うん、ぼくが言おうとしたことはわかってくれたと思ってる)

【4】（病気・痛手などから）回復する、立ち直る (= recover)

A: Do you think Linda is going to show up today?（リンダは今日くると思う？）
⇨ SHOW UP [1]

B: I doubt it. She still hasn't *gotten over* her cold.（どうかな。まだ風邪が治ってないから）

□ get through

【1】（相手に電話などで）通じる、連絡ができる

A: Could you call up George and ask him what's going on?（ジョージに電話して、どうしているのか聞いてもらえますか？）⇨ CALL UP, GO ON

B: I've been trying to call him, but I can't *get through*.（何度も電話してるんですが、つながらないんです）

【2】…をやり終える、仕上げる (= finish)

A: When do you plan on starting the new project?（新しいプロジェクトはいつから始める予定？）

B: After I *get through* my current project this week.（今週、進行中のプロジェクトをやり終えてからだ）

【3】…を通り抜ける、（水などが中へ）しみ込む、入り込む

A: When you go out, you'd better take an umbrella with you.（出かける時は傘を持っていくといいわ）⇨ GO OUT [1]

B: I don't need one. The water can't *get through* this coat.（傘はいらない。水がこのコートの中に入ることはない）

【4】（議案などが）通過する、（試験に）通る、合格する

A: Did your proposal *get through* the planning committee?（あなたの案は、計画委員会を通過した？）

B: Yes, it did. Everyone gave it the thumbs up.（ああ、通ったよ。全員一致で認めてくれた）

【5】（困難・病気などを）切り抜ける

A: I heard that your grandfather passed away.（おじいさんがお亡くなりになったそうですね）⇨ PASS AWAY

B: Yeah, he had a heart operation, but he couldn't *get through* it.（ええ、心臓の手術をしたのですが、持ちこたえられませんでした）

□ get to

【1】（人の）心にじんとくる

A: Linda's beautiful story really *got to* me.（リンダの美談にとても感動した）

B: I know. I had a hard time holding in my tears.（そうだね。涙を抑えるのが大変だった）

【2】…に取りかかる、着手する

A: Do you think we'll have enough time to get into the budget in the meeting?（会議で予算の話をする時間はあるでしょうか？）
B: No, I doubt we'll be able to *get to* that.（いや、それに手はつけられないだろう）

☐ get together （人が）集まる

A: Why don't we *get together* on Saturday and do something?（土曜日に集まって何かしようよ）
B: That sounds like fun, but I have to go into work.（楽しそうだけど、ぼくは仕事しないと）

☐ get under …の下に入る

A: What should I do if there's an earthquake?（地震がきたらどうすればいい？）
B: You need to get away from the windows and *get under* a table or something.（窓のそばから離れて、机か何かの下に入りなさい）⇨ GET AWAY［3］

☐ get up

【1】起床する、起きる

A: Why did you *get up* so early this morning?（今朝はどうしてこんなに早く起きたの？）
B: I had to get to the office and get some work done.（会社に行って、仕事を終わらせないといけないんだ）

【2】立ち［起き］上がる

A: Do you want me to *get up* and turn on the light?（起きて電気をつけようか？）⇨ TURN ON［2］
B: No, the lights will come on automatically in a few minutes.（いいよ、2、3分で自動的につくから）⇨ COME ON［3］

【3】（勇気などを）奮い起こす、かき立てる

A: Are you planning to ask your boss for a raise?（昇給を上司に頼むつもり？）
B: No, I haven't *gotten up* the courage yet.（まさか、まだそんな勇気はないよ）

☐ get up to （温度などが）…まで上がる

A: Does the temperature around here ever go over 40?（このあたりの温度は40度を超えることもある？）
B: Yeah, sometimes it *gets up to* 50.（50度まで上がることもあるよ）

give

☐ give off （煙・熱・光などを）発する、出す

A: I think your computer is *giving off* a funny smell. （あなたのコンピュータから変な匂いが出てるようだけど）

B: Yeah, I think it's about to break down. （うん、もう壊れるんじゃないかな） ⇨ BREAK DOWN [5]

☐ give out

【1】…を配給［支給］する、配る、配布する

A: Is the company going to *give out* bonuses this year? （会社は今年ボーナスを出すかしら？）

B: Yeah, but they'll probably be lower than last year. （ああ、でも去年より安くなるだろう）

【2】（力などが）尽きる、（エンジンなどが）動かなくなる

A: I'm sorry, but my legs are about to *give out*. （すみません、もう足が動きそうにありません）

B: Okay, let's sit down and take a break. （では、座って休憩しましょう）

☐ give up

【1】（犯人を）引き渡す

A: You can't hide from the police forever. Just *give* yourself *up*. （警察から永遠に逃れることはできないのよ。自首しなさい）

B: But why? I didn't do anything wrong. （どうしてだよ？ 何も悪いことしてないのに）

【2】（子供・恋人などとの）関係を絶つ、放棄する

A: Why did Linda *give up* her child? （リンダはなぜ子供を手放したの？）

B: She didn't have any way to take care of him. （育てられる術がなかったんだ）

☐ give up on （習慣などを）やめる、…を断念する (= stop)

A: Do you think the company will send me to the seminar in Hawaii? （会社は私をハワイのセミナーに行かせてくれるかな？）

B: No, you'd better *give up on* that idea. （いや、あきらめたほうがいいよ）

go

☐ go against …に逆らう、反対する

A: Can I wear jeans to work? (ジーンズで仕事してもいいかしら？)
B: I'm afraid not. They *go against* the company dress code. (だめだと思う。会社の服装規定に反するよ)

☐ go along やっていく、進んでいく

A: I can't figure out this new software. (この新しいソフト、わけがわからない)
B: Don't worry, you'll get used to it as you *go along*. (心配ないよ、使っていくうちに慣れるから)

☐ go along with …と協調する

A: Do you think Linda will *go along with* the new personnel changes? (リンダは今度の人事異動でうまくやっていけるかしら？)
B: She should. After all, they're giving her a better position. (大丈夫さ。だって、前よりいい地位に就けるんだから)

☐ go around

【1】（病気などが）はやる

A: I think I'm coming down with a fever. (熱が出てきたみたい) ⇨ COME DOWN WITH
B: You might be. The flu has been *going around* lately. (かもね。この頃インフルエンザがはやっているから)

【2】ひとまわりする

A: Darn, I can't find a parking space. (ああ、もう、駐車スペースが見つからない)
B: *Go around* the block one more time, and maybe one'll open up. (もう一度そのへんをひとまわりしてくれば、どこか空くだろう)

☐ go away

【1】立ち去る (= leave)

A: Linda sure likes to hang around your desk to chat. (あなたの机にふらふらやってきて、おしゃべりするのが好きなのよ、リンダは) ⇨ HANG AROUND [1]
B: I know. Sometimes I wish she'd *go away* and let me work. (そうなんだ。向

こうに行ってほしい、仕事をさせてほしい、と思うことがある）

【2】（痛み・問題などが）消えてなくなる

A: Do you still want some medicine for your headache?（まだ頭痛薬が必要？）
B: No, I took a nap at lunch, and it *went away*.（もういらない。昼休みに少し眠ったら痛くなくなった）

☐ go back

【1】（…まで）さかのぼる

A: Does your company have a long history?（御社の歴史は長いのですか？）
B: Yeah, we *go back* to the 19th century.（はい、19世紀までさかのぼります）

【2】（人と何年も）友人である

A: Have you known Linda for a long time?（リンダとはずっと前から知り合いなの？）
B: Oh, yeah. She and I *go back* to our high school days.（うん。彼女とは高校の頃から友だちなんだ）

☐ go back for　…を取りに戻る

A: Are you only ordering a salad from the salad bar?（サラダバーでサラダしか取らないの？）
B: Yeah, but I can *go back for* a second helping.（うん、でもおかわりするから）

☐ go back on　（約束を）破る、（人を）裏切る

A: Do you think we can trust George to help us?（ジョージが助けてくれると思う？）
B: I doubt it. He always *goes back on* his word.（どうだろう。彼はいつも約束を破るからね）

☐ go between　…のあいだに入る

A: Are George and Linda fighting again?（ジョージとリンダはまたけんかしてる？）
B: Yeah. I need to *go between* them and get them to make up.（ああ、あいだに入って仲直りさせないと）⇨ MAKE UP [2]

☐ go beyond　…を越えて進む

A: Linda did a great job on her report, didn't she?（リンダの報告書、とってもよかったわね）
B: Yeah, she *went* way *beyond* my expectations.（確かに。ぼくの期待を上回っていた）

□ go by

【1】(年月が) 経つ

A: It's hard to believe it's already December!（もう12月だなんて、うそみたい！）
B: I know! This year *went by* so fast!（そうだよね！　今年はあっというまに過ぎたなあ！）

【2】…の前［そば］を通り過ぎる

A: Is the bus to downtown coming soon?（都心に行くバスはもうすぐくる？）
B: As a matter of fact, it just *went by*.（実は、さっき通り過ぎていったよ）

【3】(機会・過失などが) 見逃される

A: How could you let the chance for that new position *go by*?（新しい地位に就けるチャンスを逃すなんて）
B: I just didn't think I was qualified to apply for it.（その地位に見合う資格がぼくにはないと思っただけです）

【4】…に立ち寄る

A: Are you *going by* the post office on your way downtown?（街に出るついでに郵便局に寄ってくれる？）
B: Yeah, do you want me to send off those packages?（いいよ、この小包を送っておく？）⇨ SEND OFF

【5】…に従って行動［判断］する

A: Do we always have to *go by* the dress code so strictly?（服装規定は常に厳守しなくてはいけないのですか？）
B: No, on Fridays we can dress casually.（いいえ、金曜日はカジュアルな服装でかまいません）

□ go down

【1】降りる、下る、(…まで) 行く

A: Isn't Linda in the office?（リンダはオフィスにいないの？）
B: No, she just *went down* to the basement to get some papers.（いないよ、書類を取りに地下に降りていったところだ）

【2】(物価・温度などが) 下がる

A: I read most farmers around here had a good harvest this year.（このあたりの農家は、ほとんどが、今年は豊作なんですって）
B: I hope that means the vegetable prices will *go down*.（そのおかげで野菜の値段が下がるといいな）

【3】(太陽・月が) 沈む

A: The sun sure *goes down* early around here.（このあたりは、日が沈むのが本当に早い）

B: I suppose it does, but don't forget it's wintertime too. (そうだね、でも冬だからってこともあるよね)

【4】(話などが) 受け入れられる

A: Did your presentation yesterday *go down* well? (昨日のプレゼン、受けた？)
B: It's hard to tell. Nobody gave much of a reaction. (どうかな。誰もあまり反応してくれなかった)

【5】(コンピュータが) ダウンする、(機械が) 故障する

A: Oh, geez, have the computers *gone down* again? (あらやだ、またコンピュータがダウンしたの？)
B: Yeah, but I called a technician to come fix them. (ああ、でも技術者に直しにきてくれるように電話したから)

□ go for

【1】…を好む、選ぶ、支持する

A: What do you say we order out for lunch today? (今日のお昼は何か取ろうよ)
B: Good idea. I could *go for* a pizza. (いいね。ピザがいいな)

【2】…を得ようとする、めざす

A: Is your son still at college? (息子さんはまだ大学に通ってるの？)
B: Yeah, he's *going for* a doctorate degree now. (ええ、博士号を取ろうとしてるんです)

【3】(物事が) …にあてはまる

A: Is the salary cut only going into effect at our office? (給料カットの影響を受けるのは、私たちの営業所だけかしら？)
B: No, it *goes for* the whole company. (いや、それは会社全体にあてはまる)

【4】…の目的に使われる

A: It must be expensive to have two kids in college. (お子さん2人を大学に通わせるのはきっと物入りでしょうね)
B: It is! I'd bet half of my savings are *going for* their tuition. (そうなんです！私の貯金の半分は子供たちの学費になるんですから)

【5】…で売られる

A: How much are those hybrid cars *going for* these days? (ああいうハイブリッドカーは今いくらぐらいする？)
B: I think you can get a cheap model for about 20,000 dollars. (低価格のタイプなら2万ドルぐらいで買えると思うよ)

☐ go in

【1】中へ入る

A: I have an appointment to see Mr. Jones. (ジョーンズさんにお目にかかるお約束なのですが)

B: Yes, he's waiting for you in his office. Please *go in*. (承知しております。ジョーンズはオフィスでお待ちしております。どうぞお入りください)

【2】(栓・鍵などが)…にぴったりはまる

A: I can't get this key to *go in* the lock. (この鍵、合わない)

B: You must have the wrong key. (鍵を間違えたんだよ)

☐ go into

【1】…の中に入る

A: Have you seen Linda? (リンダを見かけた？)

B: Yeah, she just *went into* the restroom. (ああ、彼女ならさっき化粧室に入った)

【2】…を調べる、調査する、論じる

A: Can you *go into* more detail about the new company policies? (会社の新しい規則について、さらに調べてもらえる？)

B: Well, I'll write them up and give you a copy. (はい、詳しい報告書を書いて1部お渡しします) ⇨ WRITE UP

【3】(仕事などに)就く、(職業として)…に従事する

A: What made you decide to *go into* real estate? (不動産業界に入ろうと思われた決め手は？)

B: I've just always been interested in sales. (ずっと販売に興味があったからです)

☐ go off

【1】立ち去る、出発する

A: Has today's mail *gone off* yet? (もう今日の分の郵便は出してしまったかしら？)

B: Yes, Linda took it to the post office an hour ago. (はい、リンダが1時間前に郵便局に出しに行きました)

【2】(爆薬などが)爆発する、(銃砲が)突然火を吹く

A: I heard George accidentally shot himself in the foot. (銃が暴発して、ジョージは自分の足を撃ってしまったって聞いたけど)

B: Yeah, he was loading his hunting rifle and it *went off* accidentally. (ああ、猟銃に弾を込めていたら暴発したんだ)

【3】(明かりが)消える、(ガス・水道などが)止まる

A: Last night's thunderstorm was pretty bad, wasn't it? (昨夜の雷雨はすごかったよね？)
B: Yeah, the power *went off* in my neighborhood for an hour. (うん、うちの近所では1時間停電した)

☐ go on

【1】(話などを)つづける

A: Well, I think I've told you enough about my hobbies. (あらまあ、私の趣味の言葉かりお話ししてしまったみたい)
B: No, please *go on*. I think rock-climbing is very interesting. (いえいえ、もっと話してください。ロッククライミングはとてもおもしろそうです)

【2】(催し・行事などが)行なわれる

A: What's all the noise at your neighbor's house? (お隣の家、一体何の騒ぎ？)
B: I guess some kind of party is *going on*. (パーティか何かしてるんじゃないかな)

【3】進む、つづく

A: Did you win your tennis match? (テニスの試合で勝った？)
B: No, as the match *went on*, I got really tired. (いや、試合が進むにつれて、ものすごく疲れちゃって)

【4】(明かりが)つく、(暖房・ガスなどが)つく

A: The office sure is cold in the mornings. (会社は朝、とても寒い)
B: That's because the heating doesn't *go on* until 9:00. (9時にならないと暖房がつかないからね)

☐ go out

【1】出ていく、外出する

A: Have you seen Linda around? (リンダ、このへんで見なかった？)
B: Yeah, she just *went out* to lunch. (見たよ、たった今ランチに出かけた)

【2】(異性と)付き合う、デートする

A: How long have George and Linda been *going out*? (ジョージとリンダは付き合ってどのくらい？)
B: Not long. I think their first date was just last month. (そんなに経ってないね。初めてデートしたのはまだ先月だったと思う)

【3】(火などが)消える

A: Doesn't this room seem awfully cold? (この部屋、すごく寒くない？)

B: The pilot light must have *gone out* in the furnace. (ボイラーの種火が消えてしまったに違いない)

【4】出版される、発行される、放送される、発送される

A: When does the company newsletter *go out*? (社内報はいつ出るの？)
B: We pass out copies on the first Friday of every month. (毎月第１金曜日に配布します) ⇨ PASS OUT ［1］

□ go over

【1】出かけていく、訪ねる

A: I think Linda is having trouble writing up her report. (リンダは報告書を仕上げるのが大変みたい) ⇨ WRITE UP
B: OK, I'll *go over* and help her. (わかった、リンダのところに行って、手伝ってあげるよ)

【2】（話などが）受け入れられる

A: I think your presentation yesterday *went over* really well. (あなたの昨日のプレゼン、受けがよかったわよ)
B: I hope so. I put a lot of work into it. (そうだといいな。あのプレゼンにはかなり力を入れたから)

【3】…を点検する、よく調べる

A: Could you *go over* my report and check for mistakes? (私の報告書を読んでいただいて、間違いがないかどうかご確認くださいますか？)
B: Sure. Just leave it on my desk and I'll look it over. (了解。私の机の上に置いておいてください。目を通します) ⇨ LOOK OVER ［1］

【4】…を繰り返す、復習する

A: Have you got your speech for tomorrow all memorized? (明日のスピーチ、全部覚えた？)
B: Yeah, but I want to *go over* it a few more times. (うん、でもあと何回か、繰り返しておきたい)

□ go through

【1】…を通り抜ける

A: Do you realize you just *went through* a red light? (赤信号なのに突っ切ったのよ、わかってる？)
B: Really? Oh dear, I wasn't paying attention. (ほんと？　なんてことだ、うっかりしていた)

【2】（苦しみなどを）経験する、耐え忍ぶ

A: You've really *gone through* a lot working here, haven't you? (あなたはここ

で働いて、実にいろいろなことを経験されましたよね?)

B: Yeah, I've had my share of headaches here. (ええ、私なりに悩むこともありました)

【3】(書類・数字などを)よく調べる、…をくまなく探す

A: Did the article about our company come out yet? (私たちの会社の記事、まだ出てない?) ⇨ COME OUT [1]

B: Well, *I went through* today's newspaper and didn't see it. (ああ、今日の新聞をすみずみまで読んだけど、見つからなかったよ)

【4】(衣服などを)だめにする、穴があくほど着る

A: Your son sure is growing fast, isn't he? (息子さん、成長がすごく早いわよね)

B: I'll say! He *goes through* his clothes in only a year. (まったくね! 洋服なんかせいぜい1年しか着られない)

☐ go through with (仕事などを)やり通す、…を終わりまでやり通す

A: Is Linda really going to *go through with* her divorce? (リンダはどうしても離婚する気かしら?)

B: Probably. She's really unhappy in her marriage now. (たぶんね。彼女は今とても不幸な結婚生活を送っている)

☐ go to …へ行く、通う

A: I heard you're *going to* some kind of night school. (夜学か何かに通ってるらしいわね)

B: Sort of. I'm taking a three-month business course. (まあね。3カ月間のビジネス講座に通ってる)

☐ go together つり合う、調和する、相ともなう

A: I don't think those chairs *go together*. They're different colors. (この椅子、どれもしっくり来ない感じ。全部色違いなんだもの)

B: I know. I had to get some from downstairs for today's meeting. (そうだね。今日の会議のために、下のフロアからいくつか持ってくるべきだった)

☐ go under 破産する、失敗する

A: We really had a disastrous year, didn't we? (本当にさんざんな1年だったわね)

B: Yeah, I'm worried the company is going to *go under*. (ああ、会社が倒産しそうで心配だよ)

☐ go up
【1】(物価・温度などが) 上がる、高くなる

A: Why are you buying so much ABC stock right now? (ABC 社の株を今そんなにたくさん買ってるのはなぜ？)
B: I heard it's going to start *going up* soon. (もうじき値が上がるはずだって聞いたんだ)

【2】(建物が) 建つ

A: What's that new building *going up* downtown? (ビジネス街に建設中のあの新しいビルは何なの？)
B: I think it's going to be a new bank. (新しい銀行だと思う)

☐ go up to
【1】…まで行く、…に近寄る

A: Will the waiter pick up our money at the table? (ウエイターがテーブルでお勘定してくれるの？)
B: No, you have to *go up to* the register to pay. (いや、レジに行って支払わないといけない)

【2】…まで上がる、…に達する

A: Won't it be too cold for a picnic tomorrow? (明日はピクニックには寒すぎないかな？)
B: Don't worry. It's supposed to *go up to* 25 degrees. (平気だよ。明日の気温は25度まで上がるらしい)

☐ go with
【1】…と調和する、似合う

A: Do you think these chairs *go with* the office furniture? (この椅子、オフィスの家具と合うかしら？)
B: Yeah, they match the desks really well. (ああ、机ととても合うよ)

【2】…を選ぶ

A: Have you decided which construction company you're going to use? (どの建設会社に任せるか決めましたか？)
B: Yes, we're going to *go with* ABC. They had the cheapest bid. (はい、ABC社にしました。入札価格がいちばん低かったので)

☐ go without …(すること) なしですませる、…がないのを我慢する

A: Are you going to *go without* lunch today? (今日はランチ抜き？)
B: Yeah, I had a really late breakfast. (ええ、朝食がとても遅かったので)

grow

☐ grow into

【1】成長[発展]して…になる

A: Your company has really *grown into* an impressive business. (御社はすばらしい企業になりましたね)

B: Thanks. We couldn't have done it without your help. (ありがとうございます。あなたのご尽力があったからこそです)

【2】成長して(服などが)着られるようになる

P: I bought these clothes for your new baby, but I think they're too big. (あなたの赤ちゃんに買ったお洋服なんだけど、大きすぎるかも)

S: Don't worry. She'll *grow into* them in no time. (ご心配なく。娘はすぐに着られるようになりますよ)

☐ grow on [upon]　…にとってだんだんよいと思われてくる

A: I thought you said you were going to quit your job last year. (去年、あなたは仕事を辞めるつもりだって言ってたと思うけど)

B: Well, my current job started to *grow on* me, and now I'm happy there. (まあね、当面の仕事がおもしろくなってきたんで、今はあそこでいいかなと思っている)

☐ grow out of

【1】体が成長して…が合わなくなる

A: Did you go on a diet or something? (ダイエットか何か始めた?)

B: I had to. I was *growing out of* all my clothes. (しかたなくね。太って服が全部合わなくなったんだ)

【2】([成長して]悪癖などを)やめる、…から脱皮する

A: I thought you really liked comic books. (あなたは漫画の大ファンだと思ってたけど)

B: I did, but I guess I've *grown out of* them. (確かにそうだったけど、漫画はもう卒業したって感じかな)

☐ grow up　成長する、大人になる (= mature)

A: What does your daughter want to be when she *grows up*? (あなたのお嬢さんは、大人になったら何になりたいのかしら?)

B: She says she wants to be a doctor. (医者になりたいそうです)

hand

☐ hand back （持ち主などに）…を返す、（土地などを）返還する (= return)

A: Were you able to sell your house?（あなたの家は売れましたか？）
B: No, I couldn't find a buyer, so I decided to *hand* it *back* to the bank.（いいえ、買い手が見つからなかったんです。だから銀行に返すことにしました）

☐ hand down （後世に）…を伝える、（遺産などを子孫に）残す

A: Where did you get this beautiful antique desk?（この美しいアンティークの机はどこで買ったの？）
B: It was *handed down* to me by my grandfather.（その机は祖父が私に残してくれたものです）

☐ hand in …を提出する、差し出す (= submit)

A: Have you *handed in* your report to George yet?（もうジョージに報告書を提出した？）
B: Not yet, but I'll probably finish it up by the end of the day.（まだだ。でも今日中には仕上がると思う）

☐ hand out （ビラ・印刷物などを）配る

A: Do you have an agenda for tomorrow's meeting?（明日の会議の議題一覧を持っていますか？）
B: Not yet. They'll probably *hand* them *out* at the meeting.（まだです。会議で配られるのではないでしょうか）

☐ hand over …を手渡す、引き渡す

A: I heard they're going to change the locks to the office next week.（来週、会社の鍵を付け替える予定だと聞きました）
B: They are, so you need to *hand over* your old key.（そうです。ですので、あなたが今使っている鍵を渡してください）

hang

☐ hang around

【1】…のあたりをぶらぶらする、うろつく

A: Who are all those people *hanging around* the airport lobby?（空港ロビーでうろついているあの人たちは一体誰なの？）

B: They're fans of a pop star. They're hoping to get a chance to see him.（人気歌手のファンだ。彼に会えるかもしれないって期待してるんだ）

【2】待つ、…でぐずぐずする

A: What are you still *hanging around* the office for?（どうしてまだ会社でぐずぐずしてるわけ？）

B: I have some work I need to finish before the weekend.（週末前に終わらせなくちゃいけない仕事があるんだ）

☐ hang around with （人に）つきまとう、（人と）一緒にいる

A: Have you still been *hanging around with* Linda since she quit?（リンダが退職してからも、あなたとリンダは付き合ってるの？）

B: Yeah, in fact, we're going to have dinner together tonight.（うん、実は今夜、一緒に食事することになってるんだ）

☐ hang off …から（はがれて）垂れ下がる

A: You've got some food *hanging off* your chin.（あごに何か食べ物がついている）

B: Thanks. I didn't even notice.（どうも。気づきもしなかったよ）

☐ hang on

【1】ちょっと待つ、（電話を）切らないで待つ

A: George is on the phone. He wants to talk to you.（ジョージからお電話です。あなたと話したいそうです）

B: Can you tell him to *hang on*? I'll be there in a second.（切らないで待つように伝えてもらえる？ すぐに電話に出るから）

【2】…次第である

A: Which university is best for me : Harvard or Oxford?（どの大学が私にとってベストかしら？ ハーバード、それともオックスフォード？）

B: It *hangs on* you.（きみ次第だ）

☐ hang onto
【1】…をつかまえている、…にしがみついている

A: Can you *hang onto* to my briefcase while I get the train tickets?（電車の切符を買ってくるあいだ、私のブリーフケースをしっかり持っていてくれる？）
B: Sure, but hurry up. The train is about to arrive.（わかった、でも急いで。電車はもうすぐくるよ）

【2】…を与えない［売らない］で持っている、取っておく

A: Why are you *hanging onto* such an old computer?（どうしてそんな古いコンピュータをまだ持ってるの？）
B: Why not? It still works fine.（いいじゃないか。まだよく動くんだ）

☐ hang out
【1】（外へ）垂れ下がる、突き出る

A: Is my shirt *hanging out* in the back?（私のシャツ、ウエストからはみ出してる？）
B: Yeah, it is. You'd better tuck it in.（ああ、中に入れたほうがいい）

【2】よく出入りする、たまり場にする

A: Is that bar down the street any good?（通りの先のあのバーって、いいお店？）
B: Yeah, it's really friendly. I *hang out* there all the time.（うん、居心地がいい。ぼくはいつもあそこに行くよ）

【3】付き合う、親しくする

A: Do you and George still *hang out* together?（あなたとジョージは今も親しいの？）
B: No, I haven't seen him in ages.（いや、あいつにはもう長いこと会ってない）

☐ hang over　…の上に突き出る、…ごしに身を乗り出す

A: Look at that kid *hanging over* the escalator handrail!（見て、あの子！ エスカレーターの手すりから身を乗り出してる！）
B: I hope his mother stops him. That's dangerous!（母親が止めればいいのに。危ないよ！）

☐ hang together　団結する、くっつく

A: I'm worried that the company's going to start cutting salaries.（会社は給料カットを始めるつもりじゃないかしら。心配だわ）
B: Me too. We need to *hang together* and fight for our rights.（ぼくもだよ。ぼくらは団結して権利を守るために奮闘しなければいけない）

☐ hang up

【1】（くぎ・ハンガーなどに）…を掛ける、つるす

A: Where can I put my coat?（コートはどこに置けばいいの？）
B: Just *hang* it *up* in the cloakroom.（クロークルームの中に掛けておけばいいよ）

【2】（受話器を）置く、（電話を）切る

A: Did you *hang up* on me on purpose?（私の電話をわざと切ったわけ？）
B: No, sorry, I accidentally pushed the button for another line.（違うんだ、ごめん、間違って割り込み電話のボタンを押しちゃったんだ）

【3】…の進行を妨げる、…を遅らせる

A: Why were you so late for the party?（パーティにどうしてそんなに遅れてきたの？）
B: Oh, I got *hung up* in a meeting that just wouldn't end.（なかなか会議が終わらず、時間を取られてしまったんだ）

---

column ▶▶▶ hang

hang up の逆の表現となる hang down は、高いところから物が「ぶら下がる」イメージになります。

- Icicles *hung down* from the roof.（つららが屋根からぶら下がっていた）
- Linda's head is *hanging down*. She must be depressed.（リンダがうなだれている。彼女は落ち込んでいるに違いない）
- George let his arm *hang down* into the water.（ジョージは水の中に腕を入れた）
- The branches of the tree *hang down* under the weight of the snow.（木の枝が雪の重みで垂れ下がっている）
- She let her long hair *hang down* her back.（彼女は長い髪をうしろに垂らしている）

have

☐ have against …に対して（恨み・反感などを）いだいている

A: Does the company *have* anything *against* wearing sneakers?（会社ではスニーカーをはいてはいけないのですか？）
B: Well, you probably should wear dress shoes if you can.（ええ、できればドレスシューズにしてください）

☐ have around …を手近に置く［置いている］

A: Oh, darn! I made a mistake. Do you have an eraser?（あらやだ！　間違えちゃった。消しゴム持ってる？）
B: Sure, I think I *have* one *around* here somewhere.（うん、どこかそのへんにあるはずだ）

☐ have back （貸したものを）返してもらう、取り戻す

A: Do you mind if I borrow your computer for a while?（しばらくのあいだ、あなたのコンピュータをお借りしてもいいですか？）
B: No, but I need to *have* it *back* tomorrow.（いいですよ、でも明日返してほしいです）

☐ have in （職人・医者などを）家［部屋］に入れる、呼ぶ

A: I think the air conditioner is broken.（エアコンが壊れてるみたい）
B: It is. We're *having* a repairman *in* next week to fix it.（そうだね。来週、修理工に直しにきてもらうよ）

☐ have off （ある期間・曜日などを）休みにする

A: Do you ever work on Saturdays?（土曜日も出勤することがあるの？）
B: No, I *have* the weekends *off*.（いや、週末は休みだ）

☐ have on

【1】（服・帽子・眼鏡などを）身につけている、かけている（= wear）

A: This print is so small I can't read it. Can you?（活字が小さくて読めない。あなた読める？）
B: No, sorry, I don't *have* my glasses *on*.（ごめん、眼鏡をかけてないので読めない）

□ hang up

【1】(くぎ・ハンガーなどに)…を掛ける、つるす

A: Where can I put my coat?（コートはどこに置けばいいの？）
B: Just *hang* it *up* in the cloakroom.（クロークルームの中に掛けておけばいいよ）

【2】(受話器を) 置く、(電話を) 切る

A: Did you *hang up* on me on purpose?（私の電話をわざと切ったわけ？）
B: No, sorry, I accidentally pushed the button for another line.（違うんだ、ごめん、間違って割り込み電話のボタンを押しちゃったんだ）

【3】…の進行を妨げる、…を遅らせる

A: Why were you so late for the party?（パーティにどうしてそんなに遅れてきたの？）
B: Oh, I got *hung up* in a meeting that just wouldn't end.（なかなか会議が終わらず、時間を取られてしまったんだ）

---

column ▶▶▶ hang

hang up の逆の表現となる hang down は、高いところから物が「ぶら下がる」イメージになります。

- Icicles *hung down* from the roof.（つららが屋根からぶら下がっていた）
- Linda's head is *hanging down*. She must be depressed.（リンダがうなだれている。彼女は落ち込んでいるに違いない）
- George let his arm *hang down* into the water.（ジョージは水の中に腕を入れた）
- The branches of the tree *hang down* under the weight of the snow.（木の枝が雪の重みで垂れ下がっている）
- She let her long hair *hang down* her back.（彼女は長い髪をうしろに垂らしている）

have

☐ have against …に対して（恨み・反感などを）いだいている

A: Does the company *have* anything *against* wearing sneakers?（会社ではスニーカーをはいてはいけないのですか？）
B: Well, you probably should wear dress shoes if you can.（ええ、できればドレスシューズにしてください）

☐ have around …を手近に置く［置いている］

A: Oh, darn! I made a mistake. Do you have an eraser?（あらやだ！ 間違えちゃった。消しゴム持ってる？）
B: Sure, I think I *have* one *around* here somewhere.（うん、どこかそのへんにあるはずだ）

☐ have back （貸したものを）返してもらう、取り戻す

A: Do you mind if I borrow your computer for a while?（しばらくのあいだ、あなたのコンピュータをお借りしてもいいですか？）
B: No, but I need to *have* it *back* tomorrow.（いいですよ、でも明日返してほしいです）

☐ have in （職人・医者などを）家［部屋］に入れる、呼ぶ

A: I think the air conditioner is broken.（エアコンが壊れてるみたい）
B: It is. We're *having* a repairman *in* next week to fix it.（そうだね。来週、修理工に直しにきてもらうよ）

☐ have off （ある期間・曜日などを）休みにする

A: Do you ever work on Saturdays?（土曜日も出勤することがあるの？）
B: No, I *have* the weekends *off*.（いや、週末は休みだ）

☐ have on

【1】（服・帽子・眼鏡などを）身につけている、かけている（= wear）

A: This print is so small I can't read it. Can you?（活字が小さくて読めない。あなた読める？）
B: No, sorry, I don't *have* my glasses *on*.（ごめん、眼鏡をかけてないので読めない）

【2】（ラジオ・テレビなどを）つけている

A: Who *has* the radio *on*? (誰がラジオをつけてるの？)
B: Linda. She likes to listen to music while she works. (リンダだ。仕事しながら音楽を聞くのが好きなんだよ)

【3】（約束・すべきことなどが）ある、（会などを）予定［計画］している

A: Do you *have* anything *on* for tonight? (今夜、何か予定がある？)
B: Not really. Do you want to go out for dinner or something? (何もない。食事にでも出かけようか？) ⇨ GO OUT [1]

【4】（体に）…をつけている

A: What is that that Linda *has on* her shoulders? (リンダが肩にかけているものは何かな？)
B: It looks like some kind of fur shawl. (毛皮のショールみたいだ)

□ **have out**　…を外へ出す、（歯などを）抜いてもらう、取ってもらう

A: Why is George in the hospital? (ジョージはなぜ入院しているの？)
B: I heard he's going to *have* his appendix *out*. (盲腸を取るって聞いたよ)

□ **have over**　（家に）…を客として迎える

A: Is your party tomorrow going to be very big? (明日のあなたたちのパーティはとても盛大になるのかしら？)
B: No, we're just *having* a few friends *over*. (いや、友だちを数人呼んでいるだけだよ)

---

column ▶▶▶ have

What do you have on? は、状況によりニュアンスが異なります。

「何を着ているの？」
「何の料理を作っているの？」
「テレビで何を見ているの？」
「(CDなどで) どんな音楽を聞いているの？」
「何を予定しているの？」などさまざまな意味にとれるため、前後関係から判断する必要があります。
また、次のような使い方もするので、ぜひ覚えておいてください。

・The police *have* nothing *on* me. (警察は私に不利な証拠をつかんではいない)
・He *has* nothing *on* me. (彼よりも私が弱いことはない)
・He's *having* you *on*. (彼はあなたをだましている)

hear

☐ hear about　…の噂［こと］を聞く、…について聞く

A: Did you *hear about* George's traffic accident?（ジョージの交通事故のこと、聞いた？）

B: No, what happened? Was he hurt?（いや、何があったんだ？　あいつ、けがしたのか？）

☐ hear from　（人から）便り［電話・連絡］がある［をもらう］

A: Have you *heard from* everyone you invited to the party?（パーティに呼んだ人はみんな連絡をくれた？）

B: Almost. Only Linda hasn't answered back yet.（ほとんどはね。リンダだけだよ、まだ返事がないのは）

☐ hear of

【1】…のことを聞く、…の存在を知っている

A: Have you ever *heard of* this computer brand?（このコンピュータのブランドのこと、ご存じ？）

B: Not at all. It must be a new brand.（まったく知らない。きっと新しいブランドなんだろう）

【2】…を聞き入れる、許す

A: Why don't you let me buy lunch?（ランチをおごらせて）

B: No, I won't *hear of* it. You've already paid so many times.（いや、それはだめだ。もう何度もおごってくれてるからね）

☐ hear out　（人の言うことを）最後まで聞く

A: Linda wants to tell me about some dumb idea she has for our new campaign.（新しいキャンペーンの件で、リンダは、ぱっとしない案を私に聞いてほしがってるんだけど）

B: You should *hear* her *out*. Sometimes she has good ideas.（彼女の話を最後まで聞いたほうがいい。たまにはリンダにも名案があるんだ）

help

☐ help out

【1】 …を手伝って出してやる、…を救い出す (= rescue)

A: How were you able to get out of the car? (どうやって車から出られたの？)
⇨ GET OUT OF ［2］
B: A firefighter opened the door and *helped* me *out*. (消防士がドアを開けて、救い出してくれたんだ)

【2】 (苦境にある人を) 切り抜けさせる、救い出す

A: Do you think you could *help* me *out* on the weekend? (週末は大変なんだけど、助けてもらえない？)
B: Sure, what can I do for you? (もちろん。何をすればいいかな？)

hit

☐ hit back　反撃する、しっぺ返しをする、言葉でやり返す

A: That newspaper article was really critical of our plans. Should we *hit back*? (あの新聞記事は、私たちの計画にすごく批判的だったわ。反論すべきかしら？)
B: Yes, we need to speak up to protect our reputation. (うん、ぼくたちの評判を守るために、はっきり言う必要があるよ) ⇨ SPEAK UP ［2］

☐ hit on [upon]　…をふと思いつく、…に思いあたる

A: Does anyone have any ideas to deal with this problem? (この問題への対処法について、案のある人はいる？)
B: Yes, I *hit on* a great idea when I was in the train. (はい、電車に乗っていて、ふとすごいアイデアを思いついたんだ)

hold

☐ hold against
【1】(過去の失敗を) とがめて (人に) 不利な判断をする、…を根に持って (人を) 恨む [非難する]

A: Aren't you mad at George for erasing your computer file? (ジョージにコンピュータのファイルを削除されたのに、あなたは怒らないの？)
B: No, I can't *hold* that *against* him. It was a simple mistake. (ああ、彼を非難するわけにはいかない。単純なミスだったんだから)

【2】…を〜に押しあて (てい) る

A: Why are you *holding* that cold-compress *against* your cheek? (なぜ頬にアイスパックをあててるの？)
B: I have a terrible toothache and it's all I can do until I see the dentist. (虫歯がすごく痛いんだけど、歯医者に診せるまでこうしておくしかなくてさ)

☐ hold back
【1】…を引き止める、押しとどめる、抑える、制御する

A: Linda sure is angry at George right now. (今、きっとリンダは、ジョージにかんかんに怒ってるよ)
B: I know. We'd better *hold* her *back* or she might even hit him! (ああ。リンダを抑えないと。さもないと、ジョージをぶったりするかも！)

【2】しりごみする、ためらう

A: I wonder if I should ask for a raise. (昇給を申し入れてもいいですか) ⇨ ASK FOR [1]
B: Well, don't *hold back*. You know you deserve one. (ああ、遠慮することはない。きみの働きは昇給に値するよ)

【3】(涙・感情などを) 抑える

A: That was one of the saddest movies I've ever seen. (それは私が今まで観た中でいちばん悲しい映画だったわ)
B: I know. I could barely *hold back* the tears. (そうだね。ぼくも涙を抑えるのがやっとだったよ)

【4】(進歩・成長などを) 阻む

A: How is it that you graduated from high school at age 19? (19歳で高校を卒業したのはなぜですか？)

B: I hate to admit it, but I was *held back* a year because of bad grades. (お恥ずかしいのですが、成績が悪くて1年留年したのです)

□ hold down

【1】…を押さえつける

A: Does your cat behave well when you take it to the vet? (おたくの猫ちゃんは獣医さんのところでおとなしくしてる？)

B: Heavens no! Three people have to *hold* it *down* for a vaccination. (とんでもない！ 予防接種するのに、3人がかりで押さえつけなくちゃいけないんだ)

【2】（物価・速度などを）低く抑える、抑制する

A: I heard the police patrol this street pretty heavily. (この通りを警察がかなり集中的にパトロールしてるって聞いたけど)

B: Yeah, they do, so you'd better *hold down* your speed. (うん、だからスピードを落としたほうがいいよ)

【3】（仕事・職に）とどまる、就く

A: Why is your son still living at home? (息子さんはどうしてまだ独立していないの？)

B: Well, he just can't seem to *hold down* a job. (まだ仕事に就けないみたいなんだ)

□ hold in （感情などを）抑える

A: I thought you were going to blow up at Linda when she made fun of your clothes. (リンダがあなたの服装をからかった時、あなたが怒るんじゃないかと思ったわ)
⇨ BLOW UP [4]

B: Well, with her, it's better to *hold* it *in*. That's just her personality. (うん、リンダには怒らないほうがいいんだ。あれが彼女の持ち味なんだからさ)

□ hold off

【1】…を遅らせる、延ばす (= delay, postpone)

A: I thought we were going to launch the new product next month. (新製品を来月に発売する予定と思っていました)

B: No, there are some design problems, so we're *holding* it *off* until they're fixed. (いや、デザインにいくつか問題があるので、それが解決するまで延ばすことにします)

【2】遠ざかる、さし控える

A: Don't you think you should *hold off* on those cookies? (このクッキー、あなたは食べないでおくほうがいいわよね)

B: You're right. I really need to lose some weight. (うん。ぼくはどうしても減量しなくてはいけないんだ)

☐ hold on　がんばる、踏みとどまる、（病人などが）持ちこたえる

A: I heard your grandfather is really sick.（おじいさんのお加減がとても悪いと聞きましたが）
B: That's true. I don't think he'll be able to *hold on* for much longer.（はい。もう長くはないと思います）

☐ hold onto [on to]
【1】…につかまっている

A: Wow, this escalator really goes fast!（わあ、このエスカレーター、すごく速いわね！）
B: Yeah, we'd better *hold onto* the handrail.（ああ、手すりにつかまったほうがいいよ）

【2】…を手放さないでおく、そのまま持っている

A: Do I need to turn in this report soon?（この報告書はすぐにお渡ししなければいけませんか？）⇨ TURN IN [1]
B: No, you can *hold onto* it for a while.（いいえ、しばらく持っていてかまいません）

☐ hold out
【1】（希望・見込みなどを）持たせる、与える

A: Do you think we'll get much of a bonus this year?（今年はボーナスがたくさん出ると思う？）
B: I wouldn't *hold out* much hope. We didn't have a good year.（あまり期待できないね。今年はいい年じゃなかった）

【2】（食糧などが）もつ、つづく

A: Do we need to order any coffee?（コーヒーをもっと注文しないといけない？）
B: No, we have enough to *hold out* for another month.（しなくていい。もうひと月分あるよ）

【3】抵抗する

A: Did you get everyone to agree on the new office hours?（新しい勤務時間のこと、みんなに賛成してもらえた？）
B: Almost everyone. George is still *holding out*.（大体はね。でもジョージがまだ賛成してくれない）

☐ hold over　…を続演する

A: That new comedy is really popular, isn't it?（あの新作の喜劇はすごく人気があるじゃない？）
B: Yeah. It'll probably be *held over* in theaters an extra month.（ああ、もう1カ月続演されるだろう）

☐ hold to

【1】(約束・信念などを) 堅く守る、あくまでも捨てない

A: Do you think George will *hold to* his promise to work overtime next month?（来月残業するという約束をジョージが守ると思いますか？）

B: Of course. He's never gone back on his word before.（もちろん。彼はこれまで約束を破ったことがありません）⇨ GO BACK ON

【2】(人に約束などを) 守らせる

A: I guess I'll go to your party, since you insist so strongly.（あなたのパーティに行こうかな、あなたがそんなにきてって言うなら）

B: Great! I'll *hold* you *to* your word.（やった！ 絶対だよ！）

☐ hold up

【1】…を上げ (てい) る、持ち上げる

A: Did you get any volunteers to work this Sunday?（今度の日曜日に仕事をしてくれる人、見つかった？）

B: I asked, but nobody *held up* their hands.（有志を募ったんだけど、誰も手を挙げなかったよ）

【2】(…の進行などを) 妨げる、遅らせる

A: How come you're so late this morning?（今朝はどうしてこんなに遅刻したの？）

B: I got *held up* in traffic.（渋滞に巻き込まれてしまって）

【3】(強盗などが) …を襲う、金品を強奪する

A: Aren't you afraid to work at an all-night convenience store?（終夜営業のコンビニで働くのって怖くない？）

B: Why? Nobody will *hold up* a store they know doesn't keep any cash on hand.（ちっとも。現金がまったくないとわかっている店なんて誰も襲わないよ）

jump

☐ jump around 跳ねまわる、躍りまわる

A: How do you like that novel you're reading? (今読んでる本はどんな感じ？)
B: It's really confusing. The plot *jumps around*. (すごくわかりにくい。筋書きがあちこち跳ぶんだ)

☐ jump in 話に割り込む (= interrupt)

A: I always feel so nervous about speaking out at our meetings. (会議で話そうと思うといつも不安になる) ⇨ SPEAK OUT
B: Don't be! Just *jump in* and talk like everyone else does. (心配しないで！話に割り込んで、みんなと同じように話せばいいんだよ)

☐ jump into すぐに…を始める [行なう]

A: Do you have enough people to start the project? (このプロジェクトを始めるのに、必要な人数はそろっていますか？)
B: No, we could still use some more people to *jump into* it. (いいえ、すぐに始めるには、もう少し必要です)

☐ jump on [upon] …をひどくしかる、激しく非難する (= berate)

A: Boy, Linda sure *jumped on* you for those mistakes in your report. (あら、あなたの報告書のこういうミス、リンダはきっとひどくしかったでしょうね)
B: I know. The worst thing is the mistakes weren't that bad. (ああ。最悪なのは、それほどひどいミスではなかったってことだ)

☐ jump out at (物事が)…の目を引く

A: Do you like my new business suit? (私の新しいビジネススーツ、気に入った？)
B: Well, those flashy colors really *jump out at* you. (そうだねえ、その派手な色は間違いなく人目を引くね)

keep

☐ keep after （人に…するように）うるさく言う

A: Do you think George will be able to finish this report on time? （ジョージがこの報告書を遅れずに提出できると思う？）

B: I'll *keep after* him and make sure he does it. （ぼくがうるさく言って、必ずやらせるよ）

☐ keep around …を手近に置いておく

A: Do you have an eraser I can borrow? （貸してもらえる消しゴムがありますか？）

B: I *keep* one or two of them *around*. （どこかこのへんに1個か2個あります）

☐ keep at

【1】（ある場所に）…を置いておく

A: Why do you need to *keep* a printer *at* your desk? （どうしてあなたの机にプリンタを置いておかなければいけないのですか？）

B: I use it to print out hourly reports. （1時間おきに報告書を印刷するために使うものですから）

【2】（熱心に）…をつづけてやる

A: I don't feel like my English is getting any better. （私、ちっとも英語が上達していないみたい）

B: I'm sure if you *keep at* it, you'll see a difference. （勉強をつづければ、必ず差が出ます）

☐ keep away from …に近寄らない、（物に）触れない

A: Why do I need to *keep away from* this machine? （どうしてこの機械に近寄ってはいけないの？）

B: It might fall over and hurt you. （倒れてきたら、けがをするからさ）

☐ keep back

【1】…を抑えておく

A: Why did you get so angry with Linda yesterday? （昨日リンダにあんなに怒ったのはなぜ？）

B: She kept making mistakes and I couldn't *keep back* my anger.（間違いばかりするから、怒らずにはいられなかったんだ）

【2】…を隠しておく、言わないでおく

A: Why did you *keep* this news *back* from me?（このニュースをどうして私に隠していたの？）

B: My boss told me not to tell anyone about it.（上司から誰にも話してはいけないと言われたんだ）

☐ keep down

【1】（頭・声などを）下げている

A: Please *keep* your voice *down*. Everyone's trying to concentrate.（声を小さくしてください。みんな集中しようとしているのです）

B: Oh, sorry. I'll step outside.（すみません、外に出ています）

【2】（物価などを）抑えておく

A: Are you planning on raising your prices again?（価格を再び上げる予定があるのですか？）

B: No, if possible, we'd like to *keep* our prices *down*.（いいえ、できれば下げるつもりです）

☐ keep from

【1】…に〜させない、…が〜しないようにする

A: Are you sure George is going to show up?（ジョージは本当にくるかしら？）
⇨ SHOW UP

B: I called him up this morning and he said nothing could *keep* him *from* coming.（今朝電話したら、何があってもくると言ってたよ） ⇨ CALL UP

【2】（秘密などを人に）知らせないでおく

A: Do you want me to send out a memo to all the employees?（従業員全員にメモを回せばいいでしょうか？）

B: No, let's *keep* this news *from* them for a little longer.（いや、このニュースはもうしばらく知らせないでおこう）

【3】…を〜から守る

A: I bought a lucky charm for you to *keep* you *from* harm.（あなたが災難に遭わないようにお守りを買ったわ）

B: I hope I never have to use it.（そのお世話にならないことを祈るよ）

☐ keep in （感情などを）抑える

A: I wish Linda would come out and tell me how she really feels. (リンダが思い切って本当の気持ちを打ち明けてくれればいいのに)

B: I know. She always *keeps* her feelings *in*. (ああ。彼女はいつも感情を外に出さない)

☐ keep off …を〜から離しておく、…を〜に近寄らせない (= separate)

A: Do you mind if I use your new camera? (あなたの新しいカメラを使ってもいい？)

B: Yes, I do. *Keep* your hands *off* it! (だめです。触らないでください！)

☐ keep on

【1】（服などを）身につけたままでいる

A: Is it okay if I *keep on* my shoes here? (靴をはいたままでもいいですか？)

B: No, I'm afraid you need to take them off. (いいえ、すみませんが、靴は脱いでください)
⇨ TAKE OFF [1]

【2】（人を）雇いつづける、所有［借用・使用］しつづける

A: I heard everyone got fired except for you? (あなた以外はみんなクビになるって聞いたけど)

B: Yeah, they *kept* me *on* because I do the accounting. (うん、ぼくは経理だからクビにならないんだって)

【3】…しつづける

A: How do I get to the bank from here? (銀行にはここからどうやって行けばいいですか？)

B: *Keep on* going down this street until you reach a stoplight, then turn left. (この通りをまっすぐ行って、信号のところで左折してください)

☐ keep out of

【1】…の外にいる、…から離れている

A: Do you want to go for a walk after lunch? (ランチのあとに散歩したい？)

B: No, I'd rather *keep out of* the sun. (いや、日にあたりたくない)

【2】…に関わらないでいる、（面倒などを）避けている

A: Aren't you going to help Linda with her legal problems? (法律上の問題でリンダに手を貸してあげるの？)

B: No, I definitely want to *keep out of* that. (いや、その問題には絶対に関わりたくない)

☐ keep to （コース・場所などから）離れない

A: Do you want to *keep to* the course, or just wander around the museum?

(このコースどおりに行くほうがいい？ それとも美術館をゆっくり見てまわる？)

B: We'd better stay on the course if we want to see everything. (全部見たければ、コースどおりに行くのがいい)

□ keep together　…をまとめておく、(人びとを) 協調させる

A: Do you want me to *keep* these files *together*? (この複数のファイルをまとめておいたほうがいいですか？)

B: Yeah, let's put them in the same folder. (はい、同じフォルダにまとめましょう)

□ keep under　(感情を) 抑える

A: I was so mad that I couldn't prevent myself from throwing the documents. (あんまり頭にきたので、思わず書類を投げちゃった)

B: You need to *keep* your emotions *under* control, especially at work. (きみは感情を抑えなくてはいけない。特に仕事中は)

□ keep up

【1】(活動などを) つづける、持続する (= continue, sustain)

A: Linda has been working for 15 hours now. (リンダはもう15時間も働きづめよ)

B: I don't think she'll be able to *keep* it *up* for much longer. (もうこれ以上、長くはつづけられないだろう)

【2】(人を寝かさないで) 起こしておく

A: You look really sleepy. Did you not get enough sleep? (すごく眠そうよ。十分に寝ていないの？)

B: No. My neighbor's dog *kept* me *up* last night. (うん。近所の犬のせいで昨日の夜は眠れなかったんだ)

□ keep up with　(人・情報などに) 遅れないでついて [やって] いく

A: Is Linda able to *keep up with* the other engineers? (リンダはほかのエンジニアについていけるかな？)

B: Yes, she has no problem understanding what's going on. (大丈夫さ、彼女は状況を問題なく把握しているから)　⇨ GO ON［2］

kick

☐ kick around [about]

【1】（考え・提案を）いろいろと検討する

A: Maybe we should think about getting a new logo. （ロゴを新しくすることを考えるべきかもしれません）

B: That's an interesting idea. Let's *kick* it *around*. （いいアイデアですね。検討しましょう）

【2】…を虐待する、こづきまわす（= abuse）

A: Why don't you want to work with George? （ジョージと一緒に仕事したくないの？）

B: He's always *kicking* me *around*. He treats me like dirt. （あいつ、ぼくをいつもこき使うからさ。ぼくをないがしろにしてるんだ）

☐ kick back くつろぐ（= relax）

A: Did you do anything fun on the weekend? （週末、おもしろいことをした？）

B: No, I just *kicked back* and took it easy at home. （いや、家でただのんびりくつろいでいた）

☐ kick in

【1】（ドアなどを）け破って入る

A: How did the robbers get into your house? （泥棒はどうやってあなたの家に入ったの？）

B: They *kicked in* the door. （ドアをけ破って入った）

【2】影響し出す、効き始める

A: Do you know when this new policy will *kick in*? （この新しい方針はいつから施行されるの？）

B: I heard from George that it'll take effect in April. （ジョージの話では4月からだそうだ）

☐ kick off （人を場所・組織から）追い出す

A: Why did you get *kicked off* the committee? （どうしてあなたはその委員会から追い出されたの？）

B: I think it was because I was too critical of the chairperson. （ぼくが議長にあまりにも批判的だったからだと思う）

knock

□ knock around [about] （人・物を）こづきまわす、手荒く扱う

A: Was the printer broken when it got to your office? (そのプリンタ、あなたのオフィスに届いた時に壊れてたの？)
B: Yeah, I think it got *knocked around* by the shipping company. (ああ、運送会社で手荒く扱われたんだろう)

□ knock back （仕事・人などの）進行を遅らせる

A: Why weren't you able to get this job done by Thursday? (木曜日までにこの仕事ができなかったのはなぜ？)
B: I had an emergency, and that *knocked* me *back* by a day. (急用ができて、1日遅れてしまったんです)

□ knock down

【1】（建物などを）取り壊す、解体する

A: You're not going to *knock down* that old warehouse, are you? (あの古い倉庫は壊さないですよね？)
B: We might have to. It's hard to pay for the upkeep. (壊さざるをえないでしょう。維持費を払うのが大変なのです)

【2】（値を）下げる、（人に）値をまけさせる

A: If you could *knock* the price *down* by 10 percent, we'll increase the size of our order. (御社が価格を1割引いてくださるなら、注文を増やします)
B: I'll check with my boss and see if that's possible. (上司と相談の上、可能かどうか検討いたします) ⇨ CHECK WITH

【3】（大量の酒を）一気に飲み干す

A: I got so drunk I couldn't even stand up. (飲みすぎて立ち上がることもできなかった)
⇨ STAND UP [1]
B: Really? How many beers did you *knock down*? (ほんとに？ どれだけのビールを一気に飲んだの？)

□ knock into （人・頭に知識などを）教え込む、たたき込む

A: Linda keeps forgetting that she has to fill out a daily report. (日報を書かな

けばいけないのに、リンダはずっと忘れている）　⇨ FILL OUT

B: How can we *knock* that *into* her head?（そうしなくてはいけないとリンダに教え込むには、どうしたらいいだろう？）

☐ knock off

【1】（仕事などを）やめる、中止する、切り上げる（= quit, stop）

A: What time are you planning on *knocking off* today?（今日は何時に仕事を終える予定？）

B: If possible, I'd like to head back home at around 7:00.（できれば7時頃に帰宅したい）

【2】（ある額を）割り引く、まける（= discount）

A: Could you *knock off* 15 percent from the price?（15%値引きしてもらえませんか？）

B: That's too much. The most I can give you is a 10 percent discount.（それは多すぎます。値引きできるのは10%までです）

【3】…を殺す（= kill）

A: Does George get *knocked off* at the end of the movie?（あの映画のラストでジョージは殺されるの？）

B: I'm not going to tell you. It'll spoil the movie for you.（それは言わないでおこう。映画を見る楽しみがなくなるからね）

☐ knock out

【1】（人を）へとへとにする

A: I heard you can't go golfing with us today.（今日、一緒にゴルフに行けないんですってね）

B: Yeah, I worked a double shift yesterday and it *knocked* me *out*.（ええ、昨日、二交代勤務でへとへとになってしまって）

【2】…を手早く仕上げる、…を苦労して作る

A: How many parts does this factory make?（この工場で作っている部品はいくつですか？）

B: It can *knock out* 30,000 parts a day.（ここでは1日3万個仕上げることができます）

☐ knock over　（物を）盗む（= steal）、（場所に）強盗に入る（= burglarize）

A: I heard the convenience store got *knocked over* again last night.（昨夜、またコンビニエンスストアに強盗が入ったんですって）

B: They need to invest in a better security system.（お金をかけて、もっときちんとした防犯システムを取り入れないといけない）

laugh

☐ laugh about …について笑う

A: What's everyone *laughing about*? (みんな、何を笑っているの？)
B: Linda just showed us a funny video of her cat eating ice cream. (リンダが、アイスクリームをなめる愛猫の、おもしろいビデオを見せてくれたところさ)

☐ laugh at …をあざ笑う、冷笑する (= ridicule)

A: Just tell everyone you dropped your phone in the toilet. (トイレに電話を落としたって、みんなに言ってみたら)
B: No, I don't want to be *laughed at*. (いや、笑いものにされるのはごめんだ)

☐ laugh away …を笑って払いのける、笑いとばす

A: Do you think George is ever going to pay you back? (ジョージがお金を返すとでも思っているの？)　⇨ PAY BACK [1]
B: No, I don't. I asked him about it and he just *laughed* me *away*. (いや、そうじゃない。頼んでみたけど、笑いとばされたよ)

☐ laugh off …を笑ってごまかす、一笑に付す、笑いとばす

A: I'm so embarrassed. Everyone saw me with my shoelaces untied. (とても恥ずかしいわ。靴ひもがほどけているのを、みんなが見てたの)
B: It's not that serious. Just *laugh* it *off*. (そんなに気にすることはない。笑ってすませばいいさ)

lay

☐ lay aside …をわきへ置く、中断する (= suspend)

A: Do you think we should just forget about this project? (このプロジェクトはもはや放念すべきとお考えですか？)

B: No, we just need to *lay* it *aside* for now. We'll come back to it later. (いえ、一時中断すればいいだけです。のちほど再開します) ⇨ COME BACK [3]

☐ lay back くつろぐ、リラックスする (= relax)

A: It seems like you're always doing something fun. (あなたって、いつもおもしろいことをしているみたい)

B: Some people like to *lay back* and relax, but I like to stay active. (のんびりくつろぐのが好きな人もいるけど、ぼくはいつも活動的でいたい)

☐ lay down …を下に置く、降ろす、寝かせる

A: I don't think I can keep on holding up this sofa. (このソファをずっと持ち上げてはいられないと思う) ⇨ KEEP ON [3]

B: Okay, why don't you *lay* it *down* carefully? (いいよ、注意して下に置いてもらえる？)

☐ lay off

【1】(一時的に) 従業員を解雇する、一時帰休させる

A: I heard that ABC is planning on *laying off* a lot of workers. (ABC 社は大勢の従業員を一時解雇する予定だと聞きました)

B: Yeah, it's true. I'm probably going to be out of a job soon. (ええ、そうです。もうすぐぼくは失業するでしょう)

【2】(酒・たばこなどを) やめる (= quit)

A: Hey, how about going out for a drink tonight? (ねえ、今夜飲みに行かない？) ⇨ GO OUT [1]

B: Sorry, I'm trying to *lay off* the alcohol. (ごめん、断酒するつもりなんだ)

☐ lay out

【1】(衣服などを) 広げる (= spread)、並べる

A: I'll try not to be late tomorrow, but 7:30 is really early for me. (明日は遅刻しないようにしないと。でも 7 時半は私にはすごく早いのよね)

B: Why don't you *lay out* your clothes so you can get up and get dressed in a hurry?（起きたらすぐに着られるように、服を広げて置いておけば？）⇨ GET UP [1]

【2】（仕事などの）計画を立てる、（案などを）用意する

A: What do you do at Monday morning meetings?（月曜日の朝の会議では何をするの？）
B: We *lay out* plans for the coming week.（翌週のプランを練る）

【3】（考えなど）詳しく説明する

A: I heard that you have a suggestion for bringing down our costs.（コストを下げるための案があるそうですね）⇨ BRING DOWN [3]
B: I do. If you have a few minutes, I can *lay* it *out* for you.（はい、あります。数分いただければ、それを詳しくご説明できます）

【4】（大金を）つぎ込む（= invest）

A: These new office chairs are going for only 500 dollars.（オフィス用の新しい椅子、全部でたった500ドルよ）⇨ GO FOR [5]
B: I don't think we can *lay out* that much just for chairs.（たかが椅子にそんな大金はつぎ込めないと思う）

☐ **lay up** （病気などで人を）寝込ませる

A: I haven't seen Linda in a long time. What's keeping her away?（長いことリンダに会っていない。どうしたのかな？）
B: I heard she's been *laid up* with a bad cold.（ひどい風邪で寝込んでいるそうだよ）

---

column ▶▶▶ lay

lay offは、辞書などでは「（一時的に）従業員を解雇する、一時帰休させる」と紹介されていますが、実際には一時的なものではなく、結果的に「クビにする」という意味合いで使われることがほとんどです。ただし、同義語のfire（解雇する）よりは柔らかい言い方に聞こえます。

・George would have to *lay off* his staff.（ジョージはスタッフをクビにしなくてはいけないだろう）

layoffと1語になれば「解雇、一時帰休」という名詞になり、これもまた「解雇」の意味で使われることがほとんどです。

・ABC had over 200 *layoffs* last year.（ABC社は去年200人以上を解雇した）

Lay off it!は、「やめなさい！」という意味の決まり文句で、itは「やっていること」を指します。感情的にしかりつけているように聞こえるので、そうむやみに使わないほうがいいでしょう。

leave

☐ leave behind

【1】…を置き忘れる、忘れてくる、置き去りにする

A: Why's that briefcase sitting on the floor? (このブリーフケース、どうして床に置いてあるの？)

B: Someone *left* it *behind* after the meeting. (誰かが会議のあとに忘れていったんだ)

【2】…を置いてきぼりにする、取り残す

A: How come you didn't get home until late last night? (昨日、夜遅くまで家に帰ってこなかったのはなぜ？)

B: I was late for the bus and I got *left behind*. (バスに乗り遅れて、置いてきぼりにされたんだ)

☐ leave in (字句などを) そのままにしておく

A: Do you think I should *leave in* this part of my presentation? (私のプレゼンのこの部分、残しておいたほうがいいかしら？)

B: Maybe you should take it out. It's not very relevant. (削除したほうがいいと思う。本筋とはあまり関連がないから) ⇨ TAKE OUT [2]

☐ leave off

【1】(明かりなどを) 消したままにしておく

A: Don't you want me to turn on the lights? It's getting dark. (電気をつける？暗くなってきたよ) ⇨ TURN ON [2]

B: No, I want to *leave* them *off* so I can rest my eyes. (いや、電気はつけなくていいよ。そのほうが目が休まる)

【2】…を外しておく、(名簿などに) 載せないでおく

A: Do you know why my name was *left off* the list? (私の名前が名簿に載ってなかった理由がわかる？)

B: I'm sure it was done on purpose. (きっと、わざとだよ)

☐ leave on (衣服などを) 身につけたままでいる

A: Is it okay if I *leave on* my shoes? (靴をはいたままでいいですか？)

B: No, I'm afraid you need to take them off. (いいえ、すみませんが脱いでください)
⇨ TAKE OFF [1]

☐ leave out

【1】…を外に出したままにしておく

A: Why did you throw away your rug?（どうしてあなたのラグマットを捨ててしまったの？）
  ⇨ THROW AWAY [1]
B: I *left* it *out* in the rain and it got moldy.（雨の中、外に出しっぱなしにしておいたら、かびが生えてしまったんだ）

【2】(人・物を) 抜かす、除外する

A: Who should we tell to come to the meeting tomorrow?（明日の会議は誰を呼べばいいですか？）
B: Tell everyone they have to come, and don't *leave* anyone *out*.（呼ぶ必要がある者は、全員呼んでください。誰1人省くことなく）

☐ leave up to （仕事・決定などを）…に任せる

A: Do you think we should serve coffee or tea at the meeting?（会議でコーヒーか紅茶を出したほうがいいですか？）
B: I'll *leave* that *up to* you.（きみに任せるよ）

L

---

column ▶▶▶ leave

動詞の leave には「大事なものを残してどこかへ行く」というニュアンスがあるため、自分自身に対して使うと、物悲しいイメージになります。そのため感覚的には、以下のようになるでしょう。

- He *left* me. なら、
 「彼は私を置いていった」→「彼に捨てられた (離婚された)」
- I feel *left out*. なら、
 「置いていかれたような気がする」→「仲間はずれにされたように感じる」
- I got *left behind*. なら、
 「私は置いていかれた」→「(楽しい所へ行ったが) 私は置いてきぼりにされた」

物と人の両方を目的語にとる語の場合、目的語によりニュアンスが変わることもあるので、注意が必要です。

let

☐ let by …を（そばを）通す

A: Excuse me, could you *let* me *by* so I can go to the restroom?（すみません、通していただけますか？　お手洗いに行きたいので）

B: Okay, sure. I think I'd better stand up.（はい、もちろん。立ったほうがいいですね）
⇨ STAND UP ［１］

☐ let down （人の）期待を裏切る

A: Don't be so hard on yourself. You didn't do anything wrong.（そんなに自分を責めないで。あなたは間違ったことは何もしなかったわ）

B: I feel like I *let* my company *down*.（仲間の期待を裏切ったような気がする）

☐ let in （空気・光などを）通す

A: Do you want me to open up a window and *let in* the breeze?（窓を開けて風を入れましょうか？）

B: Yeah, I think we need some fresh air.（ああ、新鮮な空気が必要だね）

☐ let off

【1】（罰・仕事などから人を）放免する

A: I'm surprised your boss didn't *lay* you *off* for stopping production.（生産を止めたあなたのことを、上司がクビにしなかったなんて、驚きだわ）

B: Yeah, me too. I guess he felt sorry for me and *let* me *off* easy.（うん、ぼくもびっくりだ。ぼくをかわいそうだと思って、軽い処分ですませてくれたんだろう）

【2】（乗り物から）…を降ろす

A: Do you think the bus driver will *let* us *off* here?（バスの運転手さんはここで降ろしてくれるかしら？）

B: No, we have to wait for the next stop.（いや、次のバス停まで乗っていくしかない）

☐ let on

【1】（…であると）漏らす（= divulge）、認める（= admit）

A: Don't *let on* to anyone that we're almost out of money.（私たちにはお金がほとんどないこと、誰にも言っちゃだめよ）

B: Okay, I'll try to keep it a secret. (うん、内緒にしておくことにするよ)

【2】 …を（乗り物に）乗せる (= put)

A: Will they *let* us *on* the train with bicycles? (電車には自転車も乗せてもらえるかな？)
B: Yeah, but we'll need to stand up the whole way. (ああ、でも、ぼくらはずっと立っていなくてはいけない) ⇨ STAND UP [1]

☐ let out

【1】 …を外に出す、解放する (= release)

A: Do you *let* your cat *out*? (あなたは猫を外に出してあげる？)
B: No, she likes to stay in where it's safe. (いや、あの子は安全なところにいるのが好きなんだ)

【2】 （叫び声・怒りなどを）発する、上げる

A: How did Linda react when she learned she won the lottery? (宝くじがあたったとわかった時、リンダはどうした？)
B: She *let out* a scream and started dancing. (叫び声を上げて、踊り出した)

☐ let through （誤りなどを）見逃す (= miss)

A: How did you *let* this defect *through*? (どうしてこの欠陥を見逃してしまったのですか？)
B: I don't know. I looked at each part carefully. (さあ、わかりません。部品はどれも注意してチェックしました) ⇨ LOOK AT

☐ let up （雨・風が）やむ (= cease)、弱まる (= weaken)

A: When do you think the rain is going to *let up*? (雨はいつやむと思いますか？)
B: Hopefully soon. I want to get out of here by 3:00. (すぐやんでほしいです。3時までにここを出たいので)

☐ let up on （人に対して）より寛大になる

A: I'm going to tell George that he has to get this project done by 5:00 today. (このプロジェクトを今日の5時までに終わらせなければいけない、とジョージに言うつもりです)
B: Maybe you should *let up on* him. He's been working really hard. (ジョージを大目に見てあげたほうがいいように思います。彼はとても懸命に仕事をしています)

lie

☐ lie ahead （物事が）…の将来に起こる、…を待ち受けている

A: How is the sales forecast for next year? （来年の販売予測はどうですか？）
B: I'd say we have a really good year *lying ahead*. （とてもよい年になると言えるでしょう）

☐ lie around [about] （物が）ちらかっている、ほったらかしてある

A: You shouldn't leave your wallet *lying around* like that. （こんなふうにお財布をほったらかしにしちゃだめよ）
B: You're probably right, but I doubt anybody in the office would steal it. （なるほど、そうかもしれないけど、オフィスでは誰かがぼくの財布を盗むとは思えない）

☐ lie back あおむけに横たわる

A: You look really tired. Why don't you go home early? （すごく疲れているみたいよ。早くうちに帰ったら？）
B: Oh, I'll be okay if I just *lie back* at lunchtime and take a short nap. （ああ、でも、昼休みに横になって、少し眠れば、大丈夫だよ）

☐ lie behind …の（隠れた）理由［原因］となっている

A: I'll bet something *lies behind* all the overtime work George is doing. （ジョージが残業をつづけているのには、隠れたわけがあるに違いないわ）
B: Me too. I'm sure he's looking for a promotion. （同感だ。きっと昇進目当てだよ）

☐ lie off （陸地・他船から）少し離れている

A: I heard you bought a beach-front summer house. （海辺の別荘を買ったんですってね）
B: Yeah, it's on a small island that *lies* just *off* the coast. （はい、海岸から少し離れた小さな島にあるんです）

live

☐ live by …を生活の指針とする

A: You always eat such healthy foods, don't you? (いつもそんなに体にいいものを食べているのですか？)

B: Well, maintaining a healthy lifestyle is something I try to *live by*. (ええ、健康的な暮らしを維持することは、ぼくが目標とする生活の指針ですから)

☐ live down (不名誉・罪・過失などを) 償う (= compensate)、(汚名を) そそぐ

A: Boy, everyone was sure shocked at how drunk you were at the party. (まったく、あなたはパーティでお酒に酔ってあんなひどいことになって、みんなほんとに驚いたわよ)

B: I know. I don't know if I can ever *live* it *down*. (わかってる。あの失態をぬぐえるかどうか、わからないよ)

☐ live for …のために生きる、…を生きがいにする

A: I can't believe Linda is taking another week of vacation leave. (リンダがもう1週間休暇を取るなんて、信じられない)

B: Yeah, she sure seems to *live for* vacations. (そうだね、確かに、彼女は休暇を楽しみにして暮らしているようだ)

☐ live off …で生計を立てる、食べていく

A: I heard you're working a second job at nights. (あなたが夜にアルバイトをしていると聞きました)

B: I don't want to, but I can't *live off* just my salary here. (したくはないのですが、ここの給料だけでは、やっていけないんです)

☐ live on …に頼って暮らす

A: You really struggled when you were in college, didn't you? (大学時代はとてもご苦労されていたんですって？)

B: Oh, yeah. I was *living on* only 50 dollars a week. (はい、そうです。1週間、わずか50ドルで暮らしていました)

☐ live out

【1】（人生・年月を）終わりまで生き抜く、終わりまで過ごす

A: Is your grandmother going to move into a retirement home?（あなたのおばあさまは、老人ホームに入られるおつもりですか？） ⇨ MOVE INTO

B: No, she wants to *live out* her days in her own house.（いいえ、祖母は自宅で最後まで過ごしたいと思っています）

【2】（夢・理想などを）実現する（= realize）

A: Have you seen George's new sports car?（ジョージの新しいスポーツカーを見た？）

B: Yeah. It's like he's *living out* his teenage fantasies.（見たよ。あいつは10代の頃の夢を実現しているようだね）

☐ live through　…を（経験して）生き延びる、切り抜ける（= survive）

A: I can't believe you had to work 12-hour days all last month.（あなたが先月ずっと12時間勤務をしなくてはいけなかったなんて、信じられない）

B: Yeah, I never want to *live through* something like that again.（ああ、もう2度とあんな経験はしたくない）

☐ live up to　（期待などに）応える（= respond）

A: I heard you once wanted to be a doctor.（医師になりたいと思っていたことがあるんですってね）

B: Well, my parents wanted that, but I couldn't *live up to* their expectations.（はい、両親の希望だったのですが、期待に応えられませんでした）

☐ live with

【1】…と一緒に暮らす、同居する、同棲する

A: Do you have an apartment all to yourself?（マンションに1人だけで住んでいるの？）

B: No, I *live with* two roommates.（いや、ルームメイト2人と同居している）

【2】…に耐える、…を我慢する（= withstand）

A: It must be hard for your father to *live with* cancer.（あなたのお父さんは、癌を受け入れて生きていらっしゃって、さぞおつらいことでしょう）

B: No, he's doing quite well, and he's even optimistic about it.（いや、父はかなり回復していますし、病気については実に楽観的なんです）

look

□ look after …の世話をする、…を管理する

A: Will you *look after* my mail while I'm on vacation?（休暇中、私宛てのメールをチェックしてもらえる?）

B: No problem. I'll even answer anything that looks important.（いいよ。重要だと思うメールには返信もしておいてあげる）

□ look ahead 将来のことを考える

A: What plans does your company have for next year?（御社は来年、どんなことをご計画されていますか?）

B: We're *looking ahead* to opening a new branch office.（新しい支店を開設しようと考えております）

□ look around

【1】（立ったままで）ぐるりと見まわす

A: Are you really giving away all the office furniture?（オフィスの家具をすべて手放してしまうって本当?）

B: Yeah. *Look around* and take what you want.（ああ、ざっと見て、気に入ったものを持っていってよ）

【2】見てまわる、（買う前などに）調べる

A: Do you know what kind of car you're going to buy?（どんなタイプの車を買うつもり?）

B: No, I'm still *looking around* at different dealers.（わからない。まだディーラーを何軒か見てまわっているところだ）

□ look at …を調べる (= investigate)、検査［診察］する (= examine)

A: I can't seem to get rid of this rash on my arm.（腕の発疹が消えそうにない）

B: You should have a doctor *look at* it.（お医者さんに診てもらったほうがいいよ）

□ look back （心の中で過去を）振り返ってみる

A: I always get bored during the New Year's holiday. There's nothing to do.（お正月休みはいつも退屈。することがないんだもの）

B: Well, it's a good time to *look back* on the year. (今年1年を振り返るいい機会だ)

☐ look down （景気・物価が）下降する

A: Linda thinks that the economy is going to start looking up. (リンダの考えでは、景気は上昇し始めているんですって) ⇨ LOOK UP [1]
B: Really? If you ask me, the economy is *looking down*. (ほんとに？ ぼくに言わせれば、景気は下降しているけどね)

☐ look down at [on] …を見くだす

A: George's family has a lot of money and they like to show it off. (ジョージの家族は裕福で、それを見せびらかすのが好きなの) ⇨ SHOW OFF
B: I know. I feel like he's always *looking down at* me. (ああ。彼はいつもぼくを見くだしているように感じる)

☐ look for 自分から（面倒などを）招く

A: I'm thinking about remodeling my house by myself. (自分で自宅をリフォームしようと思ってるの)
B: Are you sure you want to do that? I think you're *looking for* trouble. (本気でそんなことしたいの？ 自分から面倒を招くことになると思うけどね)

☐ look forward to …を楽しみにして［首を長くして］待つ

A: My plane will get in at around 5:30. (私の飛行機が着くのは5時半頃です) ⇨ GET IN [3]
B: Okay, I'll be at the airport. I'm really *looking forward to* meeting you. (了解、その頃空港にいるよ。きみに会えるのがほんとに楽しみだ)

☐ look into （…の内容［原因］を）調べる、調査する (= examine, investigate)

A: I think the air conditioner has broken down. (エアコンが壊れちゃったみたい) ⇨ BREAK DOWN [5]
B: Let me *look into* it. I might be able to fix it. (調べてあげよう。たぶん直せると思うよ)

☐ look like

【1】（様子などから）…のように見える、…のようである (= appear)

A: You *look like* you haven't gotten any sleep. (一睡もしていないみたいね)
B: Yeah, I stayed up all last night trying to finish my report. (はい、報告書を仕上げようとして、昨日は徹夜しました) ⇨ STAY UP [1]

【2】…しそうだ、…になりそうだ

A: It *looks like* we're going to be late. (遅刻しそう)
B: If we leave now, we might be able to get there on time. (今出発すれば、遅れずに到着できるだろう)

☐ look over

【1】…に（ざっと）目を通す、…を（ざっと）調べる

A: You're an accountant, are you? Could you *look over* this tax form? (あなたは税理士さんですよね？　この納税申告書に目を通していただけますか？)
B: Everything appears to be in order. (すべて問題ないようです)

【2】…を視察［点検］する

A: Was your house damaged in the earthquake? (ご自宅は地震で傷みましたか？)
B: I'm not sure. I'm going to have an expert *look* it *over*. (詳しくはわかりません。専門家に点検してもらうことになっています)

☐ look through

【1】…にざっと目を通す、（書類などを）さっと調べる (= skim)

A: Could you *look through* this report before the meeting? (会議の前に、この報告書に目を通していただけますか？)
B: Sure. I'll get right on it. (いいですよ。すぐに拝見します)

【2】（引き出しの中などを）探す、調べる (= search)

A: Were you able to find the sales report for last year? (昨年の販売報告書は見つかりましたか？)
B: I *looked through* all my drawers, but it's nowhere. (自分の引き出しを全部調べたのですが、どこにもありません)

☐ look up

【1】（景気・物価が）上昇する、（天候などが）好転する

A: I think the economy is finally starting to *look up*. (景気がようやく上昇し始めたように思います)
B: I hope you're right. This recession has been going on for too long. (あなたの考えが正しいといいのですが。今度の不況はあまりにも長引いています) ⇨ GO ON ［3］

【2】（辞書などで）…を調べる、（辞書などを）引く (= consult)

A: Do you know what "hoity toity" means? ("hoity toity" って、どういう意味？)
B: That's a strange word. I'll *look* it *up* in the dictionary. (聞き慣れない言葉だ。辞書で調べてみるよ)

make

☐ **make of** ～を…と思う

A: It seems like ABC is ignoring all our e-mail messages. (ABC 社はこっちのメールをすべて無視しているみたい)

B: What do you *make of* that? Do you think they're ignoring us? (どう思う？われわれを無視しているんだろうか？)

☐ **make off with** …を持ち去る、持ち逃げする、盗む (= steal)

A: What happened to my lunch box? I'm sure I put it right here. (私のお弁当はどうしたのかしら？ ここに置いておいたはずよ)

B: Maybe someone *made off with* it. (あるいは誰かが盗んだのかもしれない)

☐ **make out**

【1】…を（なんとか）理解する、わかる、解釈する (= understand)

A: I have a hard time *making out* Linda's writing. (リンダが書いたものを理解するのはむずかしい)

B: I know. Her writing is beautiful, but it's hard to read. (そうだね。文章は美しいけど、読むのに苦労する)

【2】（表・書類などを）作成する、書く、書き上げる (= write)

A: Would you like me to *make out* a receipt? (領収書が必要ですか？)

B: Yes, please. Could you write it to Sam Brown? (はい、お願いします。サム・ブラウン宛てでお願いできますか？)

☐ **make up**

【1】（話・うそなどを）作り出す、でっち上げる

A: Linda said that she can't come today because her uncle died. (おじさんが亡くなったから、今日はこられないってリンダが言ってたわよ)

B: I'm pretty sure she *made* that *up*. She's used that lie before. (作り話に違いない。リンダは前にも同じうそをついたことがあるんだ)

【2】仲直りする

A: They had a fight, but the next day, they kissed and *made up*. (彼らはケンカをしたけど、翌日キスをして仲直りしたわ)

B: I'm glad they were able to work things out. (うまくいってよかった)

mark

☐ mark down

【1】…を値引きする、値下げする

A: It seems like our sales are slowing down. Do we need to *mark down* our prices? (われわれの売り上げは鈍化しているようね。価格を下げる必要があるかしら？)

B: No, we need to keep our prices where they are now. (いや、今の価格を維持する必要がある)

【2】…を書き留める

A: I always lose score. Do you know who has the most points? (いつもスコアを忘れてしまう。誰がいちばんポイントが高いか、わかる？)

B: Yes, I'm *marking down* the points, so don't worry. (うん、書き留めているから心配しないで)

☐ mark off

【1】（線などで）仕切る、区切る、（土地などを）区画する

A: Why are the workers *marking off* the ground like that? (あの作業員たち、どうしてあんなふうに土地を区切っているの？)

B: That's where they're going to put the foundation. (その部分に土台を立てるんだ)

【2】（リストで）…に済みの印を付ける

A: This is a list of everyone who's invited to the meeting. (これが会議に招かれた全員のリストよ)

B: Okay, I'll *mark off* the names as people come in. (了解。きた人の名前にチェックを付けるよ)

☐ mark up （定価・商品を）値上げする

A: If we don't *mark up* our prices, we'll go into the red. (値上げしなければ、赤字になってしまうわ)

B: But higher prices might hurt our sales. (でも価格が上がると、売り上げに響くかもしれない)

meet

☐ meet up

【1】(人に) 出会う、会う、待ち合わせる (meet up with)

A: Do you have time to *meet up* with George tomorrow? (明日、ジョージに会う時間はある？)

B: Sure. I'd love to sit down with him and discuss this problem. (ああ。彼と腰を据えて、この件について話したい)

【2】(道路などが) 交わる

A: Do you know what's up ahead on this road? (この道、この先がどうなっているかわかる？)

B: Yeah, it *meets up* with the freeway about a mile from here. (ああ、ここから1マイルほどで高速道路と交わるよ)

☐ meet with

【1】…を経験する、…に遭遇する (= experience, receive)

A: It seems like George really grew a lot in America. (ジョージは、アメリカで本当にずいぶんと成長したようね)

B: Yeah, he *met with* a lot of trials that made him more mature. (ああ、さまざまな試練を経験したことで、さらに成熟したよ)

【2】…と会う、会見する (= interview)

A: If possible, I'd like to *meet with* ABC's president. (できれば、ABC社の社長にお目にかかりたい)

B: Yeah, it would be good to talk to him directly. (ああ、直接話せればいいだろうね)

---

column ▶▶▶ make

make (107ページ) のよく使われる成句を1つ紹介します。make it up to は、「…に対して (迷惑などの) 埋め合わせ [償い] をする」(= compensate) の意味で使われます。

A: It's no problem. I can give you a ride to the airport. (大丈夫。空港まで車で送るわ)

B: Thanks! I'll *make it up to* you someday. (ありがとう！ いつか埋め合わせするよ)

move

☐ move around （仕事で）転々と職場［住所］を変える

A: I heard that Linda is planning on changing jobs. (リンダは転職するつもりみたいね)
B: Again? She sure does *move around* a lot. (また？　本当にしょっちゅう仕事を変えるね)

☐ move away 立ち去る、立ちのく、転居する

A: Did you hear that George is going to *move away*? (ジョージが引っ越すって聞いた？)
B: Really? I thought that he liked living here. (本当？　ここに住むのが気に入ってると思ってたよ)

☐ move into …に引っ越す

A: Do you know when Linda is going to *move into* her new house? (リンダがいつ新しい家に引っ越すか知ってる？)
B: Pretty soon, I think. She already bought new furniture for it. (もうすぐだと思うよ。もう新居用の新しい家具も買ってるし)

☐ move on （新しい場所・活動などに）移る

A: You're not serious about quitting, are you? (辞めるなんて、本気で言ってるんじゃないよね？)
B: Actually, I am. I've been working here for a long time, so it's time that I *move on*. (実は本気なんだ。長らくここで働いたから、そろそろ移る頃だと思ってね)

☐ move over （ベンチなどで）席を詰める

A: Is there enough room for three people on this bench? (このベンチに3人座れるスペースはある？)
B: If George will *move over* just a little, there is. (ジョージがちょっと席を詰めてくれれば大丈夫だ)

open

☐ open out

【1】(ソファなどが) 広げられて…になる (open out into)

A: I don't see a bed. Where do you usually sleep? (ベッドがないわね。普段どこで寝るの？)
B: This sofa *opens out* into a bed. (このソファを広げるとベッドになるんだ)

【2】(花が) 開く、咲く

A: When's the best time to see the cherry blossoms? (桜を見るのにいちばんいい時期は？)
B: They usually *open out* in late March. (大体3月末に花が開くよ)

☐ open up

【1】(新規) 開店する

A: What time does the supermarket *open up* today? (スーパーは今日何時に開くの？)
B: It's a holiday, so they're closed for the day. (今日は休日だから、終日閉店だよ)

【2】心を開く、自由に [隠さずに] 話す

A: Do you know why Linda is crying? (どうしてリンダが泣いているのか、わかる？)
B: I asked her what was wrong, but she wouldn't *open up* to me. (どうしたのかたずねたんだけど、何も話してくれなかったよ)

pass

☐ pass around [round] …をぐるりと回す、順々に回す

A: Would you like me to *pass around* these printouts?（このプリントを回しましょうか？）

B: No, that's okay. I'll pass them out.（いえ、結構です。私が配ります）　⇨ PASS OUT [1]

☐ pass away （人が）亡くなる、息を引き取る (= die)

A: Did you hear that George's grandfather *passed away*?（ジョージのおじいさんが亡くなったって聞いた？）

B: No, I didn't know. Was it sudden?（いや、聞いてなかったな。急だったの？）

☐ pass by （そばを）通り過ぎる

A: Could you give me a ride to the shopping mall?（ショッピングモールまで車で送ってくれない？）

B: Okay, sure. I'll *pass by* there on my way to work.（もちろん、いいよ。仕事に行く時に通るから）

☐ pass in （答案・宿題などを）提出する (= submit)

A: Okay, time is up, and everyone needs to *pass in* their test sheet now.（はい、時間です。みなさん、今から答案用紙を提出してください）

B: But I'm not even half finished!（でも半分も終わってないよ！）

☐ pass on （人が）死ぬ (= die)

A: I have some bad news. Your grandmother has *passed on*.（悪い知らせがあるの。あなたのおばあさんが亡くなったわ）

B: Oh, no. I can't believe it.（えー、信じられないよ）

☐ pass out

【1】（ビラ・商品・見本などを）配る (= distribute)

A: Do you want me to *pass out* these pamphlets?（このパンフレットを配りましょうか？）

B: No, just put them on the table and let people pick them up.（いや、ただテ

ーブルの上に置いて、持っていってもらおう)

【2】意識を失う、気絶する (= faint)

A: I was so nervous I *passed out*. (緊張のあまり、気絶しちゃったわ)
B: You're kidding. How long did it take for you to come to? (冗談だろ？　正気づくまでどれぐらいかかったの？)

□ pass through　(苦しみなどを) 通り抜ける、経験する (= experience)

A: Did you have a safe flight? (安全なフライトだった？)
B: No, we *passed through* a bad storm and it was really rough. (いや、大嵐を切り抜けたよ。本当に大変だった)

□ pass up　(招待などを) 断わる、辞退する (= decline)

A: Aren't you going to go to the hot springs with everyone? (みんなと一緒に温泉に行かないの？)
B: No, I'm going to have to *pass* that *up* this time. (うん、今回は見送らないといけないんだ)

---

column ▶▶▶ pass

　pass といえば「通過する、過ぎ去る、回す」といった意味を思い浮かべるでしょうが、ネイティブはもう1つ「死ぬ」ことも想像します。
　die はあまりにも直接的に「死ぬ」を表わす言葉のため、それを避けて婉曲的に pass で表現するのです。そのため、「彼は去年死んだ」と言うのであれば、He died last year. よりも、

・He *passed away* last year.
・He *passed on* last year.

のほうが柔らかな表現となります。

　pass away と pass on はほぼ同じ意味ですが、pass away のほうがより多く使われているようです。He passed last year. でも同じような意味になりますが、これはやや古い言い方で、最近はあまり使われません。

pay

☐ pay back
【1】(人に)金を返す (= return, repay)

A: Why don't you trust George?（どうしてジョージを信用しないの？）
B: I lent him some money, but he never *paid* me *back*.（いくらかお金を貸したんだけど、決して返してくれないんだよ）

【2】…に仕返しをする、しっぺ返しをする (= requite)

A: Aren't you mad at Linda for telling rumors about you?（リンダがあなたの噂を流したのに、腹を立ててないの？）
B: Yes, I am. I'm going to *pay* her *back*.（怒ってるさ。仕返ししてやるよ）

☐ pay for …の報いを受ける

A: I have a really bad headache this morning.（今朝は本当にひどい頭痛がするの）
B: You're *paying for* drinking too much last night.（昨夜飲みすぎた報いだね）

☐ pay off (口止めなどのために)…を買収する (= buy)

A: Why didn't George get arrested? Everyone knows he's guilty.（どうしてジョージは逮捕されなかったの？ 彼に罪があるって、みんなわかってるのに）
B: I'm pretty sure he *paid off* the police.（警察を買収したに決まってるよ）

☐ pay up (滞納金などを)全額支払う

A: George took my computer, but he never gave me the money for it.（ジョージは私からコンピュータを買ったのに、ぜんぜん支払ってくれないの）
B: You're kidding? Okay, I'll get him to *pay up*.（本当かい？ よし、ぼくが全額払わせるよ）

pick

☐ pick on …のあら探しをする、…をいじめる (= tease)

A: One of my coworkers is always *picking on* me. It's really stressful. (ある同僚がいつも私のあら探しばかりするの。すごいストレスなのよ)
B: You need to complain about it to your boss. (上司に訴えるべきだよ)

☐ pick out …をつまみ［抜き］出す

A: If you see a defective part, you need to *pick* it *out*. (もし欠陥部品を見かけたら、より分けておいて)
B: Okay, I'll watch out for anything irregular. (わかった。異常がないか気をつけるよ)
⇨ WATCH OUT

☐ pick through …の中をくまなく探す、1つひとつ調べる

A: Where did you find these pretty earrings? (このすてきなイヤリング、どこで見つけた?)
B: It was in that box. I had to *pick through* it all to find them. (あの箱の中にあったんだ。これを見つけるのに、くまなく探さないとならなかったよ)

☐ pick up

【1】(車で人を) 迎えにいく

A: How can I get from the airport to your office? (空港からあなたのオフィスまで、どう行けばいいの?)
B: Don't worry. I'll go to the airport and *pick* you *up*. (心配しないで。空港まで迎えに行くから)

【2】(外国語などを) 聞き覚える、身につける (= learn)

A: Did it take you a long time to *pick up* Spanish? (スペイン語を身につけるのに、長い時間がかかった?)
B: It took about five years, but I had a good time doing it. (5年ほどかかったけど、楽しかったよ)

【3】…の支払いを引き受ける

A: That was a wonderful dinner. Let me pay for it. (すばらしいディナーだったわ。ここは私に支払わせて)
B: That's okay. My company will *pick* it *up*. (大丈夫。会社で持ちますから)

play

☐ play around [about] (人・動物が) 遊びまわる、ふざける

A: Okay, everyone, stop *playing around* and get back to work. (さあ、みんな。ふざけるのはおしまいにして、仕事に戻りましょう)

B: We're on our break and we still have five more minutes. (まだ休憩中で、あと5分あるよ)

☐ play down (物事を) 重要でないように見せる、(記事を) 小さく扱う

A: Did the newspaper report on the scandal? (このスキャンダル、新聞で報じられた?)

B: Yeah, but they really *played* it *down*. Most people never heard about it. (ああ、でも本当に小さな扱いだったから、ほとんどの人はまったく知らなかったよ)

☐ play up …を重要であるように見せる、強調する (= emphasize)

A: I was only three minutes late, but my boss really screamed at me. (たった3分遅れただけなのに、上司ったらすごく怒鳴りつけたのよ)

B: Yeah, he really *played* it *up*. He was trying to make an example out of you. (ああ、ひどく大ごとにしてたね。きみを見せしめにしようとしてたんだろう)

☐ play with …で遊ぶ、(言葉・感情などを) もて遊ぶ

A: I heard George told Linda that he loves her. (ジョージがリンダに告白したって聞いたわよ)

B: I'm sure he was just *playing with* her. He doesn't really like her. (彼女をもて遊んでるだけさ。本当は好きなんかじゃないよ)

pull

☐ pull apart （人間関係を）引き裂く、…を引き離す (= separate, tear)

A: I think my parents are trying to *pull* us *apart*. (うちの両親は、私たちの仲を引き裂こうとしてると思う)

B: Nothing can ever make me leave you. (何があっても、きみから離れないよ)

☐ pull away （車などが）出ていく、発車する (= depart)

A: Is it too late to get on the ship? (船に乗るには遅すぎますか？) ⇨ GET ON [1]

B: It's *pulling away* now. If you hurry, you might be able to get on. (今、出るところです。急げば乗れるかもしれません)

☐ pull back （人・物を）引き戻す

A: George is in London, but he's not making any progress. (ジョージはロンドンにいるんだけど、まったく進展がないの)

B: Oh, I see. Do you think we should *pull* him *back*? (ああ、そうか。彼を呼び戻すべきだと思う？)

☐ pull for …を応援する (= cheer)

A: I really don't think I can do it. I don't have the skills. (私、本当にできないと思う。スキルがないもの)

B: Don't give up. Everyone's *pulling for* you. (あきらめないで。みんな応援してるから)

☐ pull in （客などを）引きつける、呼び寄せる (= attract)

A: Why do you sell eggs for less than what they cost? (どうして卵を原価より安く売ってるの？)

B: We use them to *pull in* customers. (お客さんを引きつけるために卵を使ってるんだ)

☐ pull into （列車などが駅などに）入る、到着する (= arrive)

A: Are we too late to get on the 5:15 train? (私たち、5時15分の電車に乗るには遅すぎますか？) ⇨ GET ON [1]

B: You should be okay. The train's *pulling into* the station right now. (大丈夫ですよ。電車はちょうど今、駅に入ってきています)

☐ pull off

【1】 …を（さっと）脱ぐ、外す、引っ張って取る (= remove)

A: Could you help me *pull off* these gloves? They're too tight. (この手袋を脱ぐのを手伝ってもらえますか？ きつすぎるんです)
B: How did you ever get them on? (一体どうやってはめたの？) ⇨ GET ON [4]

【2】 …をうまくやり遂げる、見事にやってのける

A: Are you sure George can talk ABC into saying yes? (ABC 社がイエスと言うように、ジョージが説得できるって本当に思う？)
B: Don't worry. He can *pull* it *off*. (心配しないで。彼ならうまくやれるよ)

☐ pull out （歯・栓などを）抜く (= remove)

A: Why are you going to the dentist's? (なんで歯医者さんに行くの？)
B: I'm going to have them *pull out* a wisdom tooth. (親知らずを抜いてもらうんだ)

☐ pull out of （困難・契約などから）抜け出す、手を引く、(軍隊が)…から撤退する

A: I thought you were in a joint venture with ABC. (御社は ABC 社との合併事業をやっていると思っていました)
B: We were, but we decided to *pull out of* it. (そうでしたが、手を引くことにしました)

☐ pull through 元気【意識】を回復する (= recover)

A: I heard Linda was in an accident. Is she going to *pull through*? (リンダが事故に遭ったって聞いたわ。回復するの？)
B: Yeah, she's feeling better already. (ああ、もう元気になってきた)

☐ pull together 協力して働く、協力してやっていく (= cooperate)

A: I'm amazed that your team got so much work done. (あなたたちのチームがとても多くの仕事をしたので驚いたわ)
B: Yeah, everyone *pulled together* and worked really hard. (ああ、みんなで協力し合って、懸命に働いたよ)

push

☐ push back （予定などを）延ばす、遅らせる (= delay, extend)

A: I thought you were going to a big meeting today. （あなた、今日は大きな会議があると思ってたけど）
B: I did, but it got *pushed back* a week. （そうだったんだけど、1週間延びたんだ）

☐ push for …のためにがんばる

A: I heard that Linda is *pushing for* George's proposal. （ジョージの提案に対して、リンダがすごくがんばってるって聞いたわよ）
B: Really? I wonder why she likes it so much. （本当に？ どうしてリンダはそんなに気に入ってるんだろう？）

☐ push into （人に）強いて…させる

A: Why did you run for mayor? （どうして市長選に出馬したの？） ⇨ RUN FOR
B: I really didn't want to, but I got *pushed into* it. （本当はしたくなかったんだけど、立候補させられたんだ）

☐ push out …を解雇する、追い出す (= dismiss, expel)

A: Didn't you go into business with George? （ジョージと一緒に事業を立ち上げたんじゃなかったの？）
B: I did, but we disagreed on some things and I got *pushed out*. （そうだけど、いくつか合意できないことがあって、ぼくは追い出されたんだ）

☐ push up …を押し上げる

A: The president is trying to *push up* employment numbers before the election. （大統領は、選挙前に雇用者数を押し上げようとしているわね）
B: It'll be hard to increase jobs during this recession. （この不況で仕事を増やすのは大変だろうね）

put

☐ put across （計画・意見などを）…に理解させる、わからせる

A: Do you think Linda will be able to get approval for her proposal? (リンダは提案を承認してもらえると思う？)

B: Probably not. She has a hard time *putting across* her opinions. (たぶん、むり。わかってもらうのは大変だろうね)

☐ put aside （仕事などを）中断する

A: What about the plan you told me about last month? (先月話してくれた計画はどう？)

B: Well, I decided to *put* it *aside* for a couple of years. (ああ、あの計画は数年中断することにしたよ)

☐ put away

【1】（いつもの所へ）…をしまう、片づける

A: Don't forget to *put away* those tools when you're through with them. (その道具、使い終わったら忘れずに片づけてね)

B: I won't. I'll put them all back in the box. (忘れずに全部箱にしまうよ)

【2】（将来に備えて）…を蓄える、貯金する、取っておく (= save)

A: Were you able to *put* any money *away* when you were working in London? (ロンドンで働いている時、多少は貯金できたの？)

B: Yes, I saved up enough money to pay for my tuition. (うん、授業料を払えるくらい貯まったよ)

☐ put back

【1】…の進行を遅らせる (= retard)

A: Do you think this accident will have an impact on the project? (この事故でプロジェクトに影響が出ると思う？)

B: I'm sure it will. It'll *put* us *back* three months. (もちろん出るね。進行が3カ月遅れるだろう)

【2】（日付・行事などを）延期する、あとへ延ばす

A: Do you mind if we *put* our appointment *back* a couple of days? (約束を

数日延ばしてもかまいませんか？）

　B: Sure. How about meeting on Friday morning?（かまいません。金曜日の朝に会う
　　のはいかがですか？）

【3】（大酒を）飲む (= drink)

　A: I didn't know that George was such a big drinker.（ジョージがあんなに大酒飲み
　　とは知らなかった）

　B: Neither did I. He *put back* about 20 beers.（ぼくも。ビールを20杯ぐらい飲んでたよ）

□ put before …を〜より優先させる

　A: I know you want to go to a funeral, but you have to work.（葬儀に行きたい
　　のはわかるけど、仕事しないと）

　B: I'm sorry, but this time I'm going to *put* my family *before* my job.（申し訳
　　ないが、今回は仕事より家族を優先させてもらうよ）

□ put down

【1】…を（下に）置く

　A: Do you want me to put this vase up on the shelf?（この花瓶、棚の上に置けばい
　　いの？） ⇨ PUT UP [6]

　B: You'd better *put* it *down* on the floor so it won't break if it falls over.（床
　　に置いたほうがいいんじゃないかな。そうすれば、落ちて割れてしまうことはない）

【2】…を書き記す、記入する (= fill)

　A: Are you sure you *put down* everything that Linda said?（リンダが言ったこと、
　　確かに全部書き記したのね？）

　B: Yes, I'm sure I didn't miss anything.（確かだよ。ひと言も漏らさずにね）

【3】頭金［内金］として（ある金額を）払う (= pay)

　A: I think you should back out of the deal.（その契約を取り消すべきだと思う）
　　⇨ BACK OUT OF

　B: It's too late. I already *put* 500 dollars *down*.（もう遅いね。すでに頭金500ドルを
　　払ってしまったよ）

【4】…をけなす、こきおろす (= disparage)

　A: You're so slow, and you never do anything right.（まったくグズね。何１つまと
　　もにできないじゃない）

　B: Why do you enjoy *putting* me *down*?（なぜぼくをこきおろして楽しむの？）

【5】（赤ん坊を）寝かせる

　A: Hello, this is Pam. Is this a good time for you to talk?（もしもし、パムよ。今
　　話せるかしら？）

B: Let me *put* my son *down* and I'll call you right back.（息子を寝かしてから、すぐかけ直すよ）

【6】（病気や老齢の動物を）安楽死させる、殺す（= kill）

A: Are you thinking about *putting down* your dog?（あなたの犬を安楽死させるつもり？）

B: I know she's in a lot of pain, but I want to keep her alive as long as possible.（すごく苦しんでるのはわかるけど、できるだけ長く生かしておきたいんだ）

☐ **put forward** （考え・案などを）提出する、提案する（= propose）

A: That sounds like a really great idea. I'd give it my full support.（すごくすばらしいアイデアみたいね。全面的にサポートするわ）

B: Do you think I should *put* it *forward* at the next meeting?（次の会議で提案すべきだと思う？）

☐ **put into** （人を役職などに）就かせる

A: Do you think we should *put* Linda *into* a management position?（リンダを管理職に就かせるべきだと思う？）

B: Well, to tell you the truth, she's not that good at communicating.（うーん、実を言うとね、彼女はコミュニケーションがうまくないんだ）

☐ **put off**

【1】（物事・約束などを）延期する（= postpone）

A: When are you going to make up your mind? ABC is waiting for your decision.（いつ腹を決めるつもりなの？ ABC 社はあなたの決定を待ってるのよ）

B: I guess I can't *put* it *off* any longer.（これ以上延ばせないと思う）

【2】（言葉・態度が人を）不快にする

A: Why is George mad at me? I didn't say anything rude at all to him.（どうしてジョージは私に腹を立ててるの？ 失礼なことなんて何も言ってないわ）

B: I know, but your bad attitude *put* him *off*.（わかってる。でも、きみの失礼な態度が彼を不快にしたんだよ）

☐ **put on**

【1】（化粧などを）する、…を身につける（= wear）

A: Is Linda ready to leave for the airport?（リンダは空港へ出発する準備ができてる？）

B: No, she still needs to *put on* her makeup.（いや、まだメイクをしないと）

【2】（劇などを）上演する、…を催す（= stage）

A: You really *put on* a great performance last night. It was amazing!（昨夜は本当にすばらしい芝居を演じたわね。すごくよかった！）
B: Thank you! I'm glad you enjoyed it.（ありがとう！ 楽しんでくれてうれしいよ）

【3】（体重・速度などを）増す（= increase, add）

A: It looks like Linda is *putting on* a little weight. Maybe she should go on a diet.（リンダは少し体重が増えてるみたい。たぶんダイエットしたほうがいいわね）
B: Didn't you know? She's going to have a baby.（知らなかった？ 彼女、赤ちゃんが生まれるんだよ）

【4】（ブレーキ・圧力などを）かける

A: Do you think it's okay to stop here?（ここで止まっても大丈夫だと思う？）
B: Yeah, but you'd better *put on* the handbrake so we don't roll down the hill.（うん、でも坂を下らないように、サイドブレーキをかけたほうがいい）

【5】（人を）からかう、かつぐ、だます（= fool）

A: Linda told me that she's the president's daughter. Is she *putting* me *on*?（リンダは自分が大統領の娘だと言ったの。私、だまされてるのかしら？）
B: No, I'm pretty sure she's telling the truth.（いや、本当のことを言ってるに違いない）

【6】（人を電話に）出す

A: Can I talk to George directly about this?（これについてジョージと直接話せるかしら？）
B: Yeah, he's right here. Let me *put* him *on* the phone.（うん、彼はここにいるよ。電話を代わるよ）

【7】（人を仕事などに）就ける

A: Do you want me to *put* Nancy *on* this job?（この仕事にナンシーを就ける？）
B: That's okay. I can do it by myself.（いや、いいよ。自分でできる）

□ put out

【1】…を公にする、出版する（= publish）、放送する（= broadcast）

A: Isn't working for a magazine a lot of pressure?（雑誌の仕事って、すごくプレッシャーがあるんじゃない？）
B: Yeah, we have to *put out* two issues a month, so I always have a deadline.（うん、月に2回発行しないといけないから、常に締め切りがあるんだ）

【2】…を生産する（= produce）

A: Do you know what the capacity of this factory is?（この工場の生産能力がどれくらいか、わかりますか？）

B: Yes, it's 400 cars a day, but they're only *putting out* 300 cars right now.（ええ、1日に車400台ですが、現在は300台しか生産していません）

【3】（人に）面倒をかける（= inconvenience）

A: Thanks for the ride yesterday. I'm sorry if I *put* you *out*.（昨日は車に乗せていただいて、ありがとう。ご面倒だったとしたら、ごめんなさいね）

B: Oh, I was on my way to work, so it was no trouble at all.（いえいえ、仕事に向かう途中だったから、まったく問題なかったよ）

【4】…を外に出す、追い出す

A: Aren't you worried about *putting out* your cat at night?（夜に猫を外に出して心配じゃないの？）

B: Not really. She always stays in the yard.（そうでもないよ。いつも庭にいるから）

【5】（肩・ひざなどを）脱きゅうする、…の関節を外す（= dislocate）

A: Why is George walking on crutches?（どうしてジョージは松葉杖をついて歩いてるの？）

B: He went skiing and *put out* his knee.（スキーに行って、ひざを脱きゅうしたんだよ）

【6】（麻酔などで）…の意識を失わせる

A: You've been sleeping at your desk for over an hour.（机で1時間以上も眠ってたわよ）

B: Sorry, I took some cold medicine and it *put* me *out*.（申し訳ない。風邪薬を飲んだら意識をなくしちゃって）

【7】（力を）発揮する、奮い起こす（= exert）

A: I didn't have enough time to get this project done.（このプロジェクトを終わらせる時間が十分なかったの）

B: That's because you didn't *put out* enough effort.（十分に力を尽くさなかったからだよ）

□ put over （うそなどを）…に信じ込ませる（put over on）（= convince）

A: George says he knows how I can double my money in only a month.（ジョージは、私がたった1カ月でお金を2倍に増やせる方法を知っていると言っているわ）

B: It sounds like he's trying to *put* something *over* on you. Don't trust him.（きみに一杯食わせようとしているみたいだな。信用しちゃだめだよ）

□ put through

【1】（人に）…の電話をつなぐ（= connect）

A: I'd like to speak to George in Human Resources.（人事部のジョージさんとお話ししたいのですが）

B: Just one moment, and I'll *put* you *through*. (少々お待ちください。ただいまおつなぎします)

【2】（計画・改革などを）やり遂げる

A: Do you think the new president will be able to *put through* his renovation plan? (新しい社長は、彼の改革案をやり遂げられると思う？)

B: It's possible, but he's going to face a lot of resistance. (できるけど、たくさんの抵抗に遭うだろう)

【3】…に（苦しみなどを）経験させる (= experience)

A: Do you think Linda will ever get back with George? (リンダはジョージとより を戻すこともあると思う？) ⇨ GET BACK WITH

B: I hope not. He really *put* her *through* a lot. (ないと思うよ。ジョージはリンダに相当つらい思いをさせたから)

☐ put to （質問などを）…にする

A: Do you think we'll be able to expand the advertising budget? (私たちは広告予算を拡大できると思う？)

B: Let's *put* that question *to* Linda when she gets here. (リンダがここにきたら質問してみよう)

☐ put together …を集める、寄せ集めて（食事などを）作る (= gather)

A: Maybe we should have the meeting at your house, if that's okay. (もしよかったら、あなたの家で会議をしたらいいかもしれないわ)

B: No problem. I'll *put together* something to snack on while we talk. (かまわないよ。話しながら軽くつまめるよう、あり合わせで何か作るよ)

☐ put toward （金を）…の費用にあてる［使う］

A: What are you saving up for? (何か目的があってお金を貯めているの？)

B: I'm trying to *put* money *toward* starting my own company. (自分の会社を始める費用にあてようと思っている)

☐ put up

【1】（家・像などを）建てる (= build)

A: I think we should *put up* a statue of our company's founder. (会社の創業者の像を建てるべきだと思うの)

B: Well, it wouldn't be cheap to have a statue made. (うーん、像を作るのは安くないよ)

【2】 …を泊まらせる、宿泊させる（= accommodate）

A: It looks like I've missed the last train. I guess I'll have to sleep on the street.（終電を逃しちゃったみたい。路上で寝るしかないかもね）

B: Don't worry. I can *put* you *up* for the night.（心配しないで。一晩泊めてあげるよ）

【3】（資金を）提供する、融通する

A: How are you going to get the money to build a factory?（どうやって工場の建設費を調達するの？）

B: I've met an investor who's going to *put up* the capital.（資金提供してくれる投資家に会ったんだ）

【4】（家・土地などを）売りに出す

A: Why are you spending so much time fixing up your house?（どうして家の修繕にそんなに時間をかけているの？）　⇨ FIX UP

B: I'm going to *put* it *up* for sale.（売りに出すつもりなんだよ）

【5】（抵抗・戦いなどを）つづける（= continue）

A: If we cut everyone's salary, do you think they'll *put up* a protest?（みんなの給与を削減したら、彼らは抵抗すると思う？）

B: Yeah, I don't think many people will go along with that plan.（ああ、多くの人はその案を支持しないと思うね）　⇨ GO ALONG WITH

【6】（髪を）結い上げる、…を（上に）上げる（= raise）

A: When Linda *puts up* her hair, it means she has an important meeting.（リンダが髪をアップする時は、大事な会議があるってことよ）

B: I guess it does make her look more serious.（そのほうがいっそう真剣に見えるよね）

□ **put up with** …を我慢する（= tolerate）

A: I can't *put up with* that noise any longer! It's driving me crazy.（これ以上あの騒音に我慢できない！　気が変になりそうよ）

B: Okay, I'll go tell George to turn down his music.（わかった。ジョージに音楽のボリュームを下げるように言ってくるよ）　⇨ TURN DOWN [1]

read

☐ read into （物事に付加した意味を）読み込む

A: I saw George look at me funny. I think he wants me to quit. （ジョージが変な目で私を見ていた。私に辞めてもらいたいのだと思う）
B: You're *reading* too much *into* it. （考えすぎだよ）

☐ read on 読みつづける

A: Do you want me to stop reading here? （ここで読むのをやめたほうがいいかしら？）
B: No, *read on* for a few more pages. （いや、もう数ページ読んでよ）

☐ read out 声を出して読む、読み上げる

A: Is it okay if I just read it to myself? （それを黙読するだけでいいかしら？）
B: I think you'll remember it better if you *read out* loud. （大声で読んだほうがよく覚えると思うよ）

☐ read through [over] …を終わりまで読む、通読する

A: Could you *read through* this report by the meeting? （会議までに、このレポートをひととおり読んでおいてもらえますか？）
B: It's over 200 pages! I can't read that much in 30 minutes! （200ページ以上ありますよ！ そんなにたくさん、あと30分で読めません）

☐ read up on [about] （書物などで）…を集中[徹底]的に調べる、研究する (= investigate, study)

A: I've never been to Indonesia before. I don't know anything about that country. （インドネシアに行ったことないの。その国のこと、何も知らないわ）
B: Maybe you should *read up on* it before you leave. （出発までに、徹底的に調べるんだね）

run

☐ run across …に偶然出会う

A: Have you talked to Linda recently?（最近、リンダと話している？）
B: Yes, I *ran across* her a few days ago in the park.（ああ、数日前に公園でばったり会ったよ）

☐ run after …のあとを追う、追跡する (= pursue)

A: Oh, no! George left his briefcase here.（あら、やだ！ ジョージったら、ここにブリーフケースを忘れたわ）
B: Do you want me to *run after* him?（彼を追いかけたほうがいい？）

☐ run against （選挙・競走で）…に対抗する (= counter)、…と争う (= contend)

A: Are you still thinking about running for mayor?（まだ市長選への出馬を考えているの？） ⇨ RUN FOR
B: No, I would have to *run against* the current mayor, and he's really popular.（いや。現市長と争わなくてはならないだろうし、彼はとても人気があるからね）

☐ run along 去る、立ち去る

A: Why don't we have lunch today?（今日、ランチしない？）
B: I'd like to, but I'd better *run along*. I have a lot to do.（そうしたいけど、帰ったほうがいいかも。やることがいっぱいある）

☐ run around

【1】浮気する、不貞をはたらく (run around on)

A: Do you think George is *running around* on Linda?（ジョージはリンダを裏切って、浮気していると思う？）
B: I don't think so. He seems really faithful to her.（そんなことはないと思う。彼は本当に彼女ひとすじみたいだ）

【2】（あれこれと）忙しく動きまわる

A: You look tired. Did you have a busy day?（疲れてるみたいね。忙しい1日だったの？）
B: Yeah, I *ran around* all day.（ああ、終日、あれこれ忙しく動きまわっていたよ）

☐ run away

【1】逃げる、逃げ出す

A: Do you have to work again this weekend?（今週末も、また仕事しないといけないの？）

B: No, I'm going to *run away* and go somewhere where I can relax. （いや、どこかくつろげるところに逃げ出すつもりさ）

【2】駆け落ちする (= elope)

A: Did George and Linda have a big wedding?（ジョージとリンダは、盛大な結婚式を挙げたの？）

B: No, I heard they *ran away* and got married. （いや、駆け落ちして、一緒になったって聞いたよ）

☐ run back　走って戻る、急いで戻る

A: Are you going straight home from here?（これからまっすぐ帰るの？）

B: No, I need to *run back* to my office and get something. （いや、オフィスに急いで戻って、取ってこなきゃいけないものがある）

☐ run behind　（予定より）遅れる

A: Are we still *running behind* schedule?（私たち、まだ予定より遅れているの？）

B: No, I worked late last night and got caught up. （いや、昨晩遅くまで働いて、遅れを取り戻したよ）　⇨ CATCH UP

☐ run by　（意見などを求めて人に）…について話す

A: Do you know what Linda thinks? Have you spoken to her yet?（リンダが何を考えているか、わかる？　もう彼女と話したの？）

B: Yeah, I talked to her this morning and she *ran* her opinion *by* me. （ああ、今朝話して、彼女の意見を聞かせてもらったよ）

☐ run down

【1】走り下りる、急いでいく

A: Do you want me to *run down* to the grocery store and get something to drink?（食料品店までひとっぱしりして、何か飲み物を買ってきたほうがいい？）

B: That's okay. I'm sure I have something here. （いや、大丈夫。ここに何かあるはずだ）

【2】（地域・建物などが）荒廃する、さびれる

A: That hotel used to be so beautiful, but now it's really *run down*. （あのホテルは以前はすごくきれいだったのに、今はすっかりさびれてしまったわ）

B: The owners really need to fix it up. （オーナーはどうしても修繕しないといけない）

R

【3】（車・運転者が人などを）ひく、はねる

  A: I heard that George got *run down*! Is he okay?! （ジョージが車にひかれたって聞いたわ！　大丈夫なの?!）
  B: The car just knocked him over, but he's okay. （車にちょっとぶつけられたけど、大丈夫だ）

【4】…を悪く言う、けなす

  A: I feel sorry for Linda. George is always *running* her *down*. （リンダが気の毒よ。ジョージはいつも彼女をけなすから）
  B: I know. He says terrible things about her. （うん。ひどいことを言うね）

【5】（電池などを）使い果たす [使い切る]、切らす

  A: Why do you want to go to that cafe? （どうしてあのカフェに行きたいの？）
  B: My computer battery has *run down*, and they have sockets. （パソコンのバッテリーが切れているんだ。あそこに行けば、電源につなげる）

【6】（リストに）さっと目を通す

  A: Do you know if Linda came to the party? （リンダがパーティにきたか知っている？）
  B: Just a minute. Let me *run down* the list. （ちょっと待って。リストを見てみるよ）

□ run for　…に立候補する

  A: Have you ever thought about *running for* office? （選挙への出馬を考えたことはないの？）
  B: No, I'm not very interested in politics. （いや、政治にはあまり関心がない）

□ run into

【1】…にぶつかる

  A: What happened to your car? The front bumper is mashed up. （あなたの車、どうしたの？　前のバンパーがへこんでるわ）
  B: Yeah, I *ran into* the car ahead of me. （ああ、前の車両にぶつかってしまったんだ）

【2】（苦しい状況に）陥る

  A: I heard that ABC is going out of business. What happened? （ABC 社が倒産するそうね。何があったの？）
  B: They *ran into* some financial difficulties. （財政難に陥ったんだ）

【3】…に思いがけなく会う、偶然…に出くわす

  A: I *ran into* George the other day. （この前、ばったりジョージに会ったの）
  B: Oh, really?! I haven't seen him in a long time. （へー、そう？！　ぼくは長いこと会っていないな）

【4】（合計して）…に達する (= reach)

A: ABC seems to be spending a lot of money on this project. (ABC 社は、このプロジェクトに相当な額をつぎ込んでいるようね)

B: I know. Their investment will *run into* the millions. (知ってるよ。投資額は数百万に上るだろう)

【5】…に駆け込む、…の中へ走って［急いで］入る

A: I need to *run into* a drug store and get some stomach medicine. (薬局に駆け込んで、胃薬を手に入れなくちゃ)

B: There's one up ahead, so I'll stop there. (この先に1軒あるから、そこで止まろう)

□ run off

【1】走り去る、急いで立ち去る、逃げる

A: Is Linda still here? I need to talk to her. (リンダはまだいる？ 彼女と話をしないと)

B: No, she *ran off* right after the meeting. (いや、会議の直後に急いで立ち去ったよ)

【2】…を印刷する、刷る、コピーをとる

A: Could you *run off* 20 copies of this report? (この報告書を20部コピーしてもらえますか？)

B: Okay, sure, but the copy machine is being used now. (了解。でも、コピー機は今使用中だね)

【3】（機械・車などが動力・燃料などで）作動する［動く］

A: Does this machine *run off* electricity? (この機械は電気で動くの？)

B: No, it has a rechargeable battery. (いや、充電池が入っているんだ)

【4】（人などを）追い払う

A: It's too bad that Linda quit. She was a great accountant. (リンダが辞めるなんて、残念でならないわ。会計担当として、いい仕事をしていたのに)

B: I know. George put too much pressure on her and *ran* her *off*. (そうだね。ジョージが過剰にプレッシャーをかけて、追い出してしまったんだ)

□ run on

【1】（話・催し物などが予定以上に）つづく、長引く (= prolong)

A: You look really tired. Did you have a lot of meetings? (すごく疲れてるみたいね。会議がたくさんあったの？)

B: No, I just had one, but it *ran on* for hours. (いや、会議は1つだけだったけど、それが何時間も延びてしまったんだ)

【2】（機械などが電気・石油などで）動く

A: I've never seen a computer that *runs on* gasoline. (ガソリンで動くコンピュータなんて見たことないわ)

B: They say it's more convenient than electricity. (電動のものより便利だと言われている)

□ run out

【1】（在庫品・補給などが）なくなる

A: Why didn't you get any tea at the grocery store? (どうして食料品店でお茶を買ってこなかったの？)

B: They said they *ran out*, so I bought juice instead. (売り切れだって言うから、代わりにジュースを買ったよ)

【2】流れ出る (= flow)

A: Is there still water in the cooling tank? (冷却水タンクにまだ水はある？)

B: No, someone opened it up and let the water *run out*. (いや、誰かがタンクを開けたんで、流れ出ちゃったよ)

□ run out of

【1】…を使い果たす、切らす

A: It looks like we've *run out of* copy paper. (コピー用紙が切れちゃったみたい)

B: Okay, I'll put in an order for more. It should get here tomorrow. (了解。追加注文しておく。明日にはここに届くはずだ)

【2】…を〜から追い出す

A: You really don't care for George, do you? (あなた、ジョージのことあまり好きじゃないんでしょう？)

B: No, I don't. I wish I could *run* him *out of* this company. (ああ、そうだ。会社から追い出したいよ)

□ run over

【1】（車・運転者が人などを）ひく

A: I heard you got *ran over*! Are you okay? (車にひかれたそうじゃない！　大丈夫なの？)

B: Yes, the car just bumped into me. (ああ、ちょっと車がぶつかっただけだよ)

【2】（液体・容器が）あふれる

A: It's really raining hard. I'm worried about the river *running over*. (雨足が本当に強いわね。川が氾濫しないか心配だわ)

B: It's possible. The water level is getting higher and higher. (ありうるね。水位がどんどん上がっているよ)

□ run through
【1】 …を要約する、さっと復習する

A: We need to talk about the new advertising campaign. (新しい広告キャンペーンについて話す必要があります)

B: Okay, could you *run through* the basics so everyone understands the plan? (わかりました。みんなが計画を理解できるように、基本的なところを説明してもらえますか？)

【2】（金を）使い果たす、浪費する (= waste)

A: Could you help me with a loan? I'm all out of money. (ローンのことで助けていただけないでしょうか？ お金が全然ないんです)

B: How did you *run through* your entire salary so quickly?! (どうしてこんなに早く給料をみんな使ってしまうのさ？！)

□ run to （援助・助言などを求めて）…に頼る

A: Whenever Linda has a problem, she *runs to* me. (問題があると、リンダはいつも私を頼ってくるの)

B: I know. She needs to be more independent. (そうだね。彼女はもっと自立しないといけないな)

□ run up （支払額・借金などを）急に増やす、ためる

A: Wow, your entertainment expenses almost doubled last year. (わ、あなたのところの接待費、去年のほぼ倍に膨れ上がったわ)

B: Yeah, the new sales manager really *ran up* costs. (ああ、新しい営業部長が本当に出費を増やしたよ)

□ run with （人と）仲間［友だち］である、…と付き合う

A: Do Linda and George know each other well? (リンダとジョージは、おたがいよく知っているの？)

B: Yeah, they've been *running with* each other since they were kids. (ああ、子供の頃からの付き合いなんだ)

R

see

□ **see after**　…の世話をする

A: I'm stuck in a meeting, but I'm supposed to show a client around the factory.（会議から抜けられない。なのに、お客さんに工場を見せてまわることになっているの）
⇨ SHOW AROUND

B: Don't worry. I'll *see after* him.（心配しないで。ぼくがお世話するよ）

□ **see back**　（車などで人を）家まで送り届ける

A: Well, it's been a long night. I think I'll turn in.（あら、ずいぶん夜遅くなっちゃった。もう寝るわ）⇨ TURN IN ［3］

B: OK, I'll *see* you *back* to your hotel room.（ああ、ホテルの部屋まで送るよ）

□ **see in**　（人に）よい性質などを認める

A: Is Linda still dating that idiot George?（まだリンダは、あのアホなジョージと付き合ってるの？）

B: Yeah, I just can't understand what she *sees in* him.（うん、彼のどこがいいと思っているのか、わからないね）

□ **see off**　（人を）見送る、送り出す

A: Is George flying back to New York today?（ジョージは今日ニューヨークに飛行機で戻るの？）

B: Yeah. I'm going to *see* him *off* at the airport.（うん、空港まで彼を見送りに行ってくるよ）

□ **see out**　（人を）玄関まで見送る、…が外に出るのを見送る

A: Is the ABC chairman leaving now?（ABC 社の会長は、今お帰りですか？）

B: Yes. Could you *see* him *out* for me?（そうです。私の代わりに、お見送りしてもらえますか？）

□ **see over**　…の向こうが見える

A: I can't believe somebody would wear a hat in a movie theater.（映画館で

B: I know! I can't even *see over* him to watch the film.（まったくだ！　それがじゃまで映画が見えやしない）

□ see through

【1】（事業などを）最後までやり通す

A: Why don't you put Linda on the project?（どうしてリンダをプロジェクトに加えないの？）⇨ PUT ON［7］

B: I don't think she's reliable enough to *see* it *through* to the end.（最後までやり通すか信頼できないからだよ）

【2】（窓・カーテンなどを通して）向こうが見える

A: I think Linda needs to put something over her blouse.（リンダはブラウスの上に何か羽織ったほうがいいと思う）

B: I know. You can *see* right *through* it.（そうだね。中が透けちゃうよ）

□ see to （仕事などを）引き受ける、世話をする（= undertake）

A: Is somebody going to set up the meeting room for tomorrow's conference?（誰か明日の会議のために会議室を用意してくれる？）⇨ SET UP［1］

B: Yeah, George and Linda are going to *see to* it.（うん、ジョージとリンダが引き受けるよ）

---

column ▶▶▶ 句動詞はどうしてむずかしい？

「はじめに」でも書きましたが、ネイティブは、論文のような堅い文では collapse（崩壊する）を使うとしても、会話の中ではフォーマルに聞こえてしまうため、この語の使用を避けて、たとえば句動詞 break down で代用しようとします。

しかし、困ったことに、同時に日常会話でも、動詞 analyze（分析する）の代わりに、同じ break down をよく使うのです。これはなぜかといえば、短縮表現などもそうですが、ネイティブは会話などではできるだけ簡単な表現を好みます。そのため同じ句動詞を、あらゆる状況・意味で用いるのです。

これにより、句動詞が多用され、同じ表現が状況によってさまざまな意味で用いられることになります。その結果、日本人英語学習者は、句動詞はなんてむずかしいんだ、と思ってしまうようです。対応策としては、

1　同じ句動詞表現でも、状況に応じて、さまざまな意味で用いられることを認識する。

2　その意味を1つひとつ信頼できる辞書で確認し、よく使われる意味の使い方は覚える。

ということになります。2については、研究社の『ルミナス英和辞典』がおすすめです。この辞典には、各動詞の句動詞表現が枠で囲んでまとめられています。定義、例文も大変わかりやすく、本書執筆にあたっても、大いに参考にさせていただきました。

sell

☐ sell off …を手放す、(安値で) 売り払う

A: Are you going to close your downtown furniture store? (都心の家具店を閉店するつもり？)
B: Yeah. I need to start *selling off* the entire inventory. (ああ、これからすべての在庫を売り払わないといけない)

☐ sell out (店が)…を売り切る、売り尽くす

A: Did you do pretty good at yesterday's festival? (昨日の催し物は、けっこううまくいったの？)
B: Definitely. We *sold out* all of the food we prepared. (もちろん。用意した食べ物は全部売り切れたよ)

☐ sell out of …が売り切れになる

A: Did you pick up the lettuce for today's lunch? (今日のお昼ご飯のレタスは買った？)
B: No, the corner store was *sold out of* vegetables. (いや、角の店は野菜が売り切れだったよ)

send

send away
【1】 …を追い払う

A: There's somebody here trying to sell some kind of insurance. (どこかの保険の営業の方がきています)

B: I'm too busy for that. Can you *send* him *away*? (ぼくはすごく忙しいんだ。帰ってもらってよ)

【2】（品物を）注文する［取り寄せる］、通信販売で求める (send away for)

A: Did you buy this book at a bookstore? (この本は本屋さんで買ったの？)

B: No, I *sent away* for it on an online site. (いや、オンラインストアで注文したんだ)

□ send back …を戻す、(気に入らない品物などを) 送り返す (= return)

A: Oh, gross. My salad has a hair in it! (あら、やだわ。私のサラダに髪の毛が入ってる！)

B: Well, call the waiter and *send* it *back*. (ああ、ウエイターを呼んで下げてもらいなよ)

□ send for
【1】 …にくるように頼む、助けを求める (= ask)

A: I need some help making copies of this report. (この報告書をコピーするのを、誰かに手伝ってもらいたいの)

B: No problem. I'll *send for* Linda to come help. (わかった。リンダに手伝いにきてもらおう)

【2】 …を（店から）取り寄せる、…を（店に）注文する (= order)

A: Did you order all these magazines for the office? (あなたがこの雑誌を全部、オフィス用に注文したの？)

B: Not me. I think Linda must have *sent for* them. (ぼくじゃないさ。リンダが取り寄せたに違いないと思う)

□ send in
【1】（書類などを）提出する (= submit)、送付する (= send)

A: Does the head office still need my tax report? (本社では、まだ私の確定申告書が必要なの？)

B: Yeah, can you *send* it *in* by Monday? (ああ、月曜日までに送ってもらえるかい？)

【2】（警察・軍隊などを）投入する

A: It looks like a civil war is going to erupt in that country. （あの国では内戦が勃発しそうね）
B: The UN should probably *send in* some peacekeeping troops. （国連はおそらく、平和維持部隊を投入すべきだね）

□ send off （手紙・品物などを）発送する （= ship）

A: Did you *send off* the mail already? （もう郵便は送ったの？）
B: Yeah, it went out this morning. （ああ、今朝発送したよ） ⇨ GO OUT ［4］

□ send on
【1】（手紙などを）転送する （= forward）

A: I'm almost finished with my report. （報告書を大体書き終わったわ）
B: Well, when you're done, *send* it *on* to George for approval. （えーと、終わったら、ジョージに送って承認をもらってくれ）

【2】（荷物などを）先に送る、前もって送る

A: Do I have to pick up my luggage when I change planes? （飛行機の乗り換えの時、自分の荷物を引き取らなければなりませんか？）
B: No, it'll be *sent on* to your final destination. （いえ、お荷物は最終目的地まで先に送られます）

□ send out （人を）派遣する、（使いなどで）…を外へ行かせる

A: The branch office is having problems with its computer system. （支社はコンピュータシステムに問題を抱えています）
B: I know. I *sent out* George to look it over. （わかっています。調べるためにジョージを行かせました） ⇨ LOOK OVER ［2］

□ send up 上［階上］へ行かせる、上げる

A: There's a representative from ABC here to see you. （ABC 社の代表の方が、お会いしたいとこちらにお見えです）
B: Fine. Just *send* him *up* to my office. （わかりました。私のオフィスに上がってもらってください）

set

□ set about …を始める、…に取りかかる (= start)

A: When are you going to *set about* getting some new office chairs?（事務所の新しい椅子の調達には、いつ取りかかるの？）
B: I don't think we can afford them until next year.（来年まで購入する余裕がないと思うよ）

□ set aside

【1】（仕事などを）中断する、…を（一時）わきに置く

A: Do you need me to finish the budget proposal right away?（予算案を今すぐ終わらせたほうがいいですか？）
B: No, you can *set* it *aside* for now. We won't need it for a few months.（いや、今は中断してもらってかまわない。数カ月のあいだ、必要ないんだ）

【2】（ある目的［将来］のために金・時間などを）取っておく、蓄えておく (= save)

A: Why are you keeping two bank accounts?（どうして2つの銀行口座を持っているの？）
B: One is for the money I'm *setting aside* for retirement.（1つは定年後の蓄えのためなんだ）

□ set back

【1】（時計を）遅らす、戻す

A: Los Angeles is in a completely different time zone than New York, right?（ロサンゼルスはニューヨークとはまったく違う時間帯よね？）
B: Yeah, so when you fly there, be sure to *set* your watch *back*.（そうだよ。だから飛行機で行く時は、時計を遅らせるのをお忘れなく）

【2】（進行・計画などを）阻む (= hinder)、遅らせる (= delay)

A: I heard George is going to quit this project.（ジョージはこのプロジェクトをやめるって聞いたわ）
B: Yeah, that's really going to *set* us *back* unless we get someone else.（ああ、誰か見つけないと、ずいぶん計画が遅れてしまうよ）

【3】（家などを…から）引っ込めて建てる

A: Is the main office alongside the road?（本社は道路沿いにあるの？）
B: No, it's *set back* behind the factory.（いや、工場の後ろにあるんだ）

【4】（人に費用を）出費させる

A: We're going to have to replace our copy machine.（コピー機を交換する必要があるわね）
B: I see. How much is that going to *set* us *back*?（なるほど。いくらかかるんだろう？）

□ set down （基準などを）定める、規定する（= define）

A: I thought everyone would use their common sense when dressing for work.（職場の服装には、各自が常識を働かせると思っていたわ）
B: So did I, but it looks like we have to *set down* the law.（ぼくもそう思っていたけど、規範を設けないとならないようだ）

□ set forward （時計を）進める

A: It seems like you're never late for anything.（あなたは決して遅刻したことがないみたい）
B: That's because I *set* my watch *forward* by 10 minutes.（時計を10分進めているからだよ）

□ set in （悪天候などが）始まる（= start, occur）

A: Do you think we'll be able to go on a hike next weekend?（来週末、ハイキングに行けると思う？）
B: Maybe not. I heard a big storm is going to *set in*.（たぶんダメだね。激しい嵐がくるって聞いたよ）

□ set off …を引き起こす、誘発する（= cause）

A: It looks like George and Linda are fighting again.（ジョージとリンダが、またけんかしているようね）
B: Yeah, he sent her a mean e-mail and that *set off* a big fight.（ああ、ジョージが意地の悪いメールを送ったせいで、大げんかになったんだ）

□ set oneself against …に断然反対する

A: Why do you *set yourself against* hiring a new secretary?（どうして新しい秘書を雇うことにそんなに反対なの？）
B: First, we don't need one, and second, we can't afford one.（第1に必要ないし、第2にそんな余裕はないよ）

□ set out
【1】出発する、（長）旅に出る

A: Why don't you come over for the barbeque tomorrow?（明日、バーベキュー

にこない？）⇨ COME OVER [1]

B: I wish I could, but I have to *set out* for London tonight.（行きたいところだけど、今夜ロンドンに発たないとならないんだ）

【2】（…することを）企てる、（…するつもりで）動き出す

A: Why are you always making Linda angry?（どうしていつもリンダを怒らせるの？）

B: I never *set out* to make her angry, but she really gets on my nerves.（怒らせるつもりはまったくないんだけど、彼女って本当に癇に障るんだ）

【3】…を陳列する、並べる、表示［提示］する (= display, arrange)

A: Do you want me to *set out* these new books?（この新しい本を並べましょうか？）

B: Yeah, could you line them up next to the window where everyone can see them?（ええ、みんなに見えるように、窓際に並べてもらえますか？）

【4】（整然と）述べる、説明する (= describe)

A: Did George's explanation clear up everything for you?（ジョージの説明で、全部はっきりわかったかしら？）⇨ CLEAR UP [3]

B: Yes, it did. He *set out* exactly what I need to do.（ええ。ぼくが何をすべきか整然と説明してくれました）

□ set up

【1】…を用意する［準備する］

A: We need to *set up* the meeting room for 15 people.（15人用に会議室を準備しなくちゃいけないわ）

B: Okay, I'll get out the tables and chairs.（わかった、テーブルと椅子を外に出すよ）

【2】（会社・施設などを）設立する、創設［開設］する (= establish, institute)

A: Is it difficult to *set up* a company in China?（中国で会社を設立するのはむずかしい？）

B: Yeah, there's a lot of red tape you have to go through.（ああ、面倒な役所の手続きが山ほどあるよ）

【3】（人に）罪をきせる、（人を）陥れる、わなにはめる

A: Why are their drugs in your suitcase?（どうして彼らのドラッグが、あなたのスーツケースに入ってるの？）

B: A stranger paid me to carry the package for him. He *set* me *up*!（知らない人がお金をよこして、荷物を運んでくれと言ったんだ。わなにはめられたよ！）

【4】（人に）出会い［デート］の場を作る

A: Do you know how George and Linda first met?（ジョージとリンダが最初にどうやって出会ったか知ってる？）

B: Yes, I *set* them *up*, and then they started dating.（うん、ぼくがお膳立てして、それから2人は付き合い始めたんだ）

settle

☐ settle down
【1】（動いたあとで）腰を下ろす、落ち着く、ゆっくりくつろぐ (= relax)

A: I heard you're planning on changing jobs again? (あなた、また仕事を変えるつもりだって聞いたわよ)
B: No, I've decided to *settle down* and keep on working here as long as I can. (いや、腰を落ち着けて、できるだけ長くここで働くことに決めたよ)　⇨ KEEP ON [3]

【2】（結婚したりして）身を固める、定住する (= settle)

A: I heard that George is finally going to get married and *settle down*. (とうとうジョージは結婚して身を固めるらしいわね)
B: Really? Who did he get engaged to? (本当？ 誰と婚約したの？)

【3】平静になる、（騒ぎなどが）収まる

A: I heard the demonstrators got really angry. (デモ参加者は真剣に怒ってたらしいわよ)
B: They did, but now they've *settled down*. (そうだったけど、今は落ち着いたよ)

☐ settle for　…を不満足ながら受け入れる［飲む］、…に甘んじる

A: All the five-star hotels were full, so we had to *settle for* a three-star hotel. (5つ星ホテルはどこも満室だったから、3つ星ホテルで我慢しなければならなかったの)
B: Don't complain. I had to sleep in my car. (文句を言うなよ。ぼくは車で寝ないといけなかったんだよ)

☐ settle into　（新しい環境に）慣れる

A: How are you *settling into* your new job? (新しい仕事には慣れてきた？)
B: Pretty good. Everyone's helping me get used to everything. (かなりいい調子です。いろいろなことに慣れるように、みんなが助けてくれます)

☐ settle on [upon]　…を決定する、…に決める (= determine, decide)

A: Why did the meeting go for so long? (どうして会議がそんなに長引いたの？)
B: It took us a long time to *settle on* a time and place for the next meeting. (次の会議の時間と場所を決めるのに、時間がかかったんだ)

shake

☐ shake down …を振り落とす

A: That was quite an earthquake we had yesterday. (昨日、すごい地震があったわね)
B: Yeah, for a minute I thought it was going to *shake down* the building. (うん、建物が揺りたおされるかもしれないと一瞬思ったよ)

☐ shake off (病気・悪習などを) 直す、断ち切る

A: Why is the productivity at this factory so low? (この工場の生産性は、どうしてそんなに低いの？)
B: It's an old factory, so they're having a hard time *shaking off* their old ways. (古い工場だから、古い方法を断ち切るのに苦労しているんだ)

☐ shake out (…のほこりなどを) 振り落とす

A: We have to clean up this office before the president gets here on Friday. (金曜日に社長がここにくる前に、事務所をきれいに掃除しなくちゃいけないわ)
⇨ CLEAN UP [1]
B: Okay, I'll *shake out* these old rugs. (わかった。ぼくはこの古いラグマットのほこりを落とすよ)

☐ shake up (組織・人事を) 刷新する、改造する (= reform, remodel)

A: Do you think George will be able to *shake up* ABC? (ジョージは ABC 社を刷新できると思う？)
B: I hope so. They really need to shape up to stay in business. (そう願いたいね。事業継続には、改善が必要不可欠だ)

---

column ▶▶▶ set

set up (141 ページ) は、「(カメラなどを) 据え付ける」 (= install) の意味でも使われます。

A: I think someone has been sneaking into the office and downloading data. (誰かがオフィスに忍び込んで、データをダウンロードしたんだと思う)
B: Should we *set up* a camera? (カメラを取り付けるべきかな？)

shoot

☐ shoot down

【1】…を撃墜する、射落とす

A: Do you think the plane was *shot down*? (飛行機は撃墜されたんだと思う?)
B: No, I don't. I think the crash was caused by engine problems. (そうは思わないな。エンジンの問題で墜落したと思う)

【2】(提案などを)はねつける、退ける

A: Were you surprised that Linda *shot down* your proposal in the meeting? (会議でリンダがあなたの提案をはねつけたのには驚いた?)
B: Yeah, of course. She said she was behind it yesterday. (ああ、もちろん。昨日は支持していると言ってたんだ)

☐ shoot for (特に困難なことを)めざす

A: What do you think your sales will be in the coming quarter? (御社の売上げは、次期4半期にどうなると思いますか?)
B: Well, we're *shooting for* 50,000 dollars. (そうですね、5万ドルをめざしますよ)

☐ shoot up (物価・温度などが)急に上がる

A: Do you know why stock prices *shot up* after the president's speech? (どうして大統領の演説後に株価が急騰したか、わかる?)
B: Yeah, I just think investors heard what they wanted to hear. (ああ、投資家たちが聞きたかったことを聞けたからだと思う)

---

column ▶▶▶ shoot

shootはスポーツでよく用いられ、ゴルフやバスケットボールでは次のように使われます。
- He *shot* a 62 in the final round. (彼は最終ラウンドを62で回った)
- He *shot* 40 points in one game. (彼は1試合で40点挙げた)

しかし、本来は武器、特に銃を指します。次の句動詞はその代表的なものですから、覚えておきましょう。
- He *shot off* his gun. (彼は銃を撃った)
- The robbers *shot out* the lights. (泥棒が電灯を撃った)
- The enemy *shot back*. (敵が撃ち返してきた)

show

☐ show around （人を）連れて…を案内する

A: If you'd like to, I can *show* you *around* our new factory. （よろしければ、われわれの新しい工場をご案内しますよ）

B: I'd love to see it, but I don't want to take up much of your time. （ぜひそうしたいですが、あまりお時間をいただくわけにはいきません） ⇨ TAKE UP [1]

☐ show off （才能・知識・財産などを）見せびらかす

A: Makiko *showed off* her gorgeous necklace to all her guests. （真紀子は来客に自分の豪華なネックレスを見せびらかしていたわ）

B: Yeah, she wants everyone to know she's rich. （ああ、彼女は自分が金持ちだってことをみんなに知らせたいんだよ）

☐ show through （物が）透けて見える

A: It seems like Linda's blouse is *showing through*. （リンダのブラウス、透けてるみたい）

B: I know. Maybe you should say something to her about it. （うん。きみが彼女にさりげなく言ってあげるのがいいかもしれない）

☐ show up

【1】（約束の時間に）姿を現わす、（会などに）出る

A: I can't believe that George didn't *show up*. （ジョージが姿を見せなかったなんて信じられない）

B: I can't either. It's unusual for him to forget about appointments. （ぼくもだよ。ジョージが約束を忘れるなんて珍しい）

【2】目立つ

A: That new sign doesn't *show up* very well. （あの新しい標識はあまり目立たないわね）

B: Don't worry. When we turn on the light, it'll really stick out. （心配はいらない。照明をつければ、すごく目立つよ） ⇨ TURN ON [2], STICK OUT [2]

shut

☐ shut down （機械・装置を）止める (= stop)

A: I think we're just about finished for the day. (今日の仕事は大体終わりだと思うわ)

B: Okay, I'll *shut down* the press and turn off all the lights. (了解。プレス機を止めて、明かりを全部消すよ) ⇨ TURN OFF [1]

☐ shut off

【1】（電気などを）切る、…の供給を止める (= cut)

A: We need to pay the gas bill or they're going to *shut* it *off*. (ガス代を払わないと、ガスを止められちゃうわ)

B: Okay, I'll try to scrape together the money and pay it today. (わかった。お金をかき集めて今日払うよ)

【2】～から…を切り離す (shut off from)

A: Without the Internet, I feel *shut off* from the world. (インターネットがなければ、社会から切り離されたように感じる)

B: Well, for millions of years, people lived without it. (ああ、何百万年ものあいだ、人類はインターネットなしで暮らしていたのにね)

☐ shut out （人・動物を）締め出す、（考えなどを）締め出す (= exclude; block)

A: Did you try to talk Linda into changing the organization? (リンダを説得して、組織を変えさせようとしているの？)

B: Yeah, but she *shuts out* any new ideas. (ああ、でも彼女は、どんな新しい考えも締め出してしまうんだ)

☐ shut up …を黙らせる

A: George is saying all kinds of bad things about our company. (ジョージはわが社について、あらゆる悪口を言ってるわね)

B: Isn't there anything we can do to *shut* him *up*? (彼を黙らせる方法は何かないかな？)

sign

☐ sign for 署名して…を受け取る

A: How can I look at documents in the vault? (金庫室の書類を見るには、どうすればいいの？)

B: You need to *sign for* the key with the president's secretary. (署名して、社長の秘書から鍵をもらわないといけない)

☐ sign on 署名して就職［参加・加入］する

A: Do you want to *sign on* to our new research committee? (私たちの新しい調査委員会に参加したい？)

B: I'm tempted, but I'm not sure I have enough time for it. (そうしたい気分だけど、十分な時間があるか、はっきりわからないんだ)

☐ sign up 参加する、署名して加わる

A: Are you going to *sign up* for the company softball team? (会社のソフトボールチームに参加するつもり？)

B: Probably. That sounds like fun. (たぶんね。楽しそうだな)

☐ sign with 署名して（チームなどに）雇われる、（レコード会社などと）契約する

A: Did George decide what company he's going to *sign with*? (どの会社と契約するか、ジョージは決めたの？)

B: Not yet, but he's leaning toward joining ABC. (まだだけど、ABC社に傾いてるね)

---

column ▶▶▶ show

145ページで show up を紹介しましたが、この句動詞は「（人に）恥ずかしい思いをさせる」（= shame）の意味でもよく使われます。

A: Linda is mad at George for *showing* her *up*. (リンダは恥をかかされたと、ジョージにとても腹を立ててるの)

B: I know. He just joined the company, but he knows a lot more about accounting than she does. (わかるよ。ジョージはわが社にきたばかりだけど、会計についてはリンダより詳しいね)

sit

☐ sit around 何もしないでいる、漫然と（…して）過ごす

A: Why is everybody just *sitting around*?（どうしてみんな、何もしないでぶらぶらしてるの？）
B: The power went out, and we can't do anything.（停電で、何もできないんだ）
⇨ GO OUT [3]

☐ sit back のんきに構えている

A: Is George going to arrive soon?（ジョージはもうすぐ着くのかしら？）
B: He should. Just *sit back* and wait for him.（そのはずだよ。のんびりと彼を待つことにしよう）

☐ sit by 傍観する、手をこまねいている

A: George sure isn't very helpful sometimes.（ジョージってときどき、あまり役に立たないのは確かね）
B: I know. Look at him just *sit by* while everybody cleans the office.（そうなんだ。みんなが事務所の掃除をしているのに、ただ傍観している彼を見てごらんよ）

☐ sit for …の子守をする

A: Can you *sit for* my son while I work tonight?（今夜、仕事のあいだ、うちの息子を見てくれない？）
B: No problem. It's always fun taking care of him.（了解。彼の世話はいつも楽しいよ）

☐ sit in （人の）代理［代行］をする (sit in for)

A: Are you going to attend the conference tomorrow?（明日の会議に参加する予定なの？）
B: No, I'm having George *sit in* for me.（いや、ジョージにぼくの代わりを頼むよ）

☐ sit on

【1】（委員会などの）一員である

A: Does Linda *sit on* the board of directors?（リンダは重役の1人なの？）

B: She did, but she resigned last month.（そうだったけど、先月退任したよ）

【2】（報道・苦情・調査などを）押さえる、伏せておく

A: Isn't the company going to release last month's sales figures?（会社は先月の売上高を発表しないつもり？）

B: No, it's going to *sit on* them until they're fully analyzed.（いや、分析が完全に終わるまで控えるんだ）

□ sit out　ゲームに出ない

A: Aren't you going to go bowling with us?（私たちとボウリングに行かないの？）

B: No, I've got a sore hand. I'll *sit out* this time.（ああ、手が痛むから今回はやめるよ）

□ sit up　（ベッドなどの上で）起き上がる

A: Is your mother still very sick?（お母さんの調子、まだすごく悪いの？）

B: Yes, but at least now she can *sit up* and eat.（ああ、でも、少なくとも今は起き上がって食事を取れるよ）

---

column ▶▶▶ sit

sit には、「（ただ）座っている」だけでなく、「（仕事をしないでただ）座っている」という含みがあります。今のような「デスクワーク」がなかった時代は、座りながら仕事をするということはあまりなかったはずです。そのため、次のような文は、本来、→右のような意味合いになります。

- Everyone *sat around*.「みんなが座っていた」→「みんな何もしないでいた」
- I just want to *sit back*.「ただ座っていたい」→「何もしたくない」
- I think I'll *sit out* this time.「今回はゲームに出ないつもりだ」→「今回は参加しないつもりだ」
- He just *sat by*.「彼はただ座っていた」→「彼は（何かをすればいいのに）何もしなかった」

sleep

☐ sleep off …を寝て治す

A: Is that headache still bothering you?（まだ頭痛でつらいの？）
B: Yeah, but it'll be okay if I *sleep* it *off*.（ああ、でも寝れば大丈夫だよ）

☐ sleep on …の判断を翌日まで延ばす、…を一晩寝て考える

A: I hope you don't rush into signing a contract with ABC.（慌てて ABC 社と契約しなければいいけど）
B: You're right. I need to *sleep on* it.（きみの言うとおりだ。明日まで決定を延ばす必要がある）

☐ sleep over 人の家に１泊する、外泊する

A: That party at George's last night went awfully late, didn't it?（昨晩のジョージの家でのパーティ、すごく遅くなったんでしょう？）
B: Well, luckily, he let me *sleep over* that night.（ああ、幸い、ジョージが家に泊めてくれたよ）

☐ sleep through …のあいだ一度も目を覚まさず眠る

A: Do you realize you *slept* right *through* breakfast?（あなた、朝食の時間にずっと寝ていたのよ、わかってる？）
B: Well, why didn't someone call my room and wake me up?（うーん、どうして誰か部屋に電話して、起こしてくれなかったの？）

speak

☐ speak about …について話す［しゃべる］

A: I've been asked to give a speech at the conference.（会議でスピーチをするように頼まれているの）
B: What are you going to **speak about**?（何について話すつもり？）

☐ speak for …を代弁［代表］する

A: What does your company think about this proposal?（御社はこの提案についてどう思いますか？）
B: I can't **speak for** my company, but I personally think it's a good idea.（社を代表することはできませんが、個人的にはいい案だと思います）

☐ speak out 思い切って言う、遠慮なく話す

A: I really think George is making a bad decision.（本当にジョージはひどい決断をしていると思う）
B: Then you need to **speak out**.（それなら遠慮なく彼に言いなよ）

☐ speak to

【1】…と話す、…に話しかける（= talk）

A: Are you planning on **speaking to** Linda about this?（これについてリンダと話すつもり？）
B: I already talked to her and she said she'll back me up.（もう話したよ。ぼくを支持してくれるって言ってたよ） ⇨ BACK UP [1]

【2】…に忠告［注意］する、…をしかる（= admonish, scold）

A: George has missed too many days of work. Aren't you going to **speak to** him?（ジョージは仕事を休みすぎよ。彼に注意しないの？）
B: Okay, I'll give him a warning.（わかった。忠告しておくよ）

☐ speak up

【1】（もっと）大きな声で話す

A: I have a question. Why did you...?（質問があります。なぜあなたは…？）
B: I'm sorry. I can't hear you very well. Could you **speak up** a little?（すみま

せん。よく聞こえません。もう少し大きな声で話してもらえますか？）

【2】 率直に意見を述べる、遠慮なく話す

A: If you don't like this plan, you'd better *speak up*. (この計画が気に入らないなら、遠慮なく言ってください)

B: I don't think anyone would listen to me. (ぼくの意見になんか、誰も耳を傾けないよ)

☐ speak with

【1】 …と話す

A: I think George misunderstood me. (ジョージは私を誤解したと思う)

B: Do you want me to *speak with* him for you? I think I can make him understand. (ぼくから彼に話そうか？ ぼくならわかってもらえると思うよ)

【2】 …と話し合う、相談する (= discuss, talk)

A: Have you *spoken with* a lawyer about this problem? (この件について、弁護士と相談したの？)

B: No, but do you think a lawyer can help me? (いや、でも弁護士が助けてくれると思うかい？)

stand

☐ stand against …に反対［反抗］する (= oppose, resist)

A: I know you don't like the new policy, but are you going to *stand against* it?（あなたが新しい方針を気に入らないのはわかるけど、反対するつもり？）
B: No, I'll just try to live with it.（いや、受け入れるようにするよ）⇨ LIVE WITH ［2］

☐ stand around ぼんやりと立っている、何もしないでいる

A: Did George help you set up the meeting room?（ジョージは会議室の設営を手伝ってくれたの？）⇨ SET UP ［1］
B: No, he just *stood around* and did nothing.（いや、ぼんやり立っているだけで、何もしなかったよ）

☐ stand at 数値［金額］が…である

A: Do you know how the stock market did yesterday?（昨日の株価がどうだったか、わかる？）
B: Yes, at the end of trading, it *stood at* 4,500 yen.（うん、終値は4500円だった）

☐ stand behind …を支持する (= support)

A: What do you think about Linda's new strategy? Are you for it?（リンダの新戦略をどう思う？ 賛成？）
B: Yes, I *stand behind* what she's trying to do.（ああ、彼女がやろうとしていることを支持するよ）

☐ stand by

【1】何もしないで見ている、傍観する、そば［近く］にいる

A: Do you need me to help you with something?（何かお手伝いしましょうか？）
B: That's okay. Just *stand by* and I'll call you when everything's ready.（大丈夫。何もしなくていいよ。すべて準備ができたら呼ぶから）

【2】（約束・方針などを）堅く守る

A: Do you still think that the recession will end this quarter?（不況はこの4半期で終わると、まだ思っているのですか？）

B: Yes, I *stand by* what I said. Nothing has changed. （ええ、言ったことは曲げません。何も変わっていません）

☐ stand for　…を表わす、…の略語である (= represent)

A: Do you know what ASAP *stands for*? （ASAP って何の略かわかる？）
B: Sure, it *stands for* "as soon as possible." （もちろん。"as soon as possible" の略だよ）

☐ stand in　（人の）代わりをする、代理を務める (stand in for)

A: Oh, no! I can't go to the planning meeting today. What am I going to do?! （うわ、大変！　今日の企画会議に行けないわ。どうしよう？）
B: If you'd like, I can *stand in* for you. （よかったら、ぼくが代わりに出られるよ）

☐ stand out　目立つ、際立って見える

A: I can't believe that George bought pink chairs for the lobby. （ジョージったら、ロビーにピンクの椅子を買うなんて、信じられない）
B: I know. They really *stand out*. （そうだね。すごく目立つね）

☐ stand together　団結する、結束する (= unity)

A: Can Linda really force us to work on weekends? （リンダは本当に、週末の仕事を私たちに強いることができるの？）
B: No, not if we *stand together* and oppose her. （いや、ぼくたちが結束して反対すれば、できないよ）

☐ stand up

【1】立ち上がる、起立する、立っている

A: Why do we have to *stand up* during the entire meeting? （どうして会議のあいだ、ずっと立っていなくちゃいけないの？）
B: Linda thinks that if we sit down, we'll nod off. （座ると居眠りするとリンダは思っているんだ）

【2】耐える、長持ちする、持ちこたえる

A: What kind of building are you going to build? （どんなタイプの建物を作るの？）
B: We need one that will *stand up* under bad weather conditions. （悪天候でも持ちこたえる建物が必要なんだ）

【3】通用する、有効である

A: Why don't you think this contract will *stand up* in court? （どうしてこの契約が法廷で通用すると思わないの？）

B: It's so vague that no one can understand it. (あまりに不明瞭で、誰にも理解されないよ)

【4】(特に異性に)待ちぼうけをくわせる、…をすっぽかす

A: What happened? I thought you had a meeting with Linda. (どうしたの？リンダと打ち合わせなのかと思ってたわ)
B: I did, but she *stood* me *up*. (そのはずだったんだけど、彼女にすっぽかされたんだ)

☐ stand up against　　…に対して立ち向かう

A: Do you think we should *stand up against* this trade agreement? (この貿易協定に対抗すべきだと思う？)
B: Yes, I do. I think it'll destroy our economy. (ええ。われわれの経済を壊してしまうと思う)

☐ stand up for　　…を擁護[弁護]する、…の味方をする

A: Do you think the new president will *stand up for* human rights? (新しい社長は人権を擁護すると思う？)
B: I doubt it. He only thinks about helping companies make money. (そうは思わないね。会社の金儲けに役立つことしか考えていないよ)

☐ stand up to　　…に勇敢に立ち向かう、抵抗[対抗]する

A: George said that he's going to tell Linda she's wrong. (リンダが悪いと伝えるつもりだって、ジョージが言っていたわ)
B: Really? I doubt he can *stand up to* her. (本当？　ジョージはリンダに対抗できないんじゃないかな)

start

☐ start back 帰途につく、戻り始める

A: What time do you think we should *start back* to the office?（オフィスに戻るのに、何時に出発すればいいと思う？）

B: Let's leave at 5:00 so we can get back before dark.（暗くなる前に帰れるように5時に出よう） ⇨ GET BACK

☐ start in on …を始める、（人を）非難し始める

A: George is always so critical. As soon as I get to the office, he *starts in on* me.（ジョージはいつだって批判的なの。私がオフィスに着くなり、すぐに非難するの）

B: Maybe it's time that you stood up to him.（きみもそろそろ彼に立ち向かう時だよ）
⇨ STAND UP TO

☐ start off 始まる、始める

A: Why don't you *start off* first and give your presentation?（最初にあなたから始めて発表をしたら？）

B: Actually, if possible, I'd like to go on after you.（実は、できれば、きみのあとにつづけたらと思うんだけど）⇨ GO ON [1]

☐ start (off) with …から始める

A: We're going to *start with* soup, and then we'll have a salad.（スープから始めて、次にサラダをいただきます）

B: Sounds good. What's the main course?（いいね。メインディッシュは何かな？）

☐ start out

【1】出発する、出かける（= leave）

A: What time did you *start out* this morning?（今朝は何時に出発したの？）

B: I left my house at 5:30 and caught the first train.（家を5時半に出て、始発電車に乗ったよ）

【2】（…の状態で［として］）始める、活動し出す

A: It seems like George is a very liberal politician.（ジョージはとてもリベラルな政治家のようね）

B: He *started out* a conservative, but he's changed completely. (保守派から始めたんだけど、完全に変わったよ)

□ start over　やり直す

A: You didn't like my report at all? (私の報告書はまったく気に入らなかったの？)
B: No, I didn't. You need to *start over*. (ああ、そうだね。やり直す必要がある)

□ start up

【1】（事業・議論などを）始める

A: Do you think we should *start up* our own company? (私たちの会社を立ち上げるべきだと思う？)
B: That might be the best thing to do at this stage. (現段階では、それがいちばんかもしれないね)

【2】（エンジンなどが）始動する

A: The car won't *start up* for some reason. (なぜか車のエンジンがかからないの)
B: I'm pretty sure it's just out of gas. (ただのガス欠に違いないよ)

【3】（事を）始める

A: About when are you going to start working on this project? (このプロジェクトにはいつ頃取りかかるの？) ⇨ WORK ON [1]
B: We'll probably *start up* early next week. (たぶん来週早々に始めるよ)

---

column ▶▶▶ start

start というと「…し始める」を連想するでしょうが、本来の意味合いは「急に動き出す」です。
そのため名詞形で使った He gave me a *start*. は「彼が私をびっくりさせた」となり、句動詞の場合も「急に…する」という含みがあります。
似たようなニュアンスの語に、startle（[不意に] びっくりさせる、驚かせる、はっとさせる）や、その派生語 startled（びっくりする、はっとする）などがあります。

stay

☐ stay around 居着く、そばにいる

A: Do you think the new guy is going to *stay around*?（あの新人さん、居着くと思う？）
B: I doubt it. Very few people last more than a few months here.（さあ、どうかな。ここで数カ月以上つづく人は滅多にいないからね）

☐ stay away from …から離れている、…に近づかない、…を避ける (= avoid)

A: Why do you want me to *stay away from* Linda?（どうしてリンダに近づかないでほしいの？）
B: I'm worried that she'll have a bad influence on you.（彼女がきみに悪影響を及ぼすのを心配しているんだ）

☐ stay down （値段・温度などが）下がったままである

A: How long do you think land prices will *stay down*?（どれぐらいの期間、地価は下がりつづけると思う？）
B: Not very long. Inflation is starting to heat up.（さほど長くない。インフレが激しくなっているしね）

☐ stay in （外に出ないで）うちに［中に］いる

A: Do you want to go somewhere today?（今日はどこかへ行きたい？）
B: No, I'm feeling under the weather. I think I'll just *stay in*.（いや、具合がよくないんだ。うちにいようと思う）

☐ stay off （話題などを）避ける (= avoid)

A: Do you think we should talk about revising the budget at the meeting tomorrow?（明日の会議で予算の修正について話すべきだと思う？）
B: No, I'd rather *stay off* that topic.（いや、その話題は避けたほうがいいな）

☐ stay on

【1】（学校・会社などに）つづいて残る、居つづける、居残る

A: I heard that Linda is planning on *staying on* another year.（リンダはもう1年留まるつもりだそうよ）

B: Really? I was hoping she would step down. (本当？ 辞任すればいいと思っていたのに)

【2】(人・帽子・ふたなどが落ちないで) 上に乗っている

A: You need to wear your employee badge at all times. (社員バッジを常に身につけている必要があるの)

B: Yeah, but it won't *stay on.* The clip is broken. (ああ、でもくっつかないんだ。留め金具が壊れている)

☐ stay out of   …に立ち入らない、…に関わらない

A: Why do we need to *stay out of* the warehouse? (どうして倉庫に立ち入ってはいけないの？)

B: We keep a lot of toxic substances back there. (そこに大量の毒物を保管してあるから)

☐ stay up

【1】(寝ないで) 起きている

A: I saw you nodding off in the meeting. (会議中にあなたが居眠りしているのを見たわよ)

B: I'm really sleepy. I *stayed up* all night working on my presentation. (本当に眠かったよ。一晩中、寝ないでプレゼンに取り組んでいたんだ) ⇨ WORK ON [1]

【2】(絵・飾り・カーテンなどが) 掛けられたままである

A: How long do you want this poster to *stay up*? (どれぐらいのあいだ、このポスターを貼っておきたいの？)

B: Let's keep it up for about two weeks. (2週間ほど貼っておこう)

☐ stay with   (方法・態度などを変えずに) つづける

A: Do you think we should *stay with* the current policy? (今の方針をつづけるべきだと思う？)

B: No, we need to change it as soon as possible. (いや、ただちに変更すべきだよ)

stick

☐ stick around　そばを離れない（でいる）、近くで待つ

A: Why don't you *stick around* for a few more days?（あと数日いたらいいじゃないの）
B: I'd like to, but I already bought my return ticket.（そうしたいけど、帰りの切符はもう買ったんだ）

☐ stick at　（仕事などを）辛抱強くつづける

A: Do you think George will be able to repair all these computers?（ジョージはこのコンピュータを全部直せると思う？）
B: Yes, if he *sticks at* it, he can do it.（ああ、こつこつやればできるよ）

☐ stick by　…に忠実である、…を支援する、（人を）見捨てない

A: You said you think interest rates are going to rise. Do you still *stick by* that?（金利は上昇しつづけると思うって言ったわね。まだそう思っている？）
B: Yes, I don't think anything has changed at all.（ああ、まったく何も変わっていないと思うよ）

☐ stick out

【1】（いやな事態を）耐え抜く（= endure）

A: This hot weather is almost unbearable.（この暑い天気はほとんど耐えがたいわ）
B: Well, *stick* it *out* a few more days. It's supposed to cool down this weekend.（まあ、あと数日我慢しよう。週末には涼しくなるはずだ）

【2】目立つ

A: You really *stick out* in that yellow hat.（その黄色い帽子をかぶっていると、本当に目立つわ）
B: Good. I want everyone to see me.（いいね。みんなに見られたいんだ）

☐ stick out of　…から突き出（てい）る

A: Um, did you know your underwear is *sticking out of* your pants?（えーと、下着がズボンからはみ出しているんだけど、わかってる？）

B: Oh, dear. Thanks for letting me know. (おお、教えてくれてありがとう)

☐ stick to

【1】（物・肌などに）くっつく（= stick）

A: I hate it when it's so hot and humid. (蒸し暑いのって大嫌い)
B: Me too. Your clothes just *stick to* your body. (ぼくもだ。服が体にぴったりくっつくよ)

【2】（主題・論点などから）それない

A: Can we discuss this year's summer vacation period? (今年の夏季休暇期間について話さない？)
B: No, let's *stick to* the main issue of the salary adjustments. (いや、本題の給与調整からそれないようにしよう)

☐ stick together

【1】（人びとが）一緒に（くっついて）いる

A: Wow, this airport is really crowded! (わあ、この空港、ものすごく混んでる！)
B: Yeah, we'd better *stick together* so we don't lose each other. (ああ、おたがい見失わないように、一緒に固まっていたほうがいい)

【2】 団結［結束］する、かばい合う

A: I think the company is really serious about the pay cuts. (会社は真剣に賃金カットを考えていると思う)
B: Well, let's *stick together* so that doesn't happen. (うーん、そうならないように団結しよう)

☐ stick up （髪などが）突っ立つ

A: Do you realize your hair is *sticking up* in the back? (うしろの髪がはねてるって、気づいている？)
B: Well, I didn't have time to comb it this morning. (いやあ、今朝は髪をとかす時間がなかったんだ)

☐ stick with …に固執する、…をやり通す

A: Why doesn't our company ever change its advertisements? (わが社が決して広告を変えないのは、どうしてなの？)
B: Well, they've been effective so far. Why not *stick with* them? (うーん、これまでのところ効果的だからね。しばらくそれでいこう)

stop

☐ stop by …に立ち寄る

A: Can you *stop by* the paper-supply store on your way downtown?（街に行く途中で紙材店に立ち寄ってくれない？）
B: No problem. Do you need me to pick up some copy paper?（いいよ。コピー用紙を買ってくればいい？）

☐ stop in 立ち寄る

A: It was so nice to see you again.（またお会いできて、とてもうれしいです）
B: Me too! I'm glad you *stopped in* while you were in town.（こちらこそ！ 町にいるあいだに立ち寄ってくれて、うれしいです）

☐ stop off 途中でちょっと立ち寄る

A: Do you need me to mail those letters?（この手紙を投函しましょうか？）
B: Yeah, can you *stop off* at the post office on your way downtown?（ああ、街へ行く途中に郵便局に寄ってもらえる？）

☐ stop over 途中で降りる、途中下車［下船］をする

A: Did you have a direct flight here?（ここまでは直行便できたの？）
B: No, I *stopped over* in Chicago.（いや、途中シカゴで降りた）

☐ stop up （流れなどを）せき止める（= clog）

A: Can we use the kitchen sink now?（台所の流しは使える？）
B: No, the drain is *stopped up*. I'll have to call a plumber.（ううん、下水管が詰まっているんだ。配管工を呼ばないと）

take

☐ take after (容姿・性質・行動などが)…に似る (= resemble)

A: You really are fanatic about baseball, aren't you? (あなたは熱狂的な野球ファンなんでしょう？)
B: Yeah, I *take after* my father. He was crazy about the sport. (ああ、父親譲りでね。父が野球に夢中なんだ)

☐ take along (人を)連れていく、(物を)持っていく (= bring)

A: Well, I'm going to the downtown office now. (さて、今から都心のオフィスに出かけます)
B: You'd better *take along* an umbrella. It's supposed to rain. (傘を持っていったほうがいいよ。雨になるらしい)

☐ take around …を案内する (= guide)

A: What are you going to do with George while he's in town? (ジョージが町にいるあいだ、彼と何をするの？)
B: Oh, I'll *take* him *around* the city and show him the sights. (ああ、町を案内して、名所に連れていくよ)

☐ take away …を持ち去る、運び去る

A: What happened to your car? (あなたの車に何があったの？)
B: Well, I must have parked it illegally, and the police *took* it *away*. (えーと、駐車違反をしたに違いない。警察に持っていかれたよ)

☐ take back (前言を)取り消す (= cancel)

A: Did you really mean to call George an idiot? (本当にジョージをバカ呼ばわりするつもりだったの？)
B: No, I *take* that *back*. I was just in a really bad mood. (いや、撤回するよ。すごく虫の居所が悪かっただけなんだ)

☐ take down …を書きつける、書き留める

A: Can you tell me how to operate this program? (このプログラムをどうやって操作

するか、教えてもらえる？）

B: Yeah, but it's pretty complicated. You'd better *take down* some notes. (いいよ、でもそれはかなり複雑だ。メモを取ったほうがいいよ）

☐ take for　…を〜だと思う、…を〜と見なす

A: I wish Linda wouldn't *take* me *for* an idiot. (リンダが私のことをバカだと思わなければいいな）

B: Don't worry about her. She doesn't respect anybody. (彼女のことは心配しなくていいよ。彼女は誰のことも尊敬していないから）

☐ take in
【1】…をだます

A: What do you think of this offer for free Internet service? (無料インターネットサービスに関するこの申し出について、どう思う？）

B: Don't be *taken in* by that. It's obviously a scam. (それにだまされちゃいけない。それは明らかに詐欺だ）

【2】（衣服などの）幅を詰める、（帆を）たたむ

A: You've really lost a lot of weight, haven't you? (すごく痩せたわね）

B: Yeah, I've got to start *taking in* all my clothes. (ああ、全部の洋服の幅を詰めないといけないんだ）

【3】（犬・猫などを）家に入れて世話する、（客を）泊める

A: How did Linda end up having five cats? (どうしてリンダは5匹も猫を飼うことになったの？）

B: Oh, she's always *taking in* strays she finds on the street. (ああ、彼女はいつも路上で見つけた迷い猫を家に入れちゃうんだ）

☐ take off
【1】（衣類・靴を）脱ぐ、（帽子を）取る、（眼鏡を）外す（= remove）

A: I hope you don't mind me suddenly stopping by. (突然立ち寄って、ご迷惑でないといいですが）　⇨ STOP BY

B: Not at all. *Take off* your coat and sit down. I'll get you some coffee. (全然大丈夫だよ。コートを脱いで座って。コーヒーを入れるね）

【2】…を（値段などから）差し引く、まける

A: I like this computer, but it's still a little expensive. (私はこのコンピュータが好きだけど、まだ少し高いわね）

B: Well, I can *take off* another 200 dollars. (うーん、もう200ドルならまけられます）

【3】（ある期間を）仕事の休みとして取る

A: Is it all right if I *take* next week *off*?（来週、休みを取ってもいいですか？）
B: No problem. Next week will be pretty slow at work anyway.（問題ないよ。どうせ来週は仕事が忙しくないだろうから）

【4】（飛行機が［で］）離陸する、出発する（= leave）

A: Why isn't the airplane *taking off*?（どうして飛行機は離陸しないのかしら？）
B: The pilot just said there's some problem with the flight computer.（パイロットがフライトコンピュータに問題があるって言っていた）

☐ take on

【1】（仕事・責任などを）引き受ける（= undertake）

A: Can you help me with this report?（このレポートを手伝ってくれる？）
B: Yeah, I guess I have time to *take on* a little more work.（いいよ、もう少し仕事を引き受ける余裕はあるはずだ）

【2】…を雇う（= hire）

A: We're really getting flooded with work these days.（最近、本当に仕事が殺到しているわね）
B: I know. We need to *take on* some temporary workers.（そうだね。臨時のスタッフを雇う必要がある）

☐ take out

【1】…を（外に）取り出す、持ち出す

A: Are you going out to the parking lot?（駐車場に行くの？）⇨ GO OUT [1]
B: Yeah, why? Do you want me to *take out* the garbage?（うん、どうして？ ゴミを持っていってほしいの？）

【2】（盲腸などを）切除する、（しみなどを）抜き取る、…を取り除く

A: Is George going to have his appendix *taken out*?（ジョージは盲腸を取るつもり？）
B: Yeah, so he'll be absent all next week.（ああ、だから彼は来週ずっと休みだよ）

☐ take out of …を~から取り出す［取り除く］

A: Will George have to pay for his accident with the company car?（会社の車で起こした事故に対して、ジョージは支払いの義務があるの？）
B: Yeah, they're going to *take* it *out of* his salary.（ああ、会社は彼の給料から差っぴくつもりだ）

☐ take over

【1】(人から) 引き継ぐ、(人と) 交代する、(人の) 代わりをする

A: Can you *take over* for George at the cash register? (レジをジョージと交代できる？)

B: No problem. Is his shift over already? (いいよ。もう彼のシフトは終わっているの？)

【2】持って [連れて] いく (= bring)、運ぶ (= carry)

A: Can I borrow your computer tonight? (今晩、あなたのコンピュータを借りることはできる？)

B: Sure. I'll *take* it *over* to your house after work. (もちろん。仕事のあと、きみの家に持っていくよ)

【3】…を支配する (= dominate)、(会社などを) 乗っ取る (= occupy)

A: Do you really think ABC is going to *take over* our company? (ABC 社がうちの会社を乗っ取るつもりだと、本気で思っている？)

B: Well, it might be good for us. We haven't been making much profit. (まあ、ぼくらのためにはいいかもね。ずっと大した収益を上げていないから)

☐ take to …が好きになる

A: It looks like you've really *taken to* Linda. Are you going to ask her for a date? (あなた、本当にリンダのことが好きになったみたいね。彼女をデートに誘うつもり？)

B: It's not what you think. I just think she's a nice person. (きみが考えているようなことじゃないよ。彼女のことは、いい人だと思っているだけだ)

☐ take up

【1】(時間・場所などを) 取る

A: I hate to *take up* your time, but can you show me how to use this? (時間を取らせてしまって申し訳ないけど、どうやってこれを使うのか教えてくれる？)

B: Sure. It's really pretty simple. (いいよ。本当にとても簡単なんだ)

【2】(趣味などとして) 始める、…の勉強を始める

A: I heard you've *taken up* figure skating. (あなたがフィギュアスケートを始めたって聞いたけど)

B: Well, they're giving really cheap lessons at the local skating rink. (ああ、地元のスケートリンクで、すごく安い金額でレッスンをやっているんだ)

T

talk

☐ talk about …について話す、講演する (= lecture)

A: What are you going to *talk about* in your speech tomorrow? (明日のスピーチで何について話す予定？)
B: I'm just going to outline the company's plans for next year. (来年の会社の計画の概要を説明するつもりだ)

☐ talk away （時などを）話をして過ごす、しゃべって（時間を）過ごす

A: It sounds like you had a really fun date with Linda. (リンダとのデート、すごく楽しかったみたいね)
B: We did. We just *talked away* the whole night. (うん。一晩中しゃべりつづけたよ)

☐ talk back 口答えをする、言い返す

A: George really made me so mad! (ジョージは私を本当に怒らせたわ！)
B: Yeah, but he is your boss. You shouldn't have *talked back* to him so strongly. (ああ、でも彼はきみの上司だ。彼にそんなに強く口答えするべきじゃなかった)

☐ talk down to …を見くだしてしゃべる

A: George can really be arrogant, can't he? (ジョージって本当に傲慢よね)
B: Yeah, he *talks down to* everybody as if they're stupid. (ああ、彼はみんなのことをまるでバカにしているみたいに、見くだして話すね)

☐ talk out of （人を）説き伏せて…を思いとどまらせる

A: Is Linda really thinking of quitting? (リンダは本当に辞めるつもりなの？)
B: No, I finally *talked* her *out of* it. (いいや、彼女を説き伏せて、最終的には思いとどまらせたよ)

☐ talk over （くつろいで）…のことを語り合う、…について相談する

A: We could use another worker in this office. (このオフィスにもう1人ほしいわ)
B: All right. Let me *talk* it *over* with George. (わかった。ジョージに相談してみるよ)

tear

☐ tear apart
【1】…を引き裂く、(人などを) 引き離す (= divide, separate)、ひどく苦しめる (= martyr)

A: Going through a divorce must be really hard for Linda. (離婚の経験は、リンダにとってとても大変なことに違いないわ)　⇨ GO THROUGH ［2］

B: I know. I bet it's *tearing* her *apart*. (そうだね。彼女が離婚して苦しんでいるのは想像がつくよ)

【2】(探し物などのために場所を) ひっかきまわす

A: Have you found your keys yet? (もう鍵は見つかった？)

B: No, and I *tore apart* the whole office looking for them. (いや、鍵を探して事務所中をひっかきまわしたよ)

☐ tear down (建物を) 取り壊す

A: Why are they *tearing down* the old office building? (どうして古い事務所のビルを解体しているの？)

B: Well, because it was so broken down, it was dangerous. (ああ、すごく壊れていて危なかったからだよ)　⇨ BREAK DOWN ［1］

☐ tear into (食物に) がつがつ食いつく、…を猛然と始める

A: You're really *tearing into* your lunch. (ランチをずいぶんとがつがつ食べてるわね)

B: I'm really hungry today. (今日はすごくお腹がすいているんだ)

☐ tear off …を引きはがす、切り離す

A: Are you buying all of these as presents? (これらを全部プレゼントとして買うんですか？)

B: Yes, so can you please *tear off* all the price tags? (はい、だから全部の値札をはがしてもらえますか？)

☐ tear up (人の心などを) 引き裂く、(人を) 悲しい気持ちにする

A: I heard Linda just broke up with her boyfriend. (リンダが彼氏と別れたって聞いたわ)　⇨ BREAK UP ［3］

B: Yeah, she really seems *torn up* about it. (そう、彼女、それですごく悲しかったみたいだ)

think

☐ think about　…のことを（よく）考える

A: I get the feeling Linda is serious about quitting.（リンダは辞めることを真剣に考えているみたい）
B: I hope she *thinks about* it carefully. I really want her to stay.（彼女がもっとよく考えてくれるといいんだけど。彼女にはすごく残ってもらいたいよ）

☐ think back　（昔のことを）思い出す (think back to) (= remember)

A: This song sounds just like a disco song from the 80s.（この曲、まさに1980年代のディスコの曲みたい）
B: Yeah, it makes me *think back* to when I was a student.（ああ、学生の頃を思い出すよ）

☐ think of

【1】…を考えつく、思いつく

A: Do you know why Linda is so upset at me?（リンダがなぜ私にすごく怒っているか知ってる？）
B: No, I can't *think of* anything you did wrong.（いや、きみが何か間違ったことをしたとは思えないな）

【2】…を思い出す［思い起こす］(= remember)

A: These mountains are really beautiful, aren't they?（この山々はとてもきれいね）
B: Yeah, they make me *think of* the Alps.（ああ、アルプス山脈を思い出すよ）

☐ think out　（問題を）よく考える、（案・策を）慎重に検討する

A: Our sales figures were really low this year.（今年、うちの売上高はかなり低かったわね）
B: Yeah, we need to *think out* a better sales strategy for next year.（ああ、来年に向けて、慎重に販売戦略を検討する必要がある）

☐ think up　考え出す、考えつく、思いつく

A: Have you decided what food to bring to the party?（パーティに何の食べ物を持っていくか決めた？）
B: Not yet, but I'll *think up* something.（まだだけど、何かしら考えてみるよ）

throw

☐ **throw around [about]** （金を）むだ使いする (= waste)

A: You sure *throw around* a lot of money for clothes. （あなた、洋服にものすごくお金を使ったわね）

B: That's not true. I've only bought a few nice suits, that's all. （そうじゃないよ。いいスーツを何着か買っただけだよ）

☐ **throw aside** …を捨てる (= reject)

A: Do you need these old instruction manuals? （この古い指導マニュアルは必要なの？）

B: No, just *throw* them *aside* for now. （いいや、もう捨てちゃおう）

☐ **throw away**

【1】…を捨て去る、捨ててしまう (= abandon)

A: Half of the food in this refrigerator is past its expiration date. （この冷蔵庫の半分の食べ物は、賞味期限が切れているわ）

B: Well, just *throw* it *away* then, so nobody gets sick. （じゃあ、それなら捨ててしまおう。そうすれば、誰も具合が悪くなったりしないから）

【2】（金などを）浪費する (= waste, fritter)

A: I'm thinking of investing in ABC. （ABC 社に投資しようと思うの）

B: Don't *throw* your money *away*. Wait until it really establishes itself first. （むだ使いするなよ。まずは ABC 社が地歩を固めるまで待ちな）

☐ **throw back** （酒などを）勢いよく［ぐいと］飲む

A: Do you feel like going out for a drink after work? （仕事のあと、飲みに行かない？）
⇨ GO OUT ［1］

B: Yeah, I could *throw back* a few beers. （いいよ、ビールをぐいっと飲めるといいね）

☐ **throw in** （売り物などに物を）おまけ［付属品］として添える

A: You really got a good price on this computer, didn't you? （このコンピュータ、ずいぶんいい値段で手に入れたわね）

B: Yeah, and the computer store *threw in* a printer for free! （ああ、さらに店がタダでプリンタをおまけとして付けてくれたんだ）

☐ throw on …をさっと着る［はく］

A: Boy, you're really dressed up today. (ねえ、今日はずいぶんおしゃれしてるのね)
B: Are you kidding? I just *threw on* a suit like always. (冗談だろう？ いつもどおりにスーツを着ただけさ)

☐ throw open （場所を一般に）開放する

A: Is the company party only for employees? (その会社のパーティは、社員のためだけのもの？)
B: No, we'll *throw* it *open* for family and friends too. (いいや、家族や友だちにも開放するつもりさ)

☐ throw out （不要なものを）捨てる (= discard)、…を外へ投げ出す

A: Do you need the budget figures from ten years ago? (10年前の予算の数値データは必要？)
B: No, you can *throw* them all *out*. (いや、全部処分していいよ)

☐ throw together …を急いで［そそくさと］作る、（料理などを）さっと作る

A: This lunch looks fantastic! You must have spent hours making it! (このランチ、すてき！ 作るのに間違いなく何時間もかかったでしょう！)
B: Not at all. I just *threw* it *together* in a few minutes. (全然。数分でさっと作ったんだ)

☐ throw up

【1】（胃の中の物を）吐く、戻す (= vomit)

A: Oh, dear. Linda just *threw up* in the bathroom. (どうしよう。リンダが今、浴室で吐いちゃったの)
B: I wonder if she ate too much at lunch. (彼女、昼に食べすぎたんじゃない)

【2】…を急いで作る［建てる］

A: Is that new supermarket already finished? (あの新しいスーパー、もう完成したの？)
B: Yeah, they *threw* it *up* in only a month. (ああ、たった1カ月間で大急ぎで建てたんだ)

tie

☐ tie down （人を）束縛する、（責任などに）縛りつける （= bind）

A: Are you going to be free this weekend? （今週末はひまになる予定？）
B: No, I'm going to be *tied down* with extra work. （いいや、追加の仕事で身動きがとれないだろう）

☐ tie up

【1】…をしっかり縛る［縛り上げる］、（動物を）つなぐ （= bind）

A: That poor dog! Why would its owner *tie* it *up* like that? （なんてかわいそうなワンちゃん！　どうして飼い主はあんなふうにつないでいるのかしら？）
B: Yeah, it can barely even move! （そうだね、動くのがやっとだよ）

【2】（電話を）一人占めする、（話して）ふさぐ

A: Did you telephone the secretary at ABC yet? （ABC社の秘書にもう電話した？）
B: No, all their phones are *tied up* right now. （まだだよ、今向こうの電話が全部話し中なんだ）

【3】（交通などを）不通にする、（事故が人を）遅刻させる

A: Boy, you're late. Did you get *tied up* in traffic? （ねえ、遅いわよ。渋滞にでも遭ったの？）
B: Yeah, there was a big accident on the freeway. （ああ、高速道路で大事故があったんだ）

☐ tie up with …と提携する、…とタイアップする

A: Are we going to launch the new software ourselves? （うちは自社だけで新しいソフトを発売する予定？）
B: No, we're going to *tie up with* ABC and launch it together. （いや、ABC社と提携して、共同で発売する予定だ）

touch

☐ touch down　（飛行機・宇宙船が）着陸する （= land）

A: Has Bill's flight arrived yet?　（ビルの飛行機はもう到着した？）
B: Yeah, it looks like it *touched down* just now.　（ああ、たった今着陸したみたいだ）

☐ touch off　（事を）引き起こす、触発［誘発］する （= cause）

A: I'm worried that the company is going to go through with the pay cuts.
（会社が賃金カットを遂行するのを心配しているの）　⇨ GO THROUGH WITH
B: If it does, that'll *touch off* some real protests from all the workers.　（もしそうしたら、全従業員から本当に抗議が起こるだろうね）

☐ touch on [upon]　（言葉で）…に（簡単に）触れる、言及する （= mention）

A: What did the chairman's speech *touch on* yesterday?　（昨日の会長のスピーチは何について触れたの？）
B: Oh, he mostly talked about improving motivation among the employees.
（ああ、従業員のやる気を促す話がほとんどだった）　⇨ TALK ABOUT

☐ touch up　（写真・化粧などを）修正する

A: Will you excuse me a minute? I need to *touch up* my makeup.　（ちょっといい？　メイクを直さないと）
B: No problem. I'll wait for you outside the restroom.　（いいよ。トイレの外で待っているよ）

try

☐ **try on** （衣服・靴・帽子・眼鏡・指輪などを）試してみる

A: Is there someplace I can *try on* this dress? （このドレスを試着できる場所はあるかしら？）
B: Yes, our changing rooms are right over there. （はい、試着室がすぐそちらにあります）

☐ **try out** （方法・用具・人などを）実際に使ってみる、試してみる

A: Have you *tried out* our new computer? （新しいコンピュータは試してみた？）
B: Yeah, and it runs twice as fast as the old one. （ああ、古いものの2倍の速さで動くね）

☐ **try out for** （運動チーム・配役などの）適正選考会に参加する

A: Are you going to *try out for* the company baseball team? （会社の野球チームの入団テストを受けるの）
B: Yeah, I'd love to be on the team. （ああ、チームに入りたいんだ）

---

column ▶▶▶ try

try は、日本語では非常にポジティブな意味で受け取られていますが、英語では「あきらめ」のニュアンスが強い語です。そのため、次のような文も、ネイティブの感覚としては→右のイメージになります。

- I *tried* to do it.「私はそれをやろうとした」→「それをやってみたがだめだった」
- I'm going to *try* on the dress.「私はそのドレスを着るつもりだ」→「だめかもしれないが着てみる」
- Did you *try* out the computer?「そのコンピュータを試した？」→「そのコンピュータがだめかどうか使ってみた？」

turn

☐ turn around

【1】くるっと向きを変える、振り向く

　A: Do I have grass stains on the back of my clothes?（服の背中、芝生でよごれてる？）

　B: I don't know. *Turn around* and let me see.（わからないな。くるっと向きを変えて見せて）

【2】回転する、回る

　A: That's a beautiful music box you bought your wife.（奥さんにすてきなオルゴールを買ったわね）

　B: Yeah, and if you wind it up, it *turns around*.（ああ、ねじを巻くと回転するんだ）

【3】（事業・経済などが）好転する

　A: Are we expecting a better year next year?（来年はもっといい年を期待できるかしら？）

　B: Only if the general economy *turns around*.（経済全般が好転さえすればね）

☐ turn away　顔をそむける

　A: Boy, that movie was pretty violent, wasn't it?（ねえ、あの映画はかなり暴力的だったわね）

　B: Yeah, I had to *turn away* at about half of the scenes.（ああ、シーンの半分は顔をそむけなくちゃいけなかったよ）

☐ turn back

【1】引き返す、（元の状態に）戻る（= return）

　A: Oh, the car's almost out of gas.（あら、車のガソリンがほとんどないわ）

　B: Well, we'd better *turn back*. The next gas station isn't for miles.（ああ、戻ったほうがいいね。次のガソリンスタンドはしばらく先にいかないとないからね）

【2】（時計の針を）逆戻りさせる

　A: Do you have daylight savings time in the U.S.?（アメリカにサマータイムはある？）

　B: Yes, so we have to *turn back* our clocks in the fall.（ああ、だから、秋には時計の針を逆戻りさせないといけないんだ）

☐ turn down
【1】（ラジオ・テレビなどの）音を小さくする

A: Wow, your radio is really loud!（まあ、あなたのラジオ、とっても音が大きいわよ！）
B: I'm sorry. I'll *turn* it *down*.（ごめん。小さくするよ）

【2】（提案などを）はねつける、拒否する、断わる（= reject）

A: Did you get hired for the position at ABC?（ABC 社で雇ってもらえた？）
B: No, they *turned* me *down*.（いや、断られたよ）

☐ turn in
【1】（書類・宿題を）提出する（= submit）

A: Did you *turn in* your monthly report yet?（月次レポートはもう提出した？）
B: Not yet. The deadline is next week.（いいや、まだだ。締め切りは来週なんだ）

【2】（犯人を警察などに）引き渡す、密告［通報］する（= squeal）

A: How did the police catch the robber so easily?（どうやって警察は、そんなに簡単に泥棒を捕まえたの？）
B: I read that his mother actually *turned* him *in*.（泥棒の母親が引き渡したみたいだ）

【3】床に就く、寝る

A: You look really sleepy.（すごく眠そうね）
B: I am. I'm ready to *turn in*.（そうなんだ。いつでも寝られるよ）

☐ turn into　（変化して）…になる

A: This rainy weather is getting bad, isn't it?（この雨はひどくなるのよね？）
B: Yeah, it's almost *turning into* a monsoon.（ああ、ほぼモンスーンみたいになるみたいだ）

☐ turn off
【1】栓・スイッチをひねって止める［消す］、しめる

A: Somebody forgot to *turn off* the air conditioner last night.（昨晩、誰かがエアコンを消し忘れたの）
B: It must have been George. He was the last one to leave.（ジョージに違いない。会社を出たのは彼が最後だ）

【2】（人に…に対する）興味［性欲］を失わせる

A: Don't you think Linda is attractive?（リンダって、魅力的だと思わない？）
B: She could be, but all that makeup she wears *turns* me *off*.（そうだろうけど、彼女のあのメイクには引くね）

【3】（わき道などへ）それる、方向を変える

A: Aren't we getting close to the downtown area? (町の中心街に近づいているんじゃない？)
B: Yeah, you *turn off* at the next freeway exit. (ああ、次の高速道路の出口で降りて)

☐ turn on

【1】栓をひねって（水・ガスを）出す

A: Who *turned on* the heating this morning? (今朝、誰がヒーターをつけたの？)
B: I got to the office early, so I did. (早く会社にきたから、ぼくがつけたよ)

【2】（明かり・テレビ・ラジオを）つける

A: It's getting kind of dark. (ちょっと暗くなったわ)
B: Okay, I'll *turn on* the lights. (わかった、明かりをつけるよ)

【3】（急に）…を襲う、攻撃する (= attack)

A: How did you get your arm bitten? (どうやって腕をかまれたの？)
B: I was petting my neighbor's dog, and it suddenly *turned on* me. (隣の犬をなでていたら、突然襲いかかってきたんだ)

☐ turn out

【1】（ガス・火などを）消す

A: Giving Linda a surprise party was a great idea! (リンダにサプライズパーティを開くなんて、すごくいいこと思いついたね！)
B: Well, she's almost here, so hurry up and *turn out* the lights. (ええっと、彼女はもうすぐここにくるから、急いで明かりを消して)

【2】（人びとが催し物などに）集まる、姿を見せる (turn out for) (= gather, assemble)

A: Did a lot of people *turn out* for the company party? (会社のパーティに大勢集まった？)
B: Yeah, more than I expected. We even ran out of food. (ああ、予想したより多かったよ。食べ物すら足りなくなったよ) ⇨ RUN OUT OF [1]

☐ turn over

【1】…をひっくり返す

A: Oh, dear, this sofa cushion is stained! (あらまあ、このソファのクッションにしみが付いている！)
B: Just *turn it over*, and nobody'll notice. (ちょっとひっくり返せば、誰も気がつかないよ)

【2】（人を警察などに）引き渡す (= deliver)

A: What will happen to the illegal immigrants who tried to sneak into the country? （ひそかに入国しようとした密入国者はどうなるの？）
B: Well, the police will *turn* them *over* to their own embassy. （うん、警察が彼らの国の大使館に引き渡すんだ）

【3】（エンジンが）始動する、かかる

A: This darn engine won't *turn over*! （このエンジンときたら、かからないわ！）
B: It's probably too cold for it to start. （エンジンが始動するには、おそらく寒すぎるんだ）

□ turn to

【1】（本の中のあるページを）開ける

A: Can you explain the new employee work rules? （新しい就業規則を説明してくれる？）
B: Of course. *Turn to* page 15 of your company handbook, and I'll go over them. （もちろん。会社要覧の15ページを開けてくれたら、説明しなおすよ）　⇨ GO OVER [4]

【2】…に頼る、…を頼りとする

A: Who should I *turn to* if I have a problem with my computer? （パソコンに何かあったら、誰を頼ればいい？）
B: You should ask Linda. She knows everything about our computer system. （リンダに聞けばいいよ。彼女はうちのコンピュータシステムに関してすべて知っている）

□ turn up

【1】（ラジオ・テレビなどの）音を大きくする

A: Hey, our new TV commercial just came on! （ねえ、ちょうどうちの新しいテレビコマーシャルだわ！）　⇨ COME ON [2]
B: *Turn up* the volume. I can't hear it! （音を大きくして。聞こえないよ！）

【2】（なくなった物が）ひょっこり現われる、見つかる

A: Did your missing camera ever *turn up*? （行方不明のカメラは見つかったの？）
B: Yeah, it was underneath my car seat. （ああ、車のシートの下にあった）

wait

☐ wait around　ぶらぶらして待つ

A: How long did you have to **wait around** for George to come?（ジョージがくるまで、どれくらい待たなくちゃいけなかった？）

B: He finally showed up at 5:00.（やっと5時になって現われたよ）　⇨ SHOW UP [1]

☐ wait on　（人に）食事の給仕をする

A: This restaurant really needs more employees.（このレストランは、絶対もっと従業員が必要よ）

B: I know. One waiter can't **wait on** 15 different tables.（そうだね。1人のウエイターが、15のテーブルに給仕することはできないよ）

☐ wait up

【1】寝ないで待つ

A: Are you going to **wait up** until the new year rings in?（新年の鐘が鳴るまで寝ないで待つつもり？）

B: I doubt it. I'll probably fall asleep before then.（どうだろうね。たぶんその前に寝ちゃうよ）

【2】（人を呼び止めて）ちょっと待って

A: Hey, **wait up**. You're walking too fast.（ねえ、ちょっと待って。歩くの速すぎるよ）

B: You need to walk faster.（きみがもっと速く歩きなよ）

---

column ▶▶▶ wear

wear（181ページ）は「着る」が原義で、そこから「すり減る」「すこしずつだめになっていく」という意味でも使われるようになりました。当初は洋服や布に対して使っていましたが、今では The rowdy kids wore me out.（やんちゃな子供にへとへとにさせられた）のように人に対しても用いられます。

中でも wear and tear（〔通常の使用による〕摩損、摩滅、傷み）は保証書などにも記載されているため、日常的によく使われます。

・When you buy a hundred-year-old house, you have to expect a little **wear and tear**.（築100年の家を買うなら、多少傷んでいるのは覚悟しなければいけない）

walk

☐ walk into …にぶつかる (= hit)

A: How did you get that bruise on your forehead? (おでこのあざはどうしたの？)
B: I wasn't paying attention, and I **walked into** a wall. (注意力が欠けていて、壁にぶつかってしまったんだ)

☐ walk off
【1】…から歩いて立ち去る

A: How was the comedy show you went to last night? (昨晩行ったコメディーのショーはどうだった？)
B: Terrible. The comedian got booed, so he just **walked off** the stage. (ひどかったよ。コメディアンはブーイングを浴びせられて、ステージを降りたんだ)

【2】(抗議して仕事などを) 放棄する

A: I heard all the city office employees have **walked off** the job. (市の職員が全員抗議して、仕事を放棄しているって聞いたわ)
B: Yeah, they're all on strike for higher pay. (ああ、賃上げのためのストライキをしているんだ)

☐ walk off with (賞などを) さらっていく、(試合などに) 楽に勝つ

A: Did you win big gambling in Las Vegas? (ラスベガスでギャンブルをやって、大儲けしたの？)
B: I'll say! I **walked off with** 500 dollars! (そうなんだ！ 500 ドルいただいたよ！)

☐ walk through
【1】…を歩いて通り抜ける

A: Their office is on 22nd Street. (彼らのオフィスは 22 番街にある)
B: Let's **walk through** the park to get there. (公園を抜けていこう)

【2】(人に)…を丹念 [順々] に教える、手ほどきをする

A: First, let me **walk** you **through** the steps one by one. (まず、1つひとつステップを教えましょう)
B: That would be really helpful. I don't know what I'm doing. (そうしてもらえると、大変助かります。自分のしていることがわからなくて)

watch

☐ watch out　気をつける、注意する

A: You need to always *watch out* for the pickpockets here.（ここではいつもスリに注意しておかないと）
B: Yeah, I know. It's kind of dangerous.（ああ、そうだね。ちょっと危ないね）

wear

☐ wear down　（抵抗・反対などを）弱らせる、（人を）説き伏せる（= persuade）

A: How long have they been negotiating?（あの人たち、もうどれくらい交渉しているの？）
B: About 20 minutes. The client must be *worn down* by now.（20分くらいだ。そろそろクライアントは説得されている頃だ）

☐ wear out

【1】…をすり減らす、（もう使えないほど）使い古す（= spoil）

A: It looks like you've just about *worn out* those shoes.（あなたは、その靴をすり切れるほどはいているみたね）
B: You're right. I should probably throw them away soon.（そう。すぐにでも捨てないといけないんだけどね）　⇨ THROW AWAY [1]

【2】…を（すっかり）疲れさせる、まいらせる

A: Man, we've been working like dogs today.（ねえ、今日私たち、犬のようにがむしゃらに働いているわね）
B: Yeah, I'm completely *worn out*. Let's go home.（ああ、完全に疲れ切っている。家に帰ろう）

work

□ work off

【1】（カロリー・脂肪・体重などを）運動して減らす

A: Why are you going jogging at lunchtime?（どうして昼食時にジョギングをしているの？）

B: I'm trying to *work off* all the weight I put on at Christmas.（クリスマスに増えてしまった体重をすべて落とそうとしているんだ）⇨ PUT ON ［3］

【2】（うっぷんなどを）晴らす

A: Is it true you like to play video games?（あなたがビデオゲームが好きだって、本当？）

B: Yeah, why not? They're a good way to *work off* stress.（そう、なんで？ ストレスを発散にいいんだ）

【3】（負債を）働いて返済する

A: Is George getting his salary cut for damaging the company car?（ジョージは会社の車を傷つけたから、お給料を減らされているの？）

B: Yeah, but he'll *work* it *off* by next month.（ああ、でも来月には返し終わるよ）

□ work on

【1】…に取り組む（= tackle）、…（の制作に）従事する（= engage）

A: Who do you have *working on* the new advertising campaign?（誰が新しい広告キャンペーンに取り組んでいるの？）

B: I put Linda on it.（リンダにやらせているよ）⇨ PUT ON ［7］

【2】（人・感情などに）働きかける、…を説得する（= affect, persuade）

A: Do you think you can get George to agree to work more hours?（もっと長時間働くように、ジョージを納得させられると思う？）

B: Well, he's reluctant, but I think he'll agree if I *work on* him.（ああ、いやがっているけど、ぼくが説得すれば納得すると思う）

□ work out

【1】（計画・案などを）考え出す、練り上げる

A: Have you *worked out* the budget for next month yet?（来月の予算はもう立てた？）

B: Almost. I should have it finished by tomorrow.（ほぼね。明日までに仕上げないといけないんだ）

【2】（総額など）しめて［合計］…となる、（合計が）出る（= calculate）

- A: These budget figures don't *work out* right.（この予算の数値は正しく算定されていないわ）
- B: Sorry, I must have added them up wrong.（ごめん、きっと間違えて足しちゃったんだ）
  ⇨ ADD UP

【3】（スポーツなどの）練習［トレーニング］をする（= exercise）

- A: Linda is in amazing physical shape, don't you think?（リンダはすごくいい体つきをしてるわよね？）
- B: Yeah, she must *work out* at a gym or something.（ああ、彼女はジムかどこかで体を鍛えているに違いない）

□ work over （原稿などを）やり直す、手を加える

- A: Boy, George's report sure has a lot of mistakes.（ねえ、ジョージのレポートにたくさん間違いがあるわ）
- B: Don't worry. He promised to *work* it *over* before he turns it in.（心配しないで。提出する前に書き直すって、彼は約束したよ）⇨ TURN IN ［1］

□ work through （問題などを）処理する、片づける、克服する

- A: I'm having trouble figuring out the new taxes.（新しい税金を計算するのに困っているの）
- B: Well, let's see if we can *work through* them together.（じゃあ、うまく対処できるかどうか、一緒に見てみよう）

□ work toward （目標などを）めざして努力［前進］する

- A: When are we going to release our new product?（うちの新製品はいつ発売する予定？）
- B: We're *working toward* a release next month.（来月の発売をめざして努力しているよ）

□ work up

【1】（興味・食欲などを）引き起こす、生じさせる

- A: Are you ready for lunch?（お昼に行く？）
- B: Yeah, I really *worked up* an appetite with all this work this morning.（ああ、今朝はずっとこの仕事をやっていてすごく食欲が湧いたよ）

【2】…を仕上げる、（考えなどを）まとめ上げる

- A: Have you *worked up* the agenda for tomorrow's meeting?（明日の会議の予定表はまとめた？）
- B: Yeah, I just need to print out copies for everyone.（ああ、みんなのためにプリントしないと）

write

□ write down　…を書き留める、記録する (= record)

A: Were these all the issues covered at the meeting? (この問題がすべて会議で取り上げられたの？)

B: Yes, I think I *wrote down* everything. (ああ、どれも書き留めたと思うけど)

□ write off

【1】…を失敗［損失］と見なす、…をないものとあきらめる

A: Do you think Linda will ever pay back the money you lent her? (あなたが貸したお金、リンダは返してくれると思う？)

B: No, I decided to *write* that *off*. I'll never see that money again. (いや、もうあきらめた。あのお金が戻ることはない)

【2】（資産・費用などを）（減価）償却する

A: It seems like George is always buying new computers. (ジョージはいつも新しいコンピュータに買い替えているみたいね)

B: That's because he has a company and can *write* them *off*. (彼は会社を持っていて、そこで償却できるからね)

□ write out　…を詳しく［ちゃんと・正式に］書く

A: Could you send me an invoice? And please *write out* the details. (請求書を送ってくれますか？　そこに明細をご記入ください)

B: Okay, I'll list every item individually. (わかりました。全項目を個別に列挙します)

□ write up　（レポート・メモなどを）詳しく書く、仕上げる

A: Do you want me to have George *write up* a report? (ジョージに報告書を書かせましょうか？)

B: Yes, tell him to include all the details. (ああ、細かいことまで全部書くよう伝えてよ)

第2章

句動詞の問題

句動詞の問題に挑戦！

まとめとして、英語の名言の中で句動詞がどのように使われているか見ていきましょう。第1章で取り上げていない句動詞も含まれていますが、日本語訳を参考に挑戦してください。

【問題】
次の各文の下線部にあてはまる語を答えなさい。
※解答以外の句動詞があてはまる場合もありますが、ここではあくまで名言として伝わっている文中の句動詞を正解とします。

1.
A bank is a place where they lend you an umbrella in fair weather and ask _____ it back when it begins to rain.
銀行とは天気がいい時に傘を貸し、雨が降り始めると傘を返せと要求する場所だ。（ロバート・フロスト）

2.
I like pigs. Dogs look _____ to us. Cats look _____ on us. Pigs treat us as equals.
私は豚が好きだ。犬は私たちを尊敬する。猫は私たちを見下す。豚は私たちを公平に扱う。
（ウィンストン・チャーチル）

3.
No man is rich enough to buy _____ his past.
自分の過去を買い戻せるほどの金持ちはいない。（オスカー・ワイルド）

4.
Nothing is particularly hard if you divide it _____ small jobs.
小さな仕事に分けさえすれば、特に大変な仕事などない。（ヘンリー・フォード）

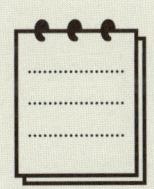

正解：for
A bank is a place where they lend you an umbrella in fair weather and *ask for* it back when it begins to rain. (Robert Frost)

正解：up, down
I like pigs. Dogs *look up to* us. Cats *look down on* us. Pigs treat us as equals.
(Winston Churchill)

正解：back
No man is rich enough to *buy back* his past. (Oscar Wilde)

正解：into
Nothing is particularly hard if you *divide* it *into* small jobs. (Henry Ford)

5.
Education is equipping our children to walk _____ doors of opportunity.
教育とは子供にチャンスを与えることだ。(L・B・ジョンソン)

6.
Education's purpose is to replace an empty mind _____ an open one.
教育の目的はからっぽの心を開かれた心へと変えることだ。(マルコム・S・フォーブス)

7.
Even if you're on the right track, you'll get run _____ if you just sit there.
たとえ正しい道にいたとしても、そこにただ座っているだけでは、車にひかれてしまう。
(ウィル・ロジャース)

8.
Happiness lies _____ the joy of achievement and the thrill of creative effort.
幸福とは達成の喜びであり、創造的に活動することの感動である。(フランクリン・D・ルーズベルト)

9.
If a man empties his purse into his head, no man can take it _____ from him.
自分の頭にお金をつぎ込めば、人から取り上げられることもない（お金は使えばなくなるが、知識を得ることに費やせばなくなりはしない）。(ベンジャミン・フランクリン)

10.
If you try hard enough to make someone else happy, you may end _____ being happy yourself.
他人を幸せにできるよう一生懸命努力すれば、最後には自分自身が幸せになるだろう。
(ジェームズ・サーバー)

正解：through
Education is equipping our children to *walk through* doors of opportunity.
(L. B. Johnson)

正解：with
Education's purpose is to *replace* an empty mind *with* an open one.
(Malcolm S. Forbes)

正解：over
Even if you're on the right track, you'll get *run over* if you just sit there.
(Will Rogers)

正解：in
Happiness *lies in* the joy of achievement and the thrill of creative effort.
(Franklin D. Roosevelt)

正解：away
If a man empties his purse into his head, no man can *take* it *away* from him.
(Benjamin Franklin)

正解：up
If you try hard enough to make someone else happy, you may *end up* being happy yourself. (James Thurber)

11.
In matters of style, swim _____ the current; in matters of principle, stand like a rock.
様式に関しては、流れに乗って泳げ。 原則に関しては、岩のように動かず立ち向かえ。
（トマス・ジェファーソン）

12.
It is easier to come _____ with new ideas than it is to let go of the old ones.
古いアイデアを手放すより新しいアイデアを考えるほうが簡単だ。（ピーター・ドラッカー）

13.
It is easier to stay _____ than to get _____ .
外出するより家に帰らないほうが簡単だ。（マーク・トウェイン）

14.
Men occasionally stumbles _____ the truth from time to time, but most pick themselves _____ and hurry _____ as if nothing happened.
人は時折真実につまずくが、ほとんどの人は起き上がり、何事もなかったかのように急いで立ち去る。
（ウィンストン・チャーチル）

15.
When you believe _____ a thing, believe _____ it all the way, implicitly and unquestionably.
あるものを信じるならば、盲目的に、疑うことなく、とことん信じなさい。（ウォルト・ディズニー）

16.
Shoot _____ the moon. Even if you miss it, you will land among the stars.
月をめざしなさい。そうすれば、たとえ失敗しても星に着陸するだろう（大きな希望を持てば、たとえ失敗してもその近くにはたどり着けるだろう）。（レス・ブラウン）

正解：with
In matters of style, *swim with* the current; in matters of principle, stand like a rock.
(Thomas Jefferson)

正解：up
It is easier to *come up with* new ideas than it is to let go of the old ones.
(Peter Drucker)

正解：out, out
It is easier to *stay out* than to *get out*. (Mark Twain)

正解：over, up, off
Men occasionally *stumbles over* the truth from time to time, but most *pick* themselves *up* and *hurry off* as if nothing happened. (Winston Churchill)

正解：in, in
When you *believe in* a thing, *believe in* it all the way, implicitly andunquestionably. (Walt Disney)

※ウォルト・ディズニーは最後の語を unquestionable と言ったと思われるが、文法的には unquestionably が正しいため、ここではそちらを採用した。

正解：for
Shoot for the moon. Even if you miss it, you will land among the stars.
(Les Brown)

17.
The best way to make your dreams come true is to wake _____ .
夢をかなえる最善の方法は、目を覚ますことです。（ポール・ヴァレリー）

18.
The future depends _____ what we do in the present.
将来は、自分が今、何をするかによる。（マハトマ・ガンジー）

19.
We cannot go _____ and make a new start, but we can start now to make a new ending.
過去に戻って新しく出直すことはできないが、新しい終わりを作るために今始めることはできる。
（スティーブン・R・コヴィー）

20.
There is nothing like a challenge to bring _____ the best in man.
人の長所を引き出すには、挑戦するのがいちばんいい。（ショーン・コネリー）

21.
There is only one thing in the world worse than being talked _____ , and that is not being talked _____ .
この世で噂をされるよりもいやなことはただ1つしかない。噂をされないことだ。（オスカー・ワイルド）

22.
Eighty percent of success is showing _____ .
成功の8割は人前に出ることで決まる。（ウディ・アレン）

23.
I never thought I'd land _____ pictures with a face like mine.
私みたいな顔で映画に出るなんて考えたこともなかったわ。（オードリー・ヘップバーン）

正解：up
The best way to make your dreams come true is to **wake up**. (Paul Valéry)

正解：on
The future **depends on** what we do in the present. (Mahatma Gandhi)

正解：back
We cannot **go back** and make a new start, but we can start now to make a new ending. (Stephen R. Covey)

正解：out
There is nothing like a challenge to **bring out** the best in man. (Sean Connery)

正解：about, about
There is only one thing in the world worse than being **talked about**, and that is not being **talked about**. (Oscar Wilde)

正解：up
Eighty percent of success is **showing up**. (Woody Allen)

正解：in
I never thought I'd **land in** pictures with a face like mine. (Audrey Hepburn)

INDEX
句動詞和英索引

- あいうえお順。
- 基本となる言い方、表現で拾った。第1章本文には「(考えなどを) 受け入れる」「(夢・理想などを) 実現する」「(橋などを) 渡る」などと各語義は記されているが、ここではそれぞれ「受け入れる」「実現する」「渡る」の形で拾った。
- 項目の頭に(　　)で囲んだ語(例:「(予定より)遅れる」)や[　　]で囲んだ語(「[…について] 聞く」)があるが、並べ変えるにあたり、前者はそれを読んで判断したが、後者はしていない。

■ あ
- あいだに入る　go between　65
- あいだに割り込む　come between　30
- 相ともなう　go together　71
- 遭う　come up against　35
- 会う　meet up　109
- 会う　meet with　109
- あおむけに横たわる　lie back　101
- 上がる　go up　72
- 明らかにする　bring out　17
- (悪天候などが) 始まる　set in　140
- あくまでも捨てない　hold to　85
- 上げ (てい) る　hold up　85
- 開ける　turn to　178
- 上げる　let out　100
- 上げる　put up　126
- 上げる　send up　138
- あざ笑う　laugh at　94
- あせる　come out　33
- 遊びまわる　play around [about]　116
- 遊ぶ　play with　116
- 与えない [売らない] で持っている　hang onto　76
- 与える　hold out　21, 84
- 頭金 [内金] として [(ある金額を)] 払う　put down　121
- あたる　fall on [upon]　49
- あちこち聞いてまわる　ask around　5
- 悪化　breakdown　15
- 扱う　do with　43
- 圧勝　blowout　10
- 集まる　get together　62
- 集まる　turn out　177
- 集める　put together　125
- あてにする　count on [upon]　37
- あてはまる　go for　67

- あとから [折り返し] 電話をする　call back　20
- あとからくる　come after　28
- 後ずさりする　back away　6
- あとで返事 [連絡] する　get back to　55
- あとへ延ばす　put back　120
- あとを追う　run after　128
- 穴があくほど着る　go through　71
- あふれる　run over　132
- 甘んじる　settle for　142
- あら探しをする　pick on　115
- 争う　run against　128
- 表わす　stand for　154
- 現われる　break through　13
- 歩いて立ち去る　walk off　180
- 歩いて通り抜ける　walk through　180
- 歩きまわる　get around　54
- あわせる　bring together　17
- 暗示する　get at　54
- 案内する　take around　163
- 安楽死させる　put down　122

■ い
- 言い返す　talk back　167
- いいかげんにしろ　come on　33
- 言う　get out　59
- 家 [部屋] に入れる　have in　78
- 家に入れて世話する　take in　164
- 家に招く　ask in, ask over, ask up, ask down　5
- 家まで送り届ける　see back　134
- 射落とす　shoot down　144
- 勢いよく [ぐいと] 飲む　throw back　170
- 生きがいにする　live for　102
- 生き延びる　live through　103
- 息を引き取る　pass away　112, 113

- 行く　go down　66
- 行く　go to　71
- 意向を探る　feel out　50
- 意識を失う　pass out　113
- 意識を失わせる　put out　124
- 意識を取り戻す　come around　29
- いじめる　pick on　115
- 急いでいく　run down　129
- 急いで立ち去る　run off　131
- 急いで [そそくさと] 作る　throw together　171
- 急いで作る [建てる]　throw up　171
- 急いで戻る　run back　129
- 忙しく動きまわる　run around　128
- いだいている　have against　78
- いたずらをする　act up　2
- 一員である　sit on　148
- 一時帰休させる　lay off　95
- 一度も目を覚まさず眠る　sleep through　150
- 一気に飲み干す　knock down　92
- 居着く　stay around　158
- 一笑に付す　laugh off　94
- 一緒にいる　hang around with　75
- 一緒に (くっついて) いる　stick together　161
- 一緒に暮らす　live with　103
- 一緒にくる [行く]　come along　28
- 一緒にする　bring together　17
- 一緒になる　fall in with　49
- 一掃する　clean out　25
- 一掃する　clear away　26
- 居つづける　stay on　158
- いないかたずねる　ask for　5
- 田舎にくる　come down　31
- 居残る　stay on　158
- 入れる　add in　3
- いろいろと検討する　kick around [about]　91

194

INDEX

言わないでおく　keep back　88
印刷する　run off　131
印象を与える　come across as　28

■う
上 [階上] へ行かせる　send up　138
上に突き出る　hang over　76
上に乗っている　stay on　159
浮かぶ　come into　32
受け入れられる　go down　67
受け入れられる　go over　70
受け入れる　buy into　19
受け継ぐ　come into　32
動かなくなる　give out　63
動き出す　set out　141
動く　run on　132
撃ち返す　shoot back　144
打ち倒す　bring down　15
うちに [中に] いる　stay in　158
打ちのめす　beat up　8
打ち負かす　beat out　7
移る　move on　110
奪い [連れ] 去る　carry off　22
うまくやっているのる　carry off　22
うまくやり遂げる　pull off　118
生む　bring in　16
埋め合わせ [償い] をする　make it up to　109
埋める　fill up　52
売れる　go for　67
売り切る　sell out　136
売り切れになる　sell out of　136
売り尽くす　sell out　136
売りに出す　put up　126
売り払う　sell off　136
うるさく言う　keep after　87
うろつく　hang around　75
浮気する　run around　128
噂 [こと] を聞く　hear about　80
運動して減らす　work off　182

■え
影響し出す　kick in　91
影響を及ぼす　get into　58
得ようとする　go for　67
選ぶ　go for　67
選ぶ　go with　72
延期する　put back　120
延期する　put off　122
延長する　draw out　45
遠慮なく話す　speak out　151
遠慮なく話す　speak up　152

■お
おいおい　come on　33
追い出す　kick off　91
追い出す　push out　119
追い出す　put out　124
[…を～から] 追い出す　run out of　132
追いつく　catch up　23
置いておく　keep at　87
置いてきぼりにする　leave behind　97, 98
追い払う　run off　131
追い払う　send away　137
応援する　pull for　117
大いに笑わせる　break up　14
大きな声で話す　speak up　151
大きな進歩　breakdown　15
大声で呼ぶ [言う]　call out　21
大儲けする　clean up　25
公にする　put out　123
起き上がる　sit up　149
置き去りにする　leave behind　97, 98
起きる　get up　21, 62
置き忘れる　leave behind　97
置く　hang up　77
置く　put down　121
遅らせる　hang up　77
遅らせる　hold off　83
遅らせる　hold up　85
遅らせる　push back　119
遅らせる　set back　139
送り返す　send back　137
送り出す　see off　134
遅れないでついて [やって] いく　keep up with　90
遅れる　drop behind　46
遅れる　fall behind　48
遅れる　get behind　55
起こしておく　keep up　90
行なわれる　go on　69
起こる　break out　13
起こる　come of　32
押さえつける　hold down　83
抑えておく　keep back　87
抑えておく　keep down　88
抑える　fight back　51
抑える　hold back　82
抑える　hold in　83
抑える　keep in　89
抑える　keep under　90
押さえる　sit on　149
収まる　settle down　142
押し上げる　push up　119
押しあて（てい）る　hold against　82
押し入り　breakdown　15
教え込む　knock into　92
押しとどめる　hold back　82
襲いかかる　come at　29
襲いかかる　come for　31

襲う　hold up　85
襲う　turn on [upon]　177
陥る　fall into　48
落ち込ませる　get down　56
落ち込む　fall in　48
落ち着く　settle down　142
陥れる　set up　141
音などが…からしてくる　come from　31
大人になる　grow up　73
躍りまわる　jump around　86
衰える　fall off　49
音を大きくする　turn up　178
音を小さくする　turn down　176
おまけ [付属品] として添える　throw in　170
思いあたる　hit on [upon]　81
思いがけなく会う　run into　130
思い切って言う　speak out　151
思い出させる　bring back　15
思い出す　think back　169
思い出す [起こす]　think of　169
思いつく　think of　169
思いつく　think up　169
思う　make of　107
思われる　come off　33
折り合っていく　get along　53
おりる　come through　35
降りる　get down　56
降りる　get off　58
降りる　get out of　60
降りる　go down　66
降ろす　bring down　16
降ろす　drop off　47
降ろす　lay down　95
降ろす　let off　99
終わらせる　break off　12
終わりまで生き抜く　live out　103
終わりまで過ごす　live out　103
終わりまでやり通す　go through with　71
終わりまで読む　read through [over]　127
終わる　break up　14
終わる　close with　27
終わる　get over　60

■か
会議に出される　come forward　31
解決する　clear up　26
会見する　meet with　109
解雇　layoff　96
解雇する　lay off　95, 96
解雇する　push out　119
解散する　break up　13
買い占める　buy up　19
解釈する　make out　107

195

外出する	go out 69
解消	breakdown 15
解消する	break up 14
改善する	shake up 143
解体する	break down 11
解体する	knock down 92
開店する	open up 111
回転する	turn around 175
該当する	fall under 49
買い取る	buy out 19
買い取る	buy up 19
外泊する	sleep over 150
回復する	get over 61
解放する	let out 100
開放する	throw open 171
買い戻す	buy back 19
返してもらう	have back 78
返す	bring back 15
返す	hand back 74
帰る	get back 55
顔をそむける	turn away 175
かかる	turn over 178
関わらない	stay out of 159
関わらないでいる	keep out of 89
書き上げる	make out 107
書き込む	fill in 52
書き込む	fill out 52
書き記す	put down 121
かき立てる	get up 62
書きつける	take down 163
書き留める	mark down 108
書き留める	take down 163
書き留める	write down 184
書き取る	get down 56
書く	make out 107
隠しておく	keep back 88
駆け落ちする	run away 129
駆け込む	run into 131
かけている	have on 78
掛けられたままである	stay on 159
掛ける	hang up 77
下降する	look down 105
加算する	add on 3
[...の]家事をする	do for 42
数を数え上げる	count up 37
稼ぐ	bring in 16
数えながら待ちわびる	count down 37
堅く守る	hold to 85
堅く守る	stand by 153
片づける	clear away 26
片づける	put away 120
片づける	work through 183
語り合う	talk over 167
がつがつ食いつく	tear into 168
がっかりさせる	bring down 16
がっかりさせる	get down 56

かつぐ	put on 123
活動し出す	start out 156
かっとなる	blow up 10
悲しい気持ちにする	tear up 168
金で丸め込む	buy off 19
金を返す	pay back 114
かばい合う	stick together 161
株や権利を買い取る	buy out 19
株を買う	buy into 19
我慢する	live with 103
我慢する	put up with 126
通う	go to 71
からかう	put on 123
体が成長して…が合わなくなる	grow out of 73
代わって答える	answer for 5
側につく	come over 35
代わりをする	stand in 154
代わりをする	take over 166
考え出す	come up with 36
考え出す	think up 169
考え出す	work out 182
考えつく	think of 169
考えつく	think up 169
考えを…へ変えさせる	bring around 15
関係を絶つ	give up 63
関節を外す	put out 124
完全にあばく	blow apart 9
完全に負かす	blow away 9
がんばる	hold on 84
管理する	look after 104

■ き

議員に選出される	get into 57
消えたくなる	go away 65
消える	come out 33
消える	come out of 34
消える	go off 69
消える	go out 69
機会[ひま]ができる	get around to 54
着飾る	do up 43
聞き入れる	hear of 80
聞き覚える	pick up 115
聞き出す	get out of 60
聞き取れない	break up 14
効きめがある	kick in 91
効く	act on [upon] 2
起床させる	get up 21
起床する	get up 21, 62
築き上げる	build up 18
気絶する	pass out 113
期待する	count on [upon] 37
期待を裏切る	let down 99
規定する	set down 140
帰途につく	start back 156

記入する	fill in 52
記入する	put down 121
機能停止	breakdown 15
決める	settle on [upon] 142
気持ちをほぐす	draw out 45
虐待する	kick around [about] 91
逆転する	come from behind 31
客として迎える	have over 79
逆戻りする	turn back 175
休暇をとる	get away 54
急に上がる	shoot up 144
急に断つ	break off 12
急に増やす	run up 133
供給を止める	cut off 40
供給を止める	shut off 146
行儀よくしない	act up 2
強行突破	breakdown 15
協調させる	keep together 90
協調する	go along with 64
強調する	play up 116
興味[性欲]を失わせる	turn off 176
興味を持つ	get into 58
協力して働く	pull together 118
協力してやっていく	pull together 118
許可を求める	check with 24
拒否する	turn down 176
ぎらぎら照りつける	beat down 7
切らす	run down 130
切らす	run out of 132
切らないで待つ	hang on 75
切り上げる	knock off 93
切り刻む	cut up 40
切り下げる	cut down 39
起立する	stand up 154
切り詰める	cut back 39
切り抜けさせる	bring through 17
切り抜けさせる	help out 81
切り抜ける	come off 33
切り抜ける	get through 61
切り抜ける	live through 103
切り離す	shut off 146
切り離す	tear off 168
着る	get on 59
着る[はく]	get into 57
切る	hang up 77
切る	shut off 146
きれいにする	clean out 25
きれいにする	do up 43
きれいに(掃除)する	clean up 25
記録する	write down 184
際立って見える	stand out 154
気をつける	watch out 181
緊急に…を必要とする	cry for 38
金品を強奪する	hold up 85

INDEX

■く
- 偶然出会う　fall in with　49
- 偶然出会う　run across　128
- 偶然…に出くわす　run into　130
- 区画する　mark off　108
- 区切る　mark off　108
- ぐずぐずする　hang around　75
- 崩れる　come down　30
- 下る　go down　66
- 口答えをする　answer back　4
- 口答えをする　talk back　167
- 口を挟む　break in　12
- くっつく　hang together　76
- くっつく　stick to　161
- （靴ひもを）結ぶ　do up　43
- くつろぐ　kick back　91
- くつろぐ　lay back　95
- 配る　give out　63
- 配る　hand out　74
- 配る　pass out　112
- くまなく探す　go through　71
- くまなく探す　pick through　115
- 暮らしていく　get along　53
- 繰り返す　go over　70
- （苦しい状況に）陥る　run into　130
- （苦しみなどを）経験させる　put through　125
- くるっと向きを変える　turn around　175
- くるように頼む　send for　137
- ぐるりと回す　pass around [round]　112
- ぐるりと見まわす　look around　104
- 苦労して作る　knock out　93
- 加える　add in　3
- 詳しい知識 [最新の情報] を人に与える　fill in　52
- 詳しく [ちゃんと・正式に] 書く　write out　184
- 詳しく書く　write up　184
- 詳しく説明する　lay out　96
- 企てる　set out　141
- 加わる　come in　32

■け
- 計画を立てる　lay out　96
- 経験する　go through　70
- 経験する　meet with　109
- 経験する　pass through　113
- 契約する　sign with　147
- ゲームに出ない　sit out　149
- 撃退する　fight off　51
- 撃墜する　shoot down　144
- 消したままにしておく　leave off　97
- 化粧する　do up　43
- （化粧などを）する　put on　122

■こ
- 消す　turn out　177
- 結果が…となる　come off　33
- 結果 [順位] が…となる　come out　34
- 結果的に…となる　add up to　3
- 結局…を意味する　add up to　3
- 結束する　stand together　154
- 決定する　settle on [upon]　142
- けなす　cry down　38
- けなす　put down　121
- けなす　run down　130
- け破って入る　kick in　91
- けんかする　fall out　49
- 玄関まで見送る　see out　134
- 元気 [意識] を回復する　pull through　118
- 元気になる　come around　29
- 研究する　read up on [about]　127
- 言及する　touch on [upon]　173
- 検査する　check over　24
- 検査 [診察] する　look at　104
- 減少させる　cut into　39
- 減少する　fall off　49
- 減退する　drop off　47

■こ
- 合意に達する　come together　35
- 講演する　talk about　167
- 合格する　get through　61
- （合計が）出る　work out　183
- 合計する　add up　3
- 合計…となる　add up to　3
- 合計…にする　bring to　17
- 攻撃する　turn on [upon]　177
- 交際を断つ　cut off　40
- 公然と [あからさまに] 言う　come (right) out and say [ask]　34
- 後退する　back away　6
- 後退する　back down　6
- 交代する　take over　166
- 好転する　look up　106
- 好転する　turn around　175
- 強盗に入る　knock over　93
- 荒廃する　run down　129
- 公表する　come out with　34
- 越えて進む　go beyond　65
- 声を出して読む　read out　127
- こきおろす　put down　121
- 克服する　break through　13
- 克服する　work through　183
- 心に浮かぶ　come to　35
- 心にじんとくる　get to　61
- 心を開く　open up　111
- 固執する　stick with　161
- 故障　breakdown　15
- 故障する　break down　11
- 故障する　go down　67

■さ
- 腰を下ろす　settle down　142
- 応える　live up to　103
- 誇張する　blow up　10
- こづきまわす　kick around [about]　91
- こづきまわす　knock around [about]　92
- ごっそり盗み出す　clean out　25
- 異なることをする　break away from　11
- 言葉でやり返す　hit back　81
- 断わる　pass up　113
- 断わる　turn down　176
- […の）ことを聞く　hear of　80
- （事を）始める　start up　157
- 粉ごなにする　break up　13
- 好む　go for　67
- コピーをとる　run off　131
- 子守りする　sit for　148
- 殺す　do for　42
- 殺す　do in　42
- 殺す　knock off　93
- 殺す　put down　122
- 転ぶ　fall down　48
- 壊す　break down　11
- 壊れる　break down　11
- （[特に]）困難なことを）めざす　shoot for　144

■さ
- 最後まで聞く　hear out　80
- 最後までやり通す　see through　135
- 探す　look through　106
- 下がったままである　stay down　158
- さかのぼる　go back　65
- 逆らう　go against　64
- 下がる　come down　30
- 下がる　go down　66
- 先立つ　come before　30
- 先に送る　send on　138
- 先に～に到着する　beat to　7
- 先にやり遂げる　beat to　7
- 咲く　come out　34
- 咲く　open out　111
- 作成する　make out　107
- 探りを入れる　feel out　50
- 避けている　keep out of　89
- 下げている　keep down　88
- 避ける　stay away from　158
- 避ける　stay off　158
- 下げる　bring down　16
- 差し出す　hand in　74
- さし控える　hold off　83
- 差し引く　take off　164
- 挫折する　fall through　49

197

日本語	英語	頁
させない	keep from	88
誘い込む	draw in	44
誘い込む	draw into	44
誘う	ask out	5
定める	set down	140
刷新する	shake up	143
さっと着る[はく]	throw on	171
さっと調べる	look through	106
さっと作る	throw together	171
さっと復習する	run through	133
さっと目を通す	run down	130
ざっと目を通す	look through	106
作動する[動く]	run off	131
さびれる	run down	129
妨げる	hold up	85
さめる	die down	41
作用する	act on [upon]	2
さらっていく	walk off with	180
去る	come away	29
去る	run along	128
騒ぎ立てる	carry on	23
参加させる	bring in	16
参加する	come in	32
参加する	sign up	147
さんざん殴りつける	beat up	8
参入する	break into	12
参入する	buy into	19

■ し

日本語	英語	頁
仕上げる	get through	61
仕上げる	work up	183
仕上げる	write up	184
強いて…させる	push into	119
支援する	get behind	55
支援する	stick by	160
仕返しをする	get back at	55
仕返しをする	pay back	114
しがみついている	hang onto	76
しかる	get after	53
しかる	speak to	151
(時間・場所などを) 取る	take up	166
仕切る	mark off	108
仕事の休みとして取る	take off	165
仕事を終える	get off	58
視察[点検]する	look over	106
支持する	back up	6
支持する	go for	67
支持する	stand behind	153
静まる	die down	41
沈む	go down	66
しそうだ	look like	106
持続する	keep up	90
したい気がする	feel like	50
辞退する	pass up	113
次第である	hang on	75
[に] 従う	act on [upon]	2

日本語	英語	頁
従って行動[判断]する	go by	66
親しくする	hang out	76
下に置く	lay down	95
下に入る	get under	62
下へ持ってくる	bring down	16
しっかり縛る[縛り上げる]	tie up	172
しつける	bring up	17
実現する	live out	103
実行する	carry out	23
実際に使ってみる	try out	174
…しつづける	keep on	89
失敗	breakdown	15
失敗[損失]と見なす	write off	184
失敗する	fall through	49
失敗する	go under	71
しっぺ返しをする	hit back	81
しっぺ返しをする	pay back	114
(質問などを) …にする	put to	125
始動する	start up	157
始動する	turn over	178
しないようにする	keep from	88
死に絶える	die out	41
死ぬ	die of	41
死ぬ	pass on	112, 113
支配する	take over	166
支払いを受ける	pick up	115
縛りつける	tie down	172
自分から (面倒などを) 招く	look for	105
しまう	put away	120
閉まる	close up	27
しみ込む	get through	61
締め出す	shut out	146
しめて [合計] …となる	work out	183
閉める	close up	27
しめる	turn off	176
しゃべって (時間を) 過ごす	talk away	167
しゃべらせる	draw out	45
習慣などが身につく	get into	57
従事する	go into	68
従事する	work on	182
修正する	touch up	173
渋滞する	back up	6
渋滞する	build up	18
重大な発見	breakdown	15
集中[徹底]的に調べる	read up on [about]	127
自由に[隠さずに]話す	open up	111
収入として入る	come in	32
重要であるように見せる	play up	116
重要でないように見せる	play down	116

日本語	英語	頁
修理する	fix up	52
終了する	close down	27
(銃を) 撃つ	shoot off	144
縮小する	cut back	39
宿泊させる	put up	126
[交替して] 出場する	come on	33
出世する	come up in the world	36
出発する	get off	58
出発する	go off	68
出発する	set out	140
出発する	start out	156
出発する	take off	165
出版される	go out	70
出版する	get out	59
出版する	put out	123
出費させる	set back	140
順々に回す	pass around [round]	112
上位にある	come before	30
上演[上映]される	come on	33
上演する	put on	123
正気づかせる	bring to	17
償却する	write off	184
生じさせる	work up	183
上昇する	look up	106
生じる	come of	32
将来に起こる	lie ahead	101
将来のことを考える	look ahead	104
除外する	leave out	98
食事の給仕をする	wait on	179
触発[誘発]する	touch off	173
徐々に聞こえなくなる	die away	41
署名して…を受け取る	sign for	147
署名して加わる	sign up	147
署名して就職[参加・加入]する	sign on	147
署名して雇われる	sign with	147
所有[借用・使用]しつづける	keep on	89
処理[処置]する	do with	43
処理する	work through	183
知らせないでおく	keep from	88
知らせる	check in	24
調べる	check into	24
調べる	check on	24
調べる	check over	24
調べる	go into	68
調べる	look around	104
調べる	look at	104
調べる	look into	105
調べる	look over	106
調べる	look through	106
調べる	look up	106
しりごみする	hold back	82

INDEX

退ける　shoot down　144
知れ渡る　get out　59
神経衰弱　breakdown　15
進行を遅らせる　knock back　92
進行を遅らせる　put back　120
進行を妨げる　hang up　77
信じ込ませる　put over　124
信じる　buy into　19
慎重に検討する　think out　169
侵入する　break into　12
辛抱強くつづける　stick at　160

■す

衰弱　breakdown　15
数値［金額］が…である　stand at　153
据え付ける　set up　143
姿を現わす　show up　145
姿を見せる　turn out　177
好きになる　take to　166
救い出す　help out　81
すぐに…を始める［行なう］　jump into　86
透けて見える　show through　145
少し離れている　lie off　101
進む　go on　69
進める　get along　53
進んでいく　go along　64
廃れる　die out　41
すっかり疲れさせる　do up　43
すっぽぬく　come out with　34
すっぽかす　stand up　155
捨て去る　do away with　42
捨て去る　throw away　170
捨ててしまう　throw away　170
捨てる　throw aside　170
捨てる　throw out　171
済みの印を付ける　mark off　108
すり減らす　wear out　179, 181
刷る　run off　131
することを免れる　get out of　60

■せ

正確であると確認される　check out　24
生活の指針とする　live by　102
制御する　hold back　82
生計を立てる　live off　102
生産する　put out　123
精神的にまいる　break down　11
成長［発展］して…になる　grow into　73
成長して（服などが）着られるようになる　grow into　73
成長する　grow up　73
せき止める　stop up　162
責任を負う　answer to　4

責任を持つ［取る］　answer for　4
席を詰める　move over　110
世間に出す　bring out　17
せずにすませる　get out of　60
絶版　breakdown　15
切除する　take out　165
窃盗　breakdown　15
説得する　bring around　15
説得する　work on　182
説明する　set out　141
絶滅する　die out　41
設立する　set up　141
迫る　come for　31
責める　beat up on　8
責める　get after　53
世話をする　look after　104
世話をする　see after　134
世話をする　see to　135
全額支払う　pay up　114
栓・スイッチをひねって止める［消す］　turn off　176
宣伝して…にする　build up　18
栓をひねって（水・ガスを）出す　turn on　177

■そ

草案を作る　draw up　45
増強する　build up　18
遭遇する　meet with　109
創設［開設］する　set up　141
相談する　speak with　152
相談する　talk over　167
送付する　send in　137
続演する　hold over　84
束縛する　tie down　172
そそぐ　live down　102
育てる　bring up　17
率直に意見を述べる　speak up　152
外にいる　keep out of　89
外に出したままにしておく　leave out　98
外に出す　let out　100
外に出す　put out　124
外に出るのを見送る　see out　134
外へ行かせる　send out　138
外へ落ちる　fall out　49
外へ出す　have out　79
外へ投げ出す　throw out　171
そのままにしておく　leave in　97
そのまま持っている　hold onto [on to]　84
そば［近く］にいる　stand by　153
そばにいる　stay around　158
そばを離れない（でいる）　stick around　160
それない　stick to　161
それる　turn off　177

存在を知っている　hear of　80
そんな　come on　33

■た

タイアップする　tie up with　172
対抗する　run against　128
退社する　get off　58
（体重・速度などを）増す　put on　123
代弁［代頭］する　speak for　151
代理［代行］をする　sit in　148
代理を務める　act for　2
代理を務める　stand in　154
ダウンする　go down　67
耐え忍ぶ　go through　70
耐え抜く　stick out　160
耐えられそうな気がする　feel up to　50
耐える　live with　103
耐える　stand up　154
倒れる　come down　30
倒れる　fall down　48
高くなる　go up　72
蓄えておく　set aside　139
蓄える　put away　120
足す　add in　3
出す　give off　63
助けを求める　send for　137
たずねる　check with　24
訪れる　go over　70
たたいて～させる　beat into　7
戦いつづける　fight on　51
たたき込む　knock into　92
たたき破って中に押し入る　beat down　7
たたむ　take in　164
立ち上がる　stand up　154
立ち［起き］上がる　get up　62
立ち入らない　stay out of　159
立ち消えになる　blow over　10
断ち切る　shake off　143
立ち去る　get away　54
立ち去る　go away　64
立ち去る　go off　68
立ち去る　move away　110
立ち去る　run along　128
立ち直る　get over　61
立ちのく　move away　110
立ち向かう　stand up against　155
立ち寄る　come by　30
立ち寄る　drop by　46
立ち寄る　drop into　46
立ち寄る　go by　66
立ち寄る　stop by　162
立ち寄る　stop in　162
経つ　go by　66
建つ　go up　72

脱きゅうする　put out　124
脱獄　breakdown　15
達する　come to　35
達する　come up to　36
達する　go up to　72
達する　run into　131
達成する　carry through　23
立っている　stand up　154
脱皮する　grow out of　73
脱落する　drop out　47
建て込ませる　build up　18
建て増す　add to　3
建物で囲む　build up　18
建てる　put up　126
[…を〜]だと思う　take for　164
楽しみにして[首を長くして]待つ
　look forward to　105
打破する　break down　11
旅に出る　set out　140
食べていく　live off　102
だまされる　fall for　48
だます　put on　123
だます　take in　164
黙らせる　shut up　146
たまりにする　hang out　76
試してみる　try on　174
試してみる　try out　174
ために生きる　live for　102
ためにがんばる　push for　119
だめにする　do for　42
だめにする　go through　71
ために尽くす　act for　2
ためらう　hold back　82
ためる　run up　133
頼って暮らす　live on　102
便り[電話・連絡]がある[をもらう]
　hear from　80
頼りとする　turn to　178
頼りにする　count on [upon]　37
頼る　draw on　45
頼る　fall back on [upon]　48
頼る　run to　133
頼る　turn to　178
垂れ下がる　hang off　75
垂れ下がる　hang out　76
団結する　hang together　76
団結する　stand together　154
団結[結束]する　stick together
　161
断然反対する　set oneself against
　140
だんだんよいと思われてくる　grow
　on [upon]　73
断念する　give up on　63
丹念[順々]に教える　walk
　through　180

■ち

小さく扱う　play down　116
小さくなる　die down　41
近くで待つ　stick around　160
近づかない　stay away from　158
近寄らせない　keep off　89
近寄らない　keep away from　87
近寄る　go up to　72
ちぎり取る　break off　12
遅刻させる　tie up　172
着手する　get to　62
着陸する　touch down　173
注意する　watch out　181
忠告[注意]する　speak to　151
中止する　call off　20
中止する　knock off　93
忠実である　stick by　160
中断する　lay aside　95
中断する　put aside　120
中断する　set aside　139
中途退学する　drop out　47
注文する　send for　137
注文する[取り寄せる]　send away
　137
調査する　go into　68
調査する　look into　105
調和する　go together　71
調和する　go with　72
貯金する　put away　120
ちょっと訪ねる　drop by　46
ちょっと立ち寄る　drop in　46, 47
ちょっと待つ　hang on　75
ちょっと待って　wait up　179
ちらかっている　lie around [about]
　101
陳列する　set out　141

■つ

追跡する　run after　128
ついていけなくなる　drop behind
　46
［…に］ついて聞く　hear about　80
［…に］ついて話す　run by　129
通過する　get through　61
通じる　get through　61
通信販売で求める　send away　137
通用する　read through [over]　127
通用する　stand up　154
使い慣らす　break in　12
使い果たす　run out of　132
使い果たす　run through　133
使い果たす［使い切る］　run down
　130
使い古す　wear out　179, 181
就かせる　put into　124
つかまえている　hang onto　76
つかまっている　hold onto [on to]

84
疲れさせる　do in　42
疲れさせる　wear out　179, 181
付き合う　go out　69
付き合う　hang out　76
付き合う　run with　133
つぎ込む　lay out　96
突き出[てい]る　stick out of　160
突き出る　hang out　76
つきまとう　hang around with　75
尽きる　give out　63
つく　come on　33
つく　go on　70
就く　go into　68
就く　hold down　83
償う　answer for　4
償う　live down　102
作り出す　make up　107
付け加える　add on　3
[ラジオ・テレビなどを]つけている
　have on　79
[体に…を]つけている　have on
　79
就ける　put on　123
つける　turn on　177
伝える　get over　60
伝える　hand down　74
伝わる　get across　53
つづいて残る　stay on　158
つづく　come after　28
つづく　go on　70
つづく　hold out　21, 84
つづく　run on　131
つづけてやる　keep at　87
つづける　carry on　22
つづける　go on　70
つづける　keep up　90
つづける　put up　126
つづける　stay with　159
突っ立つ　stick up　161
包む　do up　43
つなぐ　tie up　172
つまみ[抜き]出す　plck out　115
罪をきせる　set up　141
強く求める　cry for　38
つり合う　go together　71
つるす　hang up　77
連れていく　take along　163
連れて[持って]くる　bring along
　15
連れて…を案内する　show around
　145
連れ戻す　carry back　22

■て

出会い[デート]の場を作る　set up
　141

INDEX

出会う　come across　28
出会う　meet up　109
手荒く扱う　knock around [about]　92
提案する　put forward　122
低下する　fall off　49
提供する　put up　126
提携する　tie up with　172
抵抗 [対抗] する　stand up to　155
（抵抗・反対などを）弱らせる　wear down　181
抵抗する　fight back　51
抵抗する　hold out　84
定住する　settle down　142
提出する　get in　57
提出する　hand in　74
提出する　pass in　112
提出する　put forward　122
提出する　send in　137
提出する　turn in　176
デートする　go out　69
出かけていく　go over　70
出かける　start out　156
適性選考会に参加する　try out for　174
出くわす　come across　28
手近に置いておく　keep around　87
手近に置く [置いている] have around　78
撤退する　pull out of　118
手伝って出してやる　help out　81
でっち上げる　make up　107
徹底的にやっつける　beat up on　8
出ていく　go out　69
出ていく　pull away　117
手直しする　fix up　52
手に入れる　come by　30
手に入れる　come into　32
手に入れる　get at　54
手放さないでおく　hold onto [on to]　84
手放す　sell off　136
手早く仕上げる　knock out　93
手ほどきをする　walk through　180
出る　come out　34
出る　show up　145
手渡す　hand over　74
手を加える　work over　183
手をこまねいている　sit by　148
手を引く　back down　6
手を引く　back out of　6
手を引く　draw back　44
手を引く　pull out of　118
転居する　move away　110
点検する　check over　24

点検する　go over　70
転送する　send on　138
転々と職場 [住所] を変える　move around　110
（電灯などを）銃で撃って消す　shoot out　144
電話する　call about　20
電話する　call up　21
電話で呼ぶ　call for　20
電話に出る　put on　123
電話をつなぐ　put through　125

■ と
という状態で出てくる　come out in　34
倒壊する　come down　30
同居する　live with　103
同棲する　live with　103
逃走する　get away　54
到着する　come in　32
到着する　get in　57
到着する　get into　57
到着する　pull into　117
同調する　come over　35
同調 [同意] する　come around　29
投入する　send in　138
導入する　bring in　16
遠ざかる　hold off　83
通す　let by　99
通す　let in　99
通り過ぎる　pass by　112
通り抜ける　get by　56
通り抜ける　get through　61
通り抜ける　go through　70
通り抜ける　pass through　113
通る　get through　61
とがめて（人に）不利な判断をする　hold against　82
説き伏せて…を思いとどまらせる　talk out of　167
説き伏せる　wear down　181
解く　clear up　26
（時計を）遅らす　set back　139
（時計を）進める　set forward　140
（時計を）戻す　set back　139
床に就く　turn in　176
年を取る　get on　59
途中下車 [下船] をする　stop over　162
途中で降りる　stop over　162
途中でちょっと立ち寄る　stop off　162
突然立ち去る　break away　11
突然出る　break out　13
突然火を吹く　go off　68
突然吹き出す　break into　12

取っておく　hang onto　76
取っておく　put away　120
取っておく　set aside　139
取ってもらう　have out　79
突破する　break through　13
届く　get at　54
とどまる　hold down　83
泊まらせる　put up　126
止まる　go off　69
留める　do up　43
止める　shut down　146
泊める　take in　164
ともなって生じる　come with　36
取り入れる　bring in　16
取りかかる　get around to　54
取りかかる　get to　62
取りかかる　set about　139
取り組む　work on　182
取り消す　call off　20
取り消す　cry off　38
取り消す　take back　163
取り壊す　knock down　92
取り壊す　tear down　168
取り出す　take out　165
取り出す [取り除く]　take out of　165
とりつく　get into　58
取りにくる　come for　31
取りに戻る　go back for　65
取り残す　leave behind　97
取り除く　clear away　26
取り除く　take out　165
取り乱す　break down　11
取り戻す　have back　78
取りやめる　call off　20
取り寄せる　send for　137
取る　get off　58
取る　take off　164
取れる　come off　32

■ な
ないのを我慢する　go without　72
ないものとあきらめる　write off　184
直す　shake off　143
治る　clear up　26
仲たがいする　fall out　49
仲直りする　make up　107
中に入る　get in　56
中に入る　go into　68
長引く　run on　131
中へ入る　go in　68
中へ走って [急いで] 入る　run into　131
仲間 [友だち] である　run with　133
仲間はずれにする　leave out　98
長持ちする　stand up　154

201

仲よくやっていく　get along　53
仲よく [うまく] やっていく　get on　59
流れ出る　run out　132
仲を裂く　come between　30
なくなっていく　drop away　46
亡くなる　pass away　112, 113
なくなる　run out　132
嘆く　cry over　38
なしですませる　do without　43
なしですませる　go without　72
何もしないでいる　sit around　148, 149
何もしないでいる　stand around　153
何もしないで見ている　stand by　153
並べる　lay out　95
並べる　set out　141
なりそうだ　look like　106
なる　come to　35
なる　fall into　48
慣れる　settle into　142
なんとかやっていく [切り抜ける]　get by　56
何度もたたく　beat up　8

■に
…に（なるのに）適任である　cut out for [to be]　40
似合う　go with　72
逃げ出す　get out　59
逃げ出す　run away　129
逃げ出す [脱出する]　break out of [from]　13
逃げる　get away　54
逃げる　run away　129
逃げる　run off　131
入荷する　come in　32
似た　take after　163
認可 [承認] してもらう　clear with　26
人気を博する　catch on　23

■ぬ
抜いてもらう　have out　79
抜かす　leave out　98
抜き取る　take out　165
抜く　pull out　118
脱ぐ　get off　58
脱ぐ　get out of　60
脱ぐ　pull off　118
脱ぐ　take off　164
抜け出す　get out　59
抜け出す　pull out of　118
盗む　knock over　93
盗む　make off with　107

■ね
値上げする　mark up　108
寝かせる　lay down　95
寝かせる　put down　121
値切る　beat down　7
寝込ませる　lay up　96
値下げする　mark down　108
寝て治す　sleep off　150
（寝ないで）起きている　stay up　159
寝ないで待つ　wait up　179
根に持って（人を）恨む [非難する]　hold against　82
値引きさせる　bring down　16
値引きする　mark down　108
眠ってしまう　drop off　47
練り上げる　work out　182
寝る　turn in　176
値を下げる　knock down　92
値をまけさせる　beat down　7
値をまけさせる　knock down　92

■の
逃れる　get off　58
逃れる　get out of　60
残す　hand down　74
…のことを（よく）考える　think about　169
載せないでおく　leave off　97
乗せる　let on　100
乗っ取る　take over　166
延ばす　hold off　83
延ばす　push back　119
述べる　set out　141
飲む　put back　121
のめり込む　get into　58
乗り越える　get over　60
乗る　get in　57
乗る　get into　57
乗る　get on　58
のんきに構えている　sit back　148, 149

■は
配給 [支給] する　give out　63
廃止する　do away with　42
買収する　buy off　19
買収する　pay off　114
配布する　give out　63
入り込む　get through　61
入る　get into　57
入る　pull into　117
はかどる　get along　53
吐く　throw up　171
爆破する　blow apart　9
爆破する　blow up　10
爆発する　go off　68

激しく反対 [抗議] する　cry out against　38
激しく非難する　jump on [upon]　86
励ます　get behind　55
派遣する　send out　138
運び去る　take away　163
運ぶ　take over　166
破産する　go under　71
走って戻る　run back　129
始まる　start up　156
始める　set about　139
始める　start in on　156
始める　start off　156
始める　start (off) with　156
始める　start out　156
始める　start up　157
始める　take up　166
走り下りる　run down　129
走り去る　run off　131
走り [逃げ] 出す　break for　12
恥ずかしい思いをさせる　show up　147
外しておく　leave off　97
外す　get off　58
外す　pull off　118
外す　take off　164
働いて返済する　work off　182
働きかける　work on　182
破綻　breakdown　15
発揮する　put out　124
はっきりさせる　clear up　26
はっきり示す　bring out　17
バックアップする　back up　6
発行される　go out　70
発車する　pull away　117
発する　give off　63
発する　let out　100
罰する　do for　42
発送される　go out　70
発送する　send off　138
話し合う　speak with　152
話しかける　speak to　151
離しておく　keep off　89
（話などを）終わりにする　draw the curtain over [on]　45
話に割り込む　jump in　86
話をさえぎる　cut in　39
話をして過ごす　talk away　167
話す　speak to　151
話す　speak with　152
話す　talk about　167
話す [しゃべる]　speak about　151
離れている　keep out of　89
離れている　stay away from　158
離れない　keep to　89
離れる　get away　54

202

INDEX

はねつける　shoot down　144
はねつける　turn down　176
跳ねまわる　jump around　86
はねる　run down　130
阻む　hold back　82
阻む　set back　139
幅を詰める　take in　164
はまる　fall for　48
はやる　go around　64
晴らす　work off　182
ばらばらにする　break up　13
晴れ上がる　clear up　26
パンク　blowout　10
反撃する　fight back　51
反撃する　hit back　81
反対する　go against　64
反対［反抗］する　stand against　153
反対を表明する　come out against　34
判断を翌日まで延ばす　sleep on　150

■ひ

［カーテンなどを］引いて開ける
　draw back　44, 45
引き受ける　see to　135
引き受ける　take on　165
引き起こす　bring about　15
引き起こす　bring on [upon]　16
引き起こす　set off　87
引き起こす　touch off　173
引き起こす　work up　183
引き返す　turn back　175
引き裂く　pull apart　117
引き裂く　tear apart　168
引き裂く　tear up　168
引き継ぐ　take over　166
引きつける　pull in　117
引き止める　hold back　82
引き伸ばす　blow up　10
引き伸ばす　draw out　45
引きはがす　tear off　168
引き離す　pull apart　117
引き離す　tear apart　168
引き戻す　draw back　44
引き戻す　pull back　117
引き寄せる　draw in　44
引き渡す　give up　63
引き渡す　hand over　74
引き渡す　turn in　176
引き渡す　turn over　178
引く　look up　106
ひく　run down　130
ひく　run over　132
低く抑える　hold down　83
非常に重要である　count for much

37
ひっかきまわす　tear apart　168
ひっくり返す　turn over　177
引っ越す　move into　110
引っ込めて建てる　set back　139
引っ込める　draw back　44
ぴったりはまる　go in　68
引っ張って取る　pull off　118
引っぱり込む　draw into　44
必要とする　call for　20
ひどく苦しめる　tear apart　168
ひどくしかる　jump on [upon]　86
1つひとつ調べる　pick through　115
人の家に1泊する　sleep over　150
一晩寝て考える　sleep on　150
ひとまわりする　go around　64
一人占めする　tie up　172
（人を）裏切る　go back on　65
非難し始める　start in on　156
非難する　cry down　38
秘密にしておく　draw the curtain over [on]　45
ヒューズがとぶこと　blowout　10
病気にかかる　come down with　31
表示［提示］する　set out　141
費用にあてる［使う］　put toward　125
秒読みする　count down　37
ひょっこり現われる　turn up　178
ひょっこり姿を見せる［現わす］
　blow in　9
開く　open out　111
広げられて…になる　open out　111
広げる　lay out　95

■ふ

不快にする　put off　122
吹出物　breakdown　15
吹出物が取れる　clear up　26
吹き飛ばす　blow down　9
吹き払う　blow away　9
復習する　go over　70
ふくらませる　blow up　10
ふさぐ　tie up　172
ふざける　play around [about]　116
無事におさまる　blow over　10
伏せておく　sit on　149
再び流行する　come back　29
ぶちのめす　beat up on　8
不通にする　tie up　172
復活する　come back　29
ぶつかる　run into　130
ぶつかる　walk into　180
不貞をはたらく　run around　128

ふと思いつく　hit on [upon]　81
ふと見つける　come across　28
不法侵入　breakdown　15
不満足ながら受け入れる［飲む］
　settle for　142
踏みとどまる　hold on　84
部屋に入る　fall under　49
ぶら下がる　hang down　77
ぶらぶらして待つ　wait around　179
ぶらぶらする　hang around　75
振り落とす　shake down　143
振り落とす　shake out　143
振り返ってみる　look back　104
振り向く　turn around　175
奮い起こす　get up　62
奮い起こす　put out　124
ふるまう　act out　2
（ブレーキ・圧力などを）かける　put on　123
触れない　keep away from　87
触れる　touch on [upon]　173
分解する　break down　11
噴出　blowout　10
分析　breakdown　15
分類する　break down　11

■へ

閉鎖される　close down　27
閉鎖［遮断］する　close off　27
平静になる　settle down　142
別離　breakdown　15
へとへとにする　knock out　93
減る　drop off　47
（変化して）…になる　turn into　176
返還する　hand back　74
返却する　bring back　15
勉強を始める　take up　166

■ほ

放映される　come on　33
崩壊　breakdown　15
崩壊させる　bring down　15
傍観する　sit by　148, 149
傍観する　stand by　153
放棄する　give up　63
放棄する　walk off　180
方向を変える　turn off　177
放送される　go out　70
放送する　put out　123
放免する　let off　99
訪問する　come over　35
ボカスカたたく　beat up　8
ボコボコにたたく　beat up　8
保証する　answer for　4
発疹　breakdown　15
発する　break out　13

203

日本語	英語	ページ
ほったらかしてある	lie around [about]	101
ほのめかす	get at	54
ほれ込む	fall for	48
本気で [真剣に] 取りかかる	get down to	56
ぼんやりと立っている	stand around	153

■ま

日本語	英語	ページ
まいらせる	wear out	179, 181
前に現れる	come before	30
前もって送る	send on	138
前 [そば] を通り過ぎる	go by	66
任せる	leave up to	98
まける	knock off	93
まける	take off	164
まさか	come on	33
交わる	meet up	109
増す	add to	3
増す	build up	18
待ち合わせる	meet up	109
待ち受けている	lie ahead	101
待ちぼうけをくわせる	stand up	155
待つ	hang around	75
…まで上がる	get up to	62
…まで上がる	go up to	72
…まで行く	go up to	72
まとめ上げる	work up	183
まとめておく	keep together	90
免れる	get off	58
招き入れる	ask down	5
招き入れる	ask in	5
招き入れる	ask over	5
招き入れる	ask up	5
招く	ask out	5
招く	bring on [upon]	16
守らせる	hold to	85
守る	keep from	88
回ってくる	come around	29
回る	turn around	175
漫然と (…して) 過ごす	sit around	148, 149

■み

日本語	英語	ページ
見送る	see off	134
味方をする	stand up for	155
見くだしてしゃべる	talk down to	167
見くだす	look down at [on]	105
見事にやってのける	pull off	118
短くする	cut down	39
見捨てない	stick by	160
見せびらかす	show off	145
見つける	turn up	178
見つける	come up with	36

日本語	英語	ページ
密告 [通報] する	turn in	176
見てまわる	look around	104
認める	let on	99
[…と] 見なす	take for	164
南にくる	come down	31
身につけたままでいる	keep on	89
身につけたままでいる	leave on	99
身につけている	have on	78
身につける	get on	59
身につける	pick up	115
身につける	put on	122
見逃される	go by	66
見逃す	let through	100
身のまわりの世話をする	do for	42
身をかがめる	get down	56
身を固める	settle down	142
身を乗り出す	hang over	76

■む

日本語	英語	ページ
迎えにいく	pick up	115
迎えにくる	come for	31
報いを受ける	pay for	114
向こうが見える	see over	134
向こうが見える	see through	135
むだ使いする	throw around [about]	170
夢中にさせる	carry away	22
夢中になる	fall for	48

■め

日本語	英語	ページ
明晰	breakdown	15
めぐって（言い）争う	fight over	51
めざして努力 [前進] する	work toward	183
めざす	go for	67
目立つ	show up	145
目立つ	stand out	154
目立つ	stick out	160
めり込む	fall in	48
目を通す	look over	106
目を引く	jump out at	86
面倒をかける	put out	124

■も

日本語	英語	ページ
猛然と始める	tear into	168
もぎ取る	break off	12
目的に使われる	go for	67
持たせる	hold out	21, 84
もたらす	bring about	15
もたらす	bring on [upon]	16
持ち上げる	hold up	85
持ち歩く	carry around [about]	22
持ちこたえる	hold on	84
持ちこたえる	stand up	154
持ち去る	make off with	107
持ち去る	take away	163

日本語	英語	ページ
持ち出す	take out	165
持ち逃げする	get away with	54
持ち逃げする	make off with	107
もつ	hold out	21, 84
持っていく	take along	163
持って [連れて] いく	take over	166
もて遊ぶ	play with	116
もてはやす	build up	18
戻す	send back	137
戻す	throw up	171
[…に] 基づいて行動する	act on [upon]	2
戻ってくる	come back	29
[…を] 基に事を進める	build on	18
元の所に戻す	carry back	22
求めて叫ぶ	call for	20
求める	ask for	5
戻り始める	start back	156
戻る	come back	29
戻る	get back	55
戻る	turn back	175
物を言う	count for much	37
物を片づける	clear off	26
物を片づける	clean up	25
催す	put on	123
漏らす	come out with	34
漏らす	let on	99
漏れる	get out	59

■や

日本語	英語	ページ
躍進	breakdown	15
約束・すべきことなどがある	have on	79
約束を破る	back out of	6
(約束を) 破る	go back on	65
役を務める	act as	2
やじる	cry down	38
休みにする	have off	78
やっていく	get along	53
やっていく	get on	59
やっていく	go along	64
やっと発する	get out	59
雇いつづける	keep on	89
雇う	take on	165
やむ	let up	100
やめなさい！	Lay off it!	96
やめる	cut it [that] out	40
やめる	give up on	63
やめる	grow out of	73
やめる	knock off	93
やめる	lay off	95
やり終える	get through	61
やり通す	go through with	71
やり通す	stick with	161

INDEX

やり遂げる　put through　125
やり直す　do over　42
やり直す　start over　157
やり直す　work over　183
やれそうに思う　feel up to　50

■ゆ
結い上げる　do up　43
結い上げる　put up　126
勇敢に立ち向かう　stand up to　155
有効である　stand up　154
友人である　go back　65
融通する　put up　126
優先させる　put before　121
誘発する　set off　140
ゆっくりくつろぐ　settle down　142
由来する　come from　31
許す　hear of　80

■よ
よい性質などを認める　see in　134
酔いつぶれる　113
用意する　lay out　96
用意する[準備する]　set up　141
要求する　call for　20
擁護[弁護]する　stand up for　155
様子を見る　check on　24
ようである　look like　105
［…の］ように感じる　feel like　50
ように見える　look like　105
要約する　run through　133
よく考える　think out　169
よく調べる　go over　70
よく調べる　go through　71
抑制する　hold down　83
よく出入りする　hang out　76
よくない状態になる　get into　57
よくなる　come along　28

横切って近道をする　cut across　39
寄せ集めて（食事などを）作る　put together　125
寄せつけない　fight off　51
予想[予報]する　call for　20
予想する　count on [upon]　37
予定[計画]している　have on　79
（予定より）遅れる　run behind　129
世に出る　come out　33
呼び寄せる　call over　21
呼び寄せる　pull in　117
呼ぶ　have in　78
読み上げる　call out　21
読み上げる　read out　127
読み込む　read into　127
読みつづける　read on　127
より寛大になる　let up on　100
…より重要である　come before　30
よりどころにする　fall back on [upon]　48
よりを戻す　get back together　55
よりを戻す　get back with　55
弱まる　die out　41
弱まる　let up　100

■ら
楽に勝つ　walk off with　180
らしい　feel like　50

■り
理解させる　get over　60
理解させる　put across　120
理解する　make out　107
立候補する　run for　130
略語である　stand for　154
理由[原因]となっている　lie behind　101
利用する　draw on　45

量を減らす　cut down on　39
リラックスする　lay back　95
リリース[出版]する　bring out　17
離陸する　take off　165

■れ
冷笑する　laugh at　94
連行にくる　come for　31
練習[トレーニング]をする　work out　183
連絡ができる　get through　61
連絡する　check in　24

■ろ
浪費する　run through　133
浪費する　throw away　170
論じる　go into　68

■わ
わからせる　get across　53
わからせる　put across　120
わかる　make out　107
わきに置く　set aside　139
わき[片すみ]に連れていく　draw aside　44
わきへ置く　lay aside　95
忘れてくる　leave behind　97
渡る　get across　53
わなにはめる　set up　141
笑いとばす　laugh away　94
笑いとばす　laugh off　94
笑う　laugh about　94
笑ってごまかす　laugh off　94
笑って払いのける　laugh away　94
割り引く　knock off　93
悪く言う　run down　130
我を忘れさせる　carry away　22

205

● 著者紹介 ●

デイビッド・セイン（David A. Thayne）

　1959年アメリカ生まれ。カリフォルニア州アズサパシフィック大学（Azusa Pacific University）で、社会学修士号取得。証券会社勤務を経て、来日。日米会話学院、バベル翻訳外語学院などでの豊富な教授経験を活かし、現在までに120冊以上、累計300万部の著作を刊行している。日本で30年近くにおよぶ豊富な英語教授経験を持ち、これまで教えてきた日本人生徒数は数万人に及ぶ。英会話学校経営、翻訳、英語書籍・教材制作などを行なうクリエーター集団 AtoZ（www.atozenglish.jp）の代表も務める。著書に、『ネイティブが教える　ほんとうの英語の助動詞の使い方』『ネイティブが教える　英語の形容詞の使い分け』『ネイティブが教える　ほんとうの英語の冠詞の使い方』『ネイティブが教える　英語の動詞の使い分け』『ネイティブが教える 英語の語法とライティング』（研究社）、『爆笑！英語コミックエッセイ 日本人のちょっとヘンな英語』『CDブック　聞くだけで話す力がどんどん身につく英語サンドイッチメソッド』（アスコム）、『英語ライティングルールブック――正しく伝えるための文法・語法・句読法』（DHC）、『その英語、ネイティブにはこう聞こえます』（主婦の友社）、『ネイティブはこう使う！マンガでわかる前置詞』（西東社）など多数。

古正佳緒里（ふるしょう　かおり）

● 執筆協力 ●
Jaime Jose　　Malcolm Hendricks

● イラスト ●
今川裕右

● 編集・翻訳協力 ●
杉山まどか・小島和子・宇佐美誠

● 社内協力 ●
鈴木美和

ネイティブが教える
英語の句動詞の使い方
Natural Phrasal Verb Usage for Advanced Learners

● 2014年5月12日初版発行 ●

● 著者 ●

デイビッド・セイン（David A. Thayne）
古正 佳緒里（AtoZ）

Copyright © 2014 by AtoZ

発行者 ● 関戸雅男

発行所 ● 株式会社 研究社

〒102-8152 東京都千代田区富士見2-11-3

電話 営業 03-3288-7777（代） 編集 03-3288-7711（代）

振替 00150-9-26710

http://www.kenkyusha.co.jp/

KENKYUSHA

装丁 ● 久保和正

組版・レイアウト ● AtoZ

印刷所 ● 研究社印刷株式会社

ISBN 978-4-327-45261-2 C0082   Printed in Japan

価格はカバーに表示してあります。

本書のコピー、スキャン、デジタル化等の無断複製は、著作権法上での例外を除き、禁じられています。
また、私的使用以外のいかなる電子的複製行為も一切認められていません。
落丁本、乱丁本はお取り替え致します。
ただし、古書店で購入したものについてはお取り替えできません。

研究社の出版案内

大好評!! セイン先生がずばり教えます！

ネイティブが教える
ほんとうの英語の助動詞の使い方

デイビッド・セイン
古正佳緒里〔著〕

A5判 並製 188頁
ISBN978-4-327-45260-5

今度は「助動詞」を完全マスター！
can, could, may, might, must, shall, should, will, would の9つの助動詞を中心に、その使い分けやニュアンスの違いを解説。

ネイティブが教える
英語の形容詞の使い分け

デイビッド・セイン
古正佳緒里〔著〕

A5判 並製 224頁
ISBN978-4-327-45256-8

状況に応じた英語の形容詞の使い分けを教えます。
同じ意味の形容詞から、ネイティブがよく使うと思われる5語を選び、それぞれのニュアンスの違いを例文を示しながら説明します。

ネイティブが教える
ほんとうの英語の冠詞の使い方

デイビッド・セイン
森田 修・古正佳緒里〔著〕

A5判 並製 166頁
ISBN978-4-327-45253-7

冠詞はむずかしくない。
「山ほどの例文とネイティブの解釈」をセットにして繰り返し読むことで、感覚的に「ネイティブの冠詞の使い方」が身につきます。

ネイティブが教える
英語の動詞の使い分け

デイビッド・セイン
森田 修・古正佳緒里〔著〕

A5判 並製 288頁
ISBN978-4-327-45247-6

この状況、文脈では、どんな動詞をあてるべきか？
日本人が理解しにくいこの問題を、セイン先生が、多くのネイティブに調査したうえで教えてくれます！

ネイティブが教える
英語の語法とライティング

デイビッド・セイン〔著〕

日本人が英訳の際に間違えてしまう微妙な日本語の言いまわしを、わかりやすく英訳・解説！
文法的に正しい英文を書きたい人へ。

A5判 並製 280頁 ISBN978-4-327-45240-7